Witches, Pagans, & Magic in the New Age

WITCHES, PAGANS, & MAGIC IN THE NEW AGE

KEVIN MARRON

SEAL BOOKS
McClelland-Bantam Inc.
Toronto

WITCHES
A Seal Book/September 1989

Cover art design by Styles Design
Edited by Sarah Swartz/The Editorial Centre

ISBN 0-7704-2327-2

Seal Books are published by McClelland-Bantam, Inc. Its trademark, consisting of the words "Seal Books" and the portrayal of a seal, is the property of McClelland-Bantam, Inc., 105 Bond Street, Toronto, Ontario M5B 1Y3, Canada. This trademark has been duly registered in the Trademark Office of Canada. The trademark consisting of the words "Bantam Books" and the portrayal of a rooster is the property of and is used with the consent of Bantam Books, 666 Fifth Avenue, New York, New York 10103. This trademark has been duly registered in the Trademark Office of Canada and elsewhere.

Canadian Cataloguing in Publication Data

Marron, Kevin.
Witches, pagans and magic in the new age

ISBN 0-7704-2327-2

1. Witchcraft—Canada. 2. Demonology—Canada.
3. Magic—Canada. 4. Cults—Canada. I. Title.

BF1517.C3M37 1989 133.4′0971 C89-095084-9

PRINTED IN CANADA

0 9 8 7 6 5 4 3 2 1

"Every thing possible to be believed is an image of truth."

WILLIAM BLAKE

The Marriage of Heaven and Hell

CONTENTS

CHAPTER ONE

What Is A Witch

Witchcraft and magic have fascinated, frightened and perplexed people for centuries, and continue to enthrall the popular imagination today. But they are usually thought of as remote and mysterious practices, belonging in the realm of fantasy and folklore rather than everyday experience.

One does not expect to walk into a suburban Canadian living room and see an altar to ancient pagan gods and goddesses set up on a coffee table beside the television or stereo. Neither does one anticipate meeting bureaucrats or computer technicians who spend their spare time poring over arcane spell books and invoking spiritual entities in magical rituals.

Such encounters have become commonplace to me during the past two years, as I have studied the revival of witchcraft and pagan magical beliefs in modern Canadian society. However strange it may seem in this age of advanced technology and sophisticated communications, these ancient practices are re-emerging in Canada as new spiritual movements.

Many ecologists, and some scientists, are finding new hope for the survival of mankind in a return to the worship of Mother Earth as a living organism and source of life. Goddess worship is seen by many women as a means of re-establishing true sexual equality. Magical techniques are being used by therapists, while business people are discovering their value as motivational tools.

A wide variety of people who feel dissatisfied with the values of contemporary culture and organized religion are now turning to the old traditions of witchcraft and adapting them to suit contemporary needs. They are discovering in these traditions a respect for nature, a liberating ethical code and a reverence for psychic dimensions of human experience that modern culture ignores.

In calling themselves witches, such people inevitably confront the centuries of prejudice and confusion that history has attached to that name. It inspires fear in many people, and hatred in some quarters, since it has long been commonly linked with devil worship or satanism. This confusion is compounded by the fact that society is at present witnessing a shocking resurgence of allegations of devil worship, which has been associated with child abuse and violent crimes.

The occult, a name that refers to the mystical secrets of an underground philosophical tradition and covers a wide variety of unconventional beliefs, has suddenly become an area of public concern and a field of investigation for police and social agencies.

My own concern with these issues began with the more sensational and distressing aspects. It was sparked by allegations of satanic cult activity made during the course of a disturbing child abuse case in Hamilton, which I covered for the *Globe and Mail* and described in my previous book, *Ritual Abuse.* The case involved two young children's credible allegations of satanic rituals, which included murder, cannibalism, bestiality and sadistic sexual abuse. Similarities between this case and others in North America led to suggestions that there was some kind of network of satanic cults engaged in the abuse and exploitation of children.

I was shocked by the apparent emergence in the real world of satanic activity as terrifying as the fantasies of horror movies. I was also startled to realize that satanism was being adopted as a philosophy of life by many young people all over Canada. I began to investigate this phenomenon.

In doing research on satanism, I studied the history of witchcraft, which was commonly believed to be associated with the worship of Satan, the devil or adversary, the principle of evil in Judeo-Christian tradition. I became aware that thousands of people practice witchcraft in Canada today, and that they assert that they have no link whatsoever with satanism. They are followers of present-day versions of ancient beliefs that centred around the worship of nature-based deities.

As will soon become apparent, the word *witchcraft* is applied to a wide range of beliefs and practices. The majority of people who now call themselves witches also refer to their beliefs as "pagan." This word derives from the period when Christianity became the official religion of the Roman Empire. *Pagan* is a Latin word meaning country dweller, and was therefore used as a name for the old religious beliefs that country people continued to follow after urban populations had converted to Christianity.

The name has been adopted by present-day witches, but it is also used by other people who do not call themselves witches. Paganism is a broader category denoting all those who are engaged in re-creating pre-Christian nature religions. They often refer to themselves as "neo-pagans," which means simply new pagans, in order to distinguish the modern movement from its ancient model. While the term neo-pagan is technically a more correct description of present-day people who espouse the old religions, in everyday speech they usually refer to themselves simply as "pagans," and in this book I have chosen to do the same.

Who are the present-day pagans and witches, and what do they believe? What is the truth behind the satanist scare? Is there a link between black and white magic, witchcraft and satanism? What are the forces in contemporary society that have led to the current fascination with magic and the occult? What can we learn from this phenomenon? Do we have anything to fear from it?

These are the questions that I have set out to answer in this book. They are difficult questions since they involve confronting many deeply ingrained myths and age-old superstitions. I believe it is important that we come to grips with them, not only because of the light they shed on the more disturbing and sensational new occult-related phenomena, but also because the answers can help us see our society and our place in the world in a new light.

The task of contacting witches and other pagans was made easier for me by the fact that the Canadian pagan movement has established itself to the degree that there is now a *Directory to Canadian Pagan Resources* (published by Pagans for Peace). This provides a listing of witches from all regions of Canada, as well as other pagans, including people who describe themselves as "Druids" and "elves". Many witches, however, are more private and secretive, and I had to devote considerable energy to tracking them down and winning their confidence. I travelled widely to meet witches and attend their rituals. I studied newsletters and small magazines that are written by and for witches in various parts of the country.

As I carried out this research, my interests broadened. My original focus had been on occult-related crime, but I found that witchcraft in Canada today constitutes a very varied and vibrant movement, which merits fuller public understanding in its own right. I saw that there were valuable lessons to be learned in the way these people are seeking to reconstruct old religions in order to escape the confines of their own culture. I obtained insight into those aspects of human experience that we usually refer to as occult or magical. With respect to my original intention of obtaining a better perspective on satanism, I came to realize that one cannot fully understand the nature of black magic or the antisocial behaviour associated with the dark side of the occult without having a proper grasp of its positive side.

Canadian historian Elliot Rose, writing in 1962, lamented that witches no longer existed and that it was therefore not possible to find out anything about witchcraft by positive and direct evidence. He said this was unfortunate because everything that has been written about the subject is vague, contradictory or conjectural. Definitions of the word *witch*, he said, ride a broomstick across the wide compass of heaven and hell, ranging from a wise woman and healer to a devil-worshipping hag.

Contacts that I have made would indicate that there were in fact a few witches in Canada in the early 1960s, but that they were very much underground. Now there are certainly many witches who are quite open about what they practice and believe in, and some of those who still practice their religion in private are prepared to talk about it discreetly.

This does not make it much easier, however, to draw a clear definition of a witch, since a wide range of people who call themselves witches actually hold quite different beliefs. Those I met included teachers, journalists, therapists, computer technicians, business people, a policeman and a university professor, as well as people living on homesteads and leading alternate lifestyles. In politics they ranged from conservative to anarchist. Some contemporary witches are feminists who worship a Mother Goddess and will have nothing to do with men, let alone masculine gods. But there are others who believe that it is essential to achieve a balance between male and female principles.

I talked to some witches who claimed that their beliefs have been passed down through family traditions from generation to generation, while others said that the practices of present-day witchcraft have been largely invented in recent years. Most witches are followers of a religion based on early European pagan beliefs, but I also encountered a Roman Catholic who sees no conflict between that religion and the witchcraft he practices. All these witches adamantly maintained that their beliefs have nothing whatsoever to do with devil worship or black magic, but public confusion about that issue is understandable in view of the fact that some satanists also call themselves witches.

I have not attempted to include in this book all aspects of the occult or all groups who have adopted a magical belief system, but have concentrated primarily on people who are seeking to escape the constraints of contemporary culture by espousing a value system based on ancient pagan beliefs. Although satanists do not fit into that category insofar as their religion is primarily based on a reversal of Christian values, they are included since they do call themselves witches and practice magic, and are historically linked with witchcraft.

The popular interpretation of the word *witch* is reflected in dictionary definitions. Most dictionaries define a witch as someone, usually a woman, with malignant supernatural powers, who practices sorcery with the aid of the devil. A secondary definition is "an ugly old woman, or hag." A third meaning assigned to the word is "a seductress."

Modern witches generally reject these stereotypes contemptuously. The original meaning of the word *witch* became distorted, contemporary witches believe, as the association between witchcraft and devil worship was moulded through centuries of persecution at the hands of the Christian church. Also, they will point out, witches are both male and female. *Warlock,* which many people believe is a word for male witches, means traitor or liar. It was a name that Christians gave to heretics, who were often burned at the stake as witches.

Witch is derived from the Old English word *wicca,* and most modern witches also call themselves Wiccans. Many prefer this name as it does not have the negative associations that have come to be attached to the word *witch.* It somehow typifies the diversity of Wiccan beliefs that there is no general agreement as to the original meaning of *wicca.* Some believe that it shares a common root with the English word *wit,* which meant "wisdom" and that therefore witchcraft is "the craft of the wise." Others maintain that the derivation is from an Indo-European word meaning "to shape, bend or turn," so that a witch is one who "bends or shapes reality."

Some witches refer to their beliefs and practices as "the Old Religion." Others maintain that it is not a religion at all, but rather a craft, a set of techniques for magically manipulating reality. Witches often refer to it simply as "the Craft."

Magic is an essential element of the witches' craft. It is a hard term to define, partly because, like the word *witch,* it is laden with many different associations. Magic is used to describe conjuring tricks, feelings of emotional enchantment and fabulous tales involving such miraculous transformations as the frog being turned into the prince. The definition of magic that is most often quoted by witches themselves is that coined by British occultist Aleister Crowley, who described it as "the science and art of causing change to occur in conformity with will."

Many popular notions about witchcraft and magic are derived from fairy tale, movies and myth. Jean Kozocari, a witch from Victoria, British Columbia, complained to me: "We are the only people who are still judged by the standards of Mother Goose and Walt Disney." She admitted, though, that this might be partly the witches' own fault, because they have traditionally been secretive and have to some extent cultivated the mystique that has surrounded them in order to cover their vulnerability with the semblance of power, to inspire fear in those who might be inclined to persecute them.

Magic and the use of psychic powers are not concepts that we are comfortable with in Western society. They are not part of our religious tradition and are outside the framework of our scientific thinking. Yet magic is a key word in our folklore, poetry and popular entertainment. Its emotive power is recognized and well used by the writers of advertising slogans. They know that it is a symbol to trigger feelings in the unconscious mind, precisely because it is not something we analyze or even talk about in a mature adult way.

In the same way, we recognize, and to some extent make use of, a thing that we might call psychic ability, extra-sensory perception or telepathy. Most of us experience moments when our mind has anticipated some event or when we intuitively know what another person is thinking or feeling. The popularity of psychic fairs and newspaper astrology columns testifies to the fact that many people, at the very least, enjoy indulging the fantasy that humans can discern the unseen forces that shape their lives. There are occasions when even pragmatic police officers will call upon psychics, because their experience has taught them that it sometimes works. For example, police in Montreal consulted American psychic Irene Hughes over the Cross-LaPorte kidnapping case in 1970 and she told them the address where Cross was being held and predicted the murder of LaPorte.

But, if we vaguely and grudgingly acknowledge such powers and forces, we certainly seldom think about them. We place them in the same category as superstitions. These are childish, primitive practices that we laugh about, while secretly indulging; customs and rituals that we are scarcely aware of, although we may sometimes let them rule our lives. For example, people who joke about old superstitions such as the fear of Friday the thirteenth often avoid making important appointments on that day, and in most apartment buildings the thirteenth floor is numbered as the fourteenth.

Our conception of witches belongs in a hinterland of the intellect, where fantasy and childhood notions have never been replaced by mature analysis and experience. Confronted with the notion that there are real live witches out there in our community, our first response is likely to be that of mingled fear and fascination. With no adult experience to call upon, our child-mind responds.

Anthropologist Bronislaw Malinowski wrote in 1925 that magic "seems to stir up in everyone some hidden mental forces, some lingering hopes in the miraculous, some dormant beliefs in man's mysterious possibilities." But then, he observed, when anthropologists went out into the field and studied magic in primitive societies, they were disappointed, because what they found was a sober, prosaic and practical art.

Kozocari, the Victoria witch, told me that she will not ever perform magical rituals in public, not because they are secrets, but because they are boring. She said she can't produce special effects as well as the Hollywood movies, and is, therefore, likely to disappoint the casual onlooker.

For her, and for many other contemporary witches, what we call magic is something very ordinary and practical. It is a matter of understanding and using the natural world and natural powers that we possess but do not cultivate or fully understand. While many skeptical and rational people view occultists as lacking in common sense, the witches see it the other way round. To them, we are the superstitious ones, because we half-believe in something we do not comprehend.

The revival of interest in magic and witchcraft can be seen as part of a broader re-evaluation of contemporary culture which is often referred to as the new age movement. A comprehensive survey of the new age movement is beyond the scope of this book, but the movement must inevitably impinge on a discussion of contemporary witchcraft. The new age phenomenon encompasses a vast array of therapies, practices and beliefs that range from various forms of highly commercialized spiritual consumerism to serious new scientific and ecological thinking. Many contemporary witches do not consider themselves to be a part of this movement, and look upon "new agers" as dabblers who draw upon a variety of occult sources without seriously studying them. However, many modern witches are influenced by aspects of the new age movement and witchcraft is certainly one of the beliefs that new agers often draw upon.

Most of the people I interviewed during the course of my research were seriously engaged in attempting to create or reconstruct a set of religious beliefs that they felt more appropriate to present-day realities than the doctrines of organized religion. Whether one agrees with what the witches have to say or not, there are some valuable lessons to be learned from them, which can be helpful in adapting to the changes and problems that society now faces.

While the current resurgence of interest in witchcraft and magic can be seen as a quest for a new spiritual vision, it also reflects a deep disillusionment with our religious tradition and patriarchal social structures. The failure of twentieth century society to solve the problems that it has generated is also at the root of the extreme alienation experienced by many teenagers. Many of them are also turning to magic to compensate for their feelings of powerlessness. But for some it is magic without vision, one that is based on a religion of selfishness that they call satanism.

What most witches are doing involves taking a critical view of our society and its values. Many of them feel so out of tune with the culture in which they live that, for their own sanity, they try to step outside of it by attempting to recreate the world-view of former times. For some the emphasis is on re-establishing a reverence for nature and for female principles through the worship of a Mother Goddess who is a personification of the earth. Others concentrate more on healing and personal development using traditional techniques and psychic abilities that Western culture has tended to ignore. Satanists' responses to society tend to be negative and destructive, but it is important to appreciate what they are rejecting and why.

The French novelist J.K. Huysmans wrote in 1891, "The tail ends of all centuries are alike. They're always periods of vacillation and uncertainty. When materialism is rotten-ripe, magic takes root. This phenomenon reappears every hundred years."

As we enter the 1990s, we will inevitably become more and more conscious of the fact that we are approaching the end of a millennium. However artificial our historical division of time is, we cannot help but feel that our civilization is completing a momentous cycle. We are all acutely aware of the many threats to the life of this planet. At the end of the first millennium of the Christian age, many people were anticipating the end of the world. Some fundamentalists are saying the same thing now. It is not hard for those people, who are not eagerly awaiting the second coming of Christ, to visualize the apocalypse.

Science and consumerism, the dominant influences on the twentieth century, are providing us with fewer answers and less satisfaction. Many people are realizing that we need to develop spiritual powers and values that have long been neglected. At the same time, an unprecedented number of people are unleashing psychic energies in the chaos of madness, violence and despair. Witches and other occult practitioners can, perhaps, provide some maps of inner realms that most of us have never explored before. But we need first to assure ourselves that their purpose is not to light our way to hell.

When I went off to meet witches, many of my friends warned me to watch out. One person, who had never before shown any strong belief in or preoccupation with the occult, insisted that I wear a silver medallion for protection when I first attended a witches' ritual. I found this interesting, as no-one has ever expressed any alarm about me meeting mafia members or covering motorcycle gang gatherings during the course of my work as a journalist. I realized that fears about witchcraft and the occult run deep, even among people who do not normally regard themselves as superstitious.

I have no interest in becoming a witch or a psychic, but I have learned some things during the course of my research about the use of so-called magical techniques, which I find useful in everyday life. These involve clarifying one's intentions and focussing one's will upon desired goals and acting with confidence in one's ability to achieve them. An example of this is the technique known as visualization, by which, when faced with a difficult task, one can conjure up a vision of the task as already accomplished. One can then set about completing the assignment with the feeling of confidence that one can see the finished product already sitting there neatly bundled up in the future. One does not have to be a magician to see the value of quelling doubts and insecurities and ignoring the distractions that result from a fear of failure.

I have no doubt that one can use such techniques to heal oneself of certain stress-related ailments or to impart that kind of healing strength to others. Someone lacking in self-confidence can draw strength from another person's certainty that things will work out well for them. Spells and magical rituals often serve the purpose of reinforcing or focussing that kind of confidence.

However, the reverse of all this is also true. One can undermine oneself with doubt. One can plant such doubt in others. If there is fear of magical power and fear of malevolent intentions embodied in a curse, it is quite likely that real harm can be done.

While most of my encounters with witches were positive, I did experience situations where I believed that I was the victim of attempts at malevolent manipulation. One of these was a subtle threat made to me by the proprietor of an occult store, who was warning me that I should not write anything disparaging about him in this book. It well illustrates the kind of ambivalence that I have been describing.

The witch who issued this threat preceded it with a demonstration of his power by giving a diagnosis of my physical and emotional problems. He diagnosed non-existent pains in the neck and right shoulder, and correctly guessed a weakness in my left wrist, perhaps as a result of noticing a scar from a childhood injury. I told him that he was about fifty percent accurate. He told me that he knew he was doing better than that. He then told me that I carry around a deep pain connected with something that happened to me around the age of ten. He wondered if it had anything to do with boarding school. I said that I started boarding school at the age of thirteen. He told me that the idea of fagging (a form of initiation whereby senior boys use new boys as personal 'slaves' for the duration of their first school year) came into his mind. Given my English accent, it was a fair percentage guess and only seventy-five percent wrong: I did have some trouble at school in my first year, but there wasn't any fagging, and I don't think I was scarred for life by it.

Curious about what would happen next, I told him that there was some truth in what he was telling me. He then demonstrated how he could put energy into someone by bringing his hands together around my hand. I did not feel a thing and told him so. He told me that he wasn't really concentrating the first time and did it again with more energy. I still did not feel anything, but told him that I did. Then he told me, with an ominous ring in his voice, that just as he put energy into me, he had the power to take it out.

Most of the difficulties I have had in dealing with witches have been of a very trivial nature, such as the fact that they do not always show up for appointments, return phone calls or answer letters. The only actual harm I have suffered was at the hands of the wicked witches of Winnipeg, who cashed my $10 cheque for a subscription to their magazine but failed to send me a copy. I found most witches I dealt with to be very helpful and generous, but many were extremely cautious about agreeing to be interviewed and some insisted on reading my horoscope before deciding whether to meet me. One man, who goes by the name of Father of Mysteries, sent me some information about satanic cults with a strict admonition that I should burn the document, to which a wax seal was attached, as soon as I had read it. This I gladly did, as the information was of no value. As a reader of spy fiction, burning it satisfied some of my more childish fantasies.

One person I wanted to interview said she would have to go into a trance in my presence in order to obtain direction from her spiritual master. She was a practitioner of an African-based religion and had a wide following among members of the immigrant community in the city where she lives. She went into the trance before an altar adorned with candles, images of Christian saints and African gods and a Christian bible. Supposedly speaking the words of one of the African powers who were her masters, she told me that I was very confused about my project and needed her help to accomplish it. She then told me that I would have to pay several thousand dollars for this help.

Although I do not have much experience in haggling with African gods, I was able to persuade the woman, who said she was speaking as the vessel of the master, to withdraw this exorbitant demand. She told me that the master agreed to let me negotiate directly with herself. She was ultimately gracious in her offers to help me in exchange for fair recompense. I did not avail myself of this offer because I was skeptical of the value of knowledge that was to be sold and bargained over. Also, my original interest had been in the role this woman was playing as a spiritual advisor and unofficial therapist in her community. The incident gave me a different perspective on this role. It made me realize its great potential for abuse. If I was a believer in the woman's power and the power of her gods, I might have found it very difficult to resist the demands for money supposedly coming directly from a god, who was also telling me that I urgently needed his help.

I met many more witches and pagans who freely gave their time to help other people. I found that they did play an important role in providing both spiritual and personal practical advice to people who, for various reasons, were not finding this through organized religions.

Witchcraft and magic can certainly be misused in practical ways, just as they can be, and usually are, applied to positive ends. This insight is also valid on a more spiritual level. Those who believe in magic usually refer to it as a neutral force, like electricity, that can be used for good or ill.

My perspective is essentially a skeptical one. I do not presume to be in any position to make a judgement about the existence of supernatural powers. I can say however that I have seen the effects of magic in people I have met. I know that witchcraft has provided some spiritually profound people with a purpose and meaning in life. But dabbling in black magic has led others, particularly vulnerable and inexperienced young people, on a downward spiral towards self-destruction.

The same observations apply to the impact of the new occult revival on the society at large. Occult-related criminal activity has demonstrated that it can be a powerful negative force. But, as an earth-enhancing humanist belief, witchcraft can be a dynamic positive influence that many people find more relevant and helpful than organized religion.

How to respond to the re-emergence of witchcraft in contemporary society is ultimately a question of common sense. Unfortunately it is a topic so resonant with the fears and confusions of folklore and history that people tend to forsake many of their common sense notions when confronted with it.

The secrets of witchcraft have been preserved in an occult underground tradition for centuries. Now witches are, as they often put it, "coming out of the broom closet," and bringing their mysteries into the light of day. I believe that it is worth looking clearly and sanely at what they represent and what they have to offer.

CHAPTER TWO

The Historical Witch

Many people today look to the year 2000 with much trepidation. The present problems of our planet, which appear almost insurmountable to some, are causing more and more people to wonder about what kind of society can survive into the next millennium.

This represents a profound change after generations of common belief in technological improvement and economic growth. Until recently, history was viewed in terms of gradual human progress from the dark ages of the past to the enlightenment of the present, and the future was viewed with optimism.

Now, some people are asking, ''Where did we go wrong? When did we sow the seeds of the ecological disasters and the social crises with which we are now confronted?'' They are looking at history in a new light and drawing lessons from it that are far different from those that were taught to generations of school children.

That is the kind of questioning that lies at the root of the current revival of ancient pagan ways. It represents a frantic search through the scattered remnants of the past for values and beliefs that might be of use in an uncertain and changing world.

This quest is made more difficult by the fact that Western civilization did not merely discard its old beliefs but systematically destroyed them in a campaign of terror that lasted more than two hundred years. Hundreds of thousands, and possibly millions, of people were burned at the stake or hanged during the witch-hunts of the sixteenth and seventeenth centuries. Our culture was brutally severed from its pagan past and memories of a former way of life were either lost or hopelessly distorted.

When I first read the histories of the witch-hunts, one of the things that I found hardest to come to terms with was the fact that this time of hysteria and sadistic terror came during the period of the Renaissance and the Scientific Revolution. This was the age of Newton and Galileo, Shakespeare and Leonardo da Vinci. It was a time that we now see as a great flowering of our arts and culture, and it marked the birth of the concept of scientific progress that has dominated our thinking ever since.

In my research, I had set out to consider witchcraft and the relationship between white and black magic. I was suddenly confronted with the possibility that the great achievements and ideals of Western civilization are also inextricably linked with systematic torture, casual brutality and uncontrolled destructiveness. One can see from history and from looking at the present-day world that the notion of a light side and a dark side, which is commonly applied to the occult, is also quite obviously applicable to organized religion, politics and technology.

It is with this kind of insight that many people today are engaged in trying to recapture the pagan traditions that the witch-hunts attempted to destroy. In doing this they have to piece together fragments of information gleaned from archeological research, historical records, poetry, myth and oral traditions supposedly handed down from those witches who survived the persecution. It is hard to say whether the alternative history of the human race that results from this kind of inquiry really reflects our ancient cultural roots, or whether it is a modern myth. Even if it is only a myth, however, it is a very powerful one, which a growing number of people are finding helpful in dealing with the problems of today.

A twelve-thousand-year-old painting found in a cave at Trois Frères in France depicted a masked human figure with a long beard, the face and antlers of a stag, a horse's tail and human feet. The painting, which has become known as "The Sorcerer," was at the end of a cave, the other walls of which were covered with paintings of animals. Just beneath the Sorcerer was a stone ledge, which formed a natural pulpit.

The setting suggests that the painting was a focal point for magical or religious rites. The most common interpretation is that the figure represented what anthropologists now call a shaman, someone who makes an inner journey into the spirit world for a magical purpose. The spirits of animals would usually be enlisted as guides or helpers in this journey. In this earliest form of magic, mankind learned from nature and imitated it, seeking success in hunting and other techniques for survival, also perhaps trying to ward off sickness or other calamities.

Another early form of what is believed to be religious art was a carved stone female figure with a swollen belly and augmented breasts. Several similar figures have been founded in situations that suggest they served a ritual purpose. They are usually interpreted as icons of cults that worshipped a fertility goddess.

Little is known about humanity's earliest religious practices. Anthropologists, often extrapolating from their knowledge of primitive cultures that survived into the twentieth century in remote parts of the world, see them as a mixture of religion and magic. Religion, in this context, is defined as a system of myth and ritual directed at propitiating and worshipping the forces of nature and the spirits of ancestors, while magic is an attempt to manipulate those forces and spirits for practical ends.

Both magic and religion were present in the culture of the early Greeks and Egyptians, and those of the Norse and Celtic tribes of Northern and Western Europe, which came to be labelled pagan at the beginning of the Judeo-Christian era. One can also find in the recorded myths of these cultures various forms of the two earliest religious icons, the Horned God of the Hunt and the Mother Goddess, the fertility figure who became the patroness of agriculture. These two deities of witchcraft are still worshipped by witches today.

It is almost an article of faith among many feminist witches that the early pagan cultures were matriarchal. Much anthropological research points to other conclusions, but anthropology has mostly been written by men, and some archeological information and myth can be seen as supporting the feminists' arguments. Whether one sees women as having been the leaders of primitive societies or partners with men in the struggle for survival, the ancient myths, and our modern myths about pagan cultures, certainly provide strong images of the female that are scarce in Judeo-Christian theology.

To modern witches, the most important difference between pagan religions and the organized religions like Judaism, Christianity and Islam, which came to replace them, lay in the fact that the new religions substituted the notion of a single, all-powerful male God for that of a God and Goddess. This hierarchical God was seen as existing outside of his creation, and nature was no longer held sacred. The organized religions that spread throughout the Western world robbed the earth and women of their divinity, and, in the view of most present-day pagans, paved the way for exploitation.

This is something that often tends to be oversimplified. The complexity of modern urban society and its estrangement from the rhythms of the earth leads some people to look to the past for a simpler, more natural attitude to life. In doing this many people, including many witches, choose to ignore those parts of earlier cultures that do not fit their own preconceptions. The important role of war and human sacrifice in such cultures is sometimes forgotten. The gods are cast as nature spirits and their role as emblems of human technology is often downplayed. Any goddesses that can be found in the mythology tend to be elevated to the status of Earth Mother irrespective of what the warrior tribes considered them to be.

Currently a popular notion of primitive societies is that they were all peaceful, matriarchal and in tune with the earth, combining the principles of feminism and ecology. The fact that early cultures contained the seeds of our patriarchal society and our exploitation of nature is frequently overlooked. Often that is simply blamed on the Judeo-Christian ethic, as if Moses brought violence and patriarchy down on the tablet handed to him from the sky. People tend to forget that the Greeks kept slaves and chopped down forests, that the Vikings were more famous for sword-making than weaving, and the Celts were as interested in warfare as agriculture.

The notion that the Mother Goddess was once worshipped all over Europe was advanced by several writers in the first half of this century. Although this idea has been rejected by many historians and anthropologists, it is still one of the main inspirations behind much present-day pagan and feminist thought. Most pagans worshipped Goddesses and considered them to be equals of the Gods, but it is unlikely that they all gave a nature Goddess the prime position in their cosmologies. There is, in fact, some evidence that in early British paganism the God of the Hunt was the primary deity.

By the beginning of the Christian era, human society was more than 10,000 years old. The ancient beliefs that present-day pagans are trying to piece together were already fragmented, partially lost, adapted and distorted by the time they first began to be written down and recorded in history.

The pagan cultures of Western Europe had become relatively sophisticated. For example, the Druids, a priestly caste in Celtic society, were philosophers, poets, judges, magicians and mystics.They impressed the conquering Romans with the depth of their learning. They had gleaned mathematical, philosophical and magical knowledge from Greek and Middle Eastern sources and combined these with their native culture, in which different species of trees formed the basis of an alphabet and calendar. They had some knowledge of astrology, a system of Egyptian or early Greek origin for correlating human characteristics with the movement of planets in relation to the sun. The stone circles built by European pagans, of which Stonehenge is the most famous example, probably represented a form of astrological calculation.

Some historians believe that some Stone Age tribes survived in isolated pockets of Northern Europe and Britain, just as a few primitive peoples can still be found in remote parts of the world today. These were the original elves or fairies, the "little people" who were fabled in folklore for their magical powers and their ability to make themselves invisible. They may, indeed, have been little people, as archeological evidence indicates that Stone Age people were small in stature. They were said to have the gift of making themselves invisible, because, like most primitive people, they were shy and elusive, good at running silently in the forest and hiding.

Fairies and witches were linked together in folklore. It is likely that some of the witches' beliefs were derived from the pagan practices of these primitive people. According to one theory, the fairies were the original witches. As they were conquered or dispossessed of their land by other races, some became absorbed into the new rural society and passed on their traditions, their magical practices and their knowledge of the natural secrets of the forest.

The whole picture became more confusing as Christianity began to assimilate pagan beliefs and practices. Pagan Gods and Goddesses were turned into Christian saints and their sacred places became shrines. The Virgin Mary came to take on an increased significance in Christianity in order to wean people away from the worship of the Mother Goddess. Churches and cathedrals incorporated carvings of figures from pagan mythology. Pagan celebrations and myths became merged with Christianity observances.

The old pagan religions were centred around the cycles of nature — changes of the seasons, the birth, death and rebirth of crops — with human reincarnation often playing an important role. The important religious festivals were seasonal ones, the solstices and equinoxes, and the times for planting and harvesting, for bringing livestock in to shelter for the winter and for putting them out to pasture in the spring. Seasonal changes were marked with rituals in which myths were acted out. In these myths, death and regeneration were celebrated in the symbolic sacrifice of a deity representing the old year and birth of a God of the new year.

The Christian myth of the birth, death and resurrection of Jesus Christ can be seen as a variation on this theme. Historically the birth of Christ would most likely have occurred in the autumn, which is when the census was taken in Israel, since the New Testament states that Mary and Joseph had gone to Bethlehem for the census. But the church came to celebrate Christ's birth close to the time of the winter solstice when pagans held the festival of Yule to mark the rebirth of the Sun God.

Similarly, the pagan celebration of death and reincarnation, which marked the beginning of winter, became All Souls' Day in the Christian calendar, a time for remembrance of dead souls, immediately followed by All Saints' or All Hallows Day, celebrating everlasting happiness of those souls who were believed to be in heaven. The traditions of the pagan festival have lived on in our culture under the Christianized name of Halloween, the eve of All Hallows Day.

In spite of the church's efforts at assimilation, pagan traditions continued to hold their sway in the countryside away from the centres of commerce and learning, and it is out of these traditions that witchcraft grew. At its simplest level, witchcraft is a phenomenon known all over the world in the practice of folk magic or sorcery. The folk magician uses herbs, spells and charms in attempts to heal or harm, and influence the weather or other natural processes, in much the same way as the shamans of the most primitive cultures. Wherever these kinds of witches exist, they are respected and feared. They are often resorted to in times of trouble but blamed when things go badly.

European witchcraft evolved as a combination of pagan religious observances and the practice of folk magic. It also incorporated more sophisticated magic and mysticism derived from the Druids, the learned priestly class of the Celtic culture that dominated Europe before the Roman conquest. Other influences on witchcraft included ideas that were brought back from the Middle East by people who went there on the Christian Crusades against Islam. Among these were the Knights Templar, a fraternal order of noblemen that was originally established to rebuild the temple of Jerusalem. They became saturated in occult traditions and eventually the leaders of the order were accused of witchcraft and executed.

Witches used astrology to calculate the best times for gathering herbs and administering potions. Such calculations would be based on a complex system of correspondences by which it was believed that certain plants, elements, colours and perfumes were associated with particular spiritual and emotional forces. They practiced divination with runes, stones on which were written the letters of an early magical alphabet. For fortune telling, they used a variety of methods including palm reading and numerology, a method invented by the Greek mathematician Pythagoras for assigning a numerical value to the letters in a person's name and using this to read their character.

The persecution of witches grew out of the Inquisition, a brutal investigatory body established by the Papacy in the thirteenth century to stamp out heretical sects that were attacking corruption in the church and challenging its spiritual and political power. Many of these sects rejected Christian notions of good and evil, claiming that both were attributes of God. Some sects came to be known as Gnostic (from the Greek word *gnosis,* which means "knowledge") because they emphasized a quest for personal knowledge of divinity. The Gnostics profoundly influenced Western occult traditions by promulgating the idea of the existence of a secret, forbidden body of knowledge that has been falsely associated with evil. They maintained that the knowledge that Satan offered Adam and Eve in the Garden of Eden was the way to enlightenment and was being withheld from mankind by a jealous God.

Mountainous regions, where Christian influences had not yet penetrated and paganism was widely practiced, also became strongholds for heresy and political rebellion. The association between witchcraft and satanism was forged in the Church's attempts to purge these regions of heretical influences.

The Dominicans were an order of friars who were prosecutors for the Inquisition and by means of ruthless torture, accused heretics and witches of devil worship and sexual licence. The Christian notion of the devil as a serpent became transformed into that of a horned goat, and the worshippers of the Horned God were portrayed as paying reverence to Satan.

In 1484, Pope Innocent VIII declared war on witches by saying, "It has come to our ears that numbers of both sexes do not avoid to have intercourse with the infernal fiends, and that by their sorceries they afflict both man and beast; they blight the marriage-bed, destroy the births of women, and the increase of cattle; they blast the corn of the ground, the grapes of the vineyard, the fruits of the trees, and the grass and herbs of the field."

The Pope gave the Inquisition the power to imprison, convict and punish anyone charged with these offences. The *Malleus Maleficarum* or "The Hammer of Witches," a treatise written by two Dominican priests, set the pattern for a vicious persecution that lasted two hundred years. The church had been relatively tolerant towards witches until this time and some theologians had argued that witchcraft did not exist. But the *Malleus Maleficarum* stated that Christians must believe that witchcraft exists and do everything in their power to stamp it out. The document carried the motto, ''To disbelieve in witches is the greatest of heresies.'' It warned that the end of the world was approaching and that this involved a desperate battle between the followers of Christ and the forces of Satan. It maintained that mere accusation of witchcraft was sufficient cause for arrest, and that anyone arrested who did not confess freely should be put to torture.

Although they were set in motion by the Catholic Church, the witch-hunts were also enthusiastically endorsed by Protestant leaders, whose literal interpretation of the Bible would accept as a commandment from God the passage in Genesis that states, ''Thou shalt not suffer a witch to live.''

While many of the people executed in the subsequent witch-hunts were possibly followers of traditional witchcraft or paganism, most historians believe that the majority were in fact heretics, rebels or people whom those in authority wanted to get rid of for political or commercial reasons. Once people were accused of witchcraft, it was almost inevitable that they would be subjected to brutal torture and forced to confess to the alleged crime. They would also be made to implicate others, who would in turn be arrested. Sometimes accused witches would name their enemies as accomplices, but records would seem to indicate that often names of friends and neighbours were given, simply in order to satisfy the Inquisitors and put an end to the torture. In Scotland and most parts of Europe, people who confessed to witchcraft were burned at the stake, while in England they were hanged.

People told the torturers what they wanted to hear and their confessions were used as evidence for the pervasiveness and perniciousness of devil worship. The confessions usually conformed to a pre-determined formula, a set of definitions of what witches were supposed to do. This included the acts of sorcery described in the papal pronouncement and also involved making a pact with the devil, flying through the air to attend a witches' gathering, defiling Communion Hosts, and indulging in sex with incubi and succubi, the devil in a female or male form.

It was commonly believed that witches kept small animals called familiars, which were demonic magical helpers. These were often thought to be cats and many cats were burned with witches at the stake. One writer has suggested that mass killings of cats assisted the spread of the Black Plague, which was carried by rats. Witches were believed to feed their familiars with an extra nipple, a "Devil's teat," and witch hunters would eagerly search women's bodies for such a mark, seizing on any wart or malformation as proof of witchcraft.

The myth of the evil witch who made a pact with Satan and swore enmity with the church became so powerful that many non-conformists or rebels came to espouse the image of devil worshipper. As one historian has noted, this image gave psychopaths a theme around which they could make sense of their delusions, while sadists "dignified their brutalities by giving them a satanic impulse."

Historians differ as to how many people were burned at the stake in Europe, or hanged under English law, for witchcraft. They also disagree about whether these people were witches, heretics or simply politically undesirable people. Although both men and women were executed as witches, the vast majority were women. This is partly a reflection of the fact that many of the practitioners of folk magic and leaders of pagan religious groups were female, but there are also other reasons. Powerful women, like Joan of Arc, were branded as witches. Midwives and herbal healers were regarded as a threat to the growing body of professional male physicians.

Many of those killed as witches were widows whose husbands had been killed in war. They were seen as surplus women and they were persecuted, either because other people coveted their property or, if they had no property, because they were regarded as a burden on the community.

Genuine witches were persecuted for religious reasons, but underlying the religious bigotry was the fact that a male clergy was threatened by a religion that worshipped a goddess and had a female priesthood. Another common thread in the church's attitude to witches was an extreme misogyny, which expressed most clearly in *Malleus Maleficarum*. "When a woman thinks alone she thinks evil," the tract stated. "Women act through carnal desire, which is insatiable in their case: hence, to sate their lust, they have dealings even with demons."

Witches' seasonal gatherings came to be called "Sabbats", a derivation of Sabbath. The Witches' Sabbat was a fearful and fascinating legend in Europe for hundreds of years. People believed that the witches flew to these gatherings on broomsticks, engaged in gross sexual acts with the devil, ate human flesh and danced obscenely round a foul-smelling cauldron.

The reality behind this myth was probably less frightening, but still quite exotic. The Sabbats were seasonal festivals, survivals of the old pagan ways. They were times for dancing, feasting and performing the rituals that would make the seasons turn and the crops grow. One historian described a Sabbat as "a religious feast, the meeting of a secret society, an institute picnic, a drunken orgy and a carnival."

An English Puritan gave this eyewitness description of a Sabbat: "They fall to banquet and feast, dance and leap about it, as the heathen people did at the dedication of their idols."

These unruly pagan gatherings upset the Catholic Church. According to Gerald Gardner, a twentieth century witch who was also a historian of the Craft, the Church spread the story that "the meat and drink of the witches were actually all kinds of horrible and disgusting substances, in order to make the Sabbat sound repulsive, so that people would not wish to go to it."

The sabbats gave people who normally led harsh and brutal lives a chance to let off steam and have a good time.

A medieval church official complained to his superior about people in one region where witchcraft was prevalent, "They talk of nothing but the last Sabbat. They look forward to nothing but the next."

There is a traditional belief among witches that thousands of innocent people were tortured and burnt for every witch killed during what they refer to as "the burning times." According to these traditions, witches responded to this by going underground, avoiding public attention and using skillful propaganda to make themselves into figures of fun—old women with black cats flying on broomsticks—so that eventually they would be forgotten.

Some witches themselves believed that they flew on broomsticks — usually after rubbing themselves with an ointment that incorporated hemlock and belladonna, dangerous poisons that would have had hallucinogenic effects if absorbed into the body in mild doses.

For two hundred years after the systematic persecutions ended, few people paid attention to witchcraft, except as material for fantasy and fairy tales. However, in the late nineteenth and early twentieth centuries a renewed interest in folklore and myth emerged. Various writers and scholars began to study and research pagan traditions, and came to see witchcraft as a survival of old religions, based on seasonal fertility rites and the worship of the Mother Goddess. These ideas struck a chord with people who were searching for alternatives to the Judeo-Christian religious tradition. There is much debate among present-day witches and observers of modern witchcraft as to whether these folklorists and anthropologists actually reflected a surviving tradition or helped to create a new one.

In 1899, Charles Leland, an American folklorist, published *Aradia: The Gospel of the Witches,* which was an account of the beliefs of an Italian peasant woman, who said she was a follower of the "Old Religion," a worshipper of the Goddess Diana, the God Lucifer, the light-bringer and their daughter Aradia. According to the legend told in this book, Aradia was sent down into the underworld to learn the arts of sorcery, including poisoning and ruining crops, in order to use these in a peasant revolt against the aristocracy. Many witches see Leland's book as a fraud, an expression of his own revolutionary ideas, and something that tends to feed negative concepts of witchcraft as a form of black magic. Nevertheless, it is often referred to and quoted by witches today and is valued by some feminist witches who see themselves as part of a guerilla war against patriarchy.

There was also a resurgence of interest in magic in the nineteenth century, which although not directly linked to witchcraft did strongly influence its subsequent revival in the second half of this century. This was a revival, not of the popular folk magic of witchcraft, but of something of a more intellectual nature. It came to be known as ceremonial magic or ritual magic. It drew upon ancient Greek, Egyptian and Jewish mystical writings, and traditions that had supposedly been secretly preserved by Freemasons and other similar orders, some claiming to have inherited the occult knowledge of the Knights Templar.

One of the most important aspects of this occult revival, in terms of its influence on modern witchcraft, was its rediscovery and popularization of the Tarot and the Kabbala. Many modern witches maintain that the use of Tarot cards for divination and the Kabbala, an ancient heretical Jewish system for understanding the nature of divinity, have been a part of Wiccan traditions for centuries. This is possible, but there is little evidence for it, and it is more likely that both came to be adopted by witches in the twentieth century.

The Tarot is a deck of cards, the forerunners of modern playing cards. The four suits in the Tarot are swords, cups, wands and pentacles, all of which are ancient magical tools. In addition to the 56 cards in these four suits, there are 22 cards, called the Major Arcana, that depict some basic elements of human life and consciousness. These include the sun, moon and stars, death, justice, love, strength, temperance, the emperor and empress, the high priestess, the magician and the devil.

Tarot cards probably originated in ancient Egypt and, according to some legends, were brought to Europe by the Gypsies, a nomadic people who have always had a reputation for fortune telling. The Gypsies' own legends say that they were entrusted with the occult secrets of many different groups who were being persecuted by the Christians during the Middle Ages. The Tarot is now used by witches as a tool for tapping into the symbolism of the unconscious mind and as a way of organizing or focussing extra-sensory perception. The cards are commonly used in psychic readings, which are often incorrectly understood as fortune telling, but are more precisely an attempt to discern the patterns of energy and emotion that contribute to a person's present situation in life and the direction in which it is moving.

The Kabbala, also known as the Tree of Life, is an immensely complex way of understanding the universe. It is often used as a guide for mystical exploration of the so-called astral plane. It is made up of ten basic symbols that are arranged in a tree-like pattern that is also sometimes seen as corresponding to the human body. The Crown at the top represents the pure light of creation, the closest one ever gets to comprehending the deity. The notion of the deity is of an all-inclusive being that contains all the contradictions and polarities of the universe. The Crown divides into a series of different symbols representing male and female attributes, various spiritual qualities and cosmic forces, each symbol including positive and negative aspects. There are 22 paths that connect the ten symbols together and these correspond to the 22 Tarot cards of the Major Arcana.

The nineteenth century magicians also studied astrology, numerology and alchemy, an ancient art designed to liberate the spirit that was believed to reside in all matter with the ultimate end of converting base metals into gold. They rediscovered Grimoires, medieval texts that often purported to be translations of Hebrew magical works. A belief in the magical power of words and the practice of concealing the secret names for deities and demons was present in Hebrew and pagan traditions. Riddles were used for this purpose in pagan cultures and some Jewish sects believed that the Bible contained hidden meanings that could be interpreted, if one knew the secret code. The Grimoires contained instructions on performing magical rituals, and details of incantations and charms in which names of demons and other words of mysterious origin were arranged in geometric forms.

Much of this research seems absurdly esoteric and one would be inclined to dismiss it as obscurantist self-indulgent nonsense. However, it also involved a quest to rediscover a mystical form of spirituality that had almost disappeared from Western religious traditions. This quest was embodied in a secret magical society founded in 1888 called the Order of the Golden Dawn, whose members included the poet W.B. Yeats, the dancer Isadora Duncan and many other highly influential writers, artists and social activists. The order was dedicated to achieving enlightenment, oneness with the forces of nature and, ultimately, control or manipulation of those forces. It used magical practices and occult systems of knowledge together with elaborate rituals and ceremonial costumes as ways of awakening the imagination, cultivating inner spiritual discipline and focussing both these on the attempt to transform reality.

A prominent member of the Golden Dawn was Aleister Crowley, who assiduously cultivated a reputation as the wickedest man in the world and called himself "The Great Beast." Crowley was generally regarded in magical circles as probably the greatest occultist of modern times and his influence is such that he figures prominently in the history of present-day witchcraft and also that of satanism. This has not escaped the attention of those who argue that the two phenomena are inextricably linked.

It is generally agreed that Crowley was not a paragon of virtue. He was born in 1875 in an extremely puritanical family and acted out a life-long rebellion against this narrow upbringing. He was a great mountain climber, whose reputation as such was ruined by an incident in which he refused to help comrades who were dying in an avalanche because he had quarrelled with them over his sadistic treatment of Sherpas, their guides. He attracted many lovers, whom he exploited financially and emotionally, abused physically and in possibly two cases drove to insanity. He filed two of his teeth into the form of fangs and reputedly enjoyed biting women with these until he drew blood. He was a heroin addict who somehow lived to the age of 72. Even one of his greatest admirers conceded that he was sometimes "a nasty, petty, vicious louse."

However, Crowley wrote several significant works on magic and occult knowledge, to which he brought important modern insight. It does not matter, he theorized, whether spirits, Gods or other psychic entities exist, because what counts is the practical effect of pursuing magical disciplines. In *The Book of Law,* which he claimed was dictated to him by a spiritual entity in 1904, Crowley proclaimed the dawning of a new age, an age of the will. He wrote that the motto of this age was "Do what thou wilt shall be the whole of the law."

Crowley was a friend of Gerald Gardner, the first public witch of the twentieth century and the greatest single influence on present-day witchcraft. Gardner was born in the north of England in 1884 of wealthy parents. He travelled widely in the Far East, where he worked as a rubber planter and a British customs officer. He had a lifelong interest in anthropology and the occult, and when he returned to England in the 1930s he became a member of a secret magical order called the Ordo Templis Orientis, the Order of the Eastern Temple, of which Crowley was the leader.

In 1939, at a meeting of another occult organization which he belonged to, Gardner met some people who he later learned were members of a secret witches' coven, which operated in the New Forest in the south of England. A coven is the name for a group of witches, traditionally thirteen people. Gardner was eventually initiated into the New Forest coven and believed it to be one of the last surviving remnants of a tradition that had survived through centuries of persecution. The witches had a traditional requirement that their practices be kept secret. This was also a practical necessity as it was still illegal to practice witchcraft in Great Britain. Gardner became concerned that the members of the coven were all elderly and that their traditions would die with them.

When British laws against witchcraft were repealed in 1951, Gardner decided, much to the disgust of many traditional witches, to disclose some of the secrets of the Craft in two books, which he published in 1954 and 1957. He still maintained that he was keeping the essential ingredients of witchcraft secret, and he shared these only with students whom he initiated into the new covens he established.

Gardner personally initiated hundreds of people into witchcraft. After he died in 1964 the covens that he established continued to grow into what became known as the Gardnerian tradition of witchcraft. Although Gardner was public about his involvement in witchcraft, his covens adhered to the tradition of secrecy. However, some Gardnerian witches did follow his example and continue to publicize the Craft. Among these was Raymond Buckland, who brought Gardnerian traditions to North America and wrote about them in books published in the United States. Covens formed in Canada both as a result of Buckland's influence and through the immigration of other Gardnerians from Britain.

Another form of witchcraft identical in most respects to Gardner's was popularized by Alex Sanders in Britain in the 1960s. It became known as the Alexandrian tradition and it also found its way to Canada through the immigration of some of its followers. Sanders had tried to join several Gardnerian covens but had been refused. So he started his own coven, claiming that he had been initiated as a witch by his grandmother in 1933 when he was seven years old. He was more of a showman and a popularizer than Gardner and achieved notoriety after proclaiming himself to be the King of the Witches. After his death in 1988, his followers, who now represent a strong world-wide tradition, were supposed to be electing a new king. If they have done so, they have apparently decided to keep it a secret.

Critics of Gardner have claimed that the New Forest coven never existed and that most of its rituals were actually made up by Crowley. There is little evidence to either support or refute such claims. What evidence there is, and the quality and nature of Gardner's material itself, would seem to point to the probability that Gardner did learn traditional teachings, but in a fragmented form. He then apparently supplemented this with material he drew from his own wide occult knowledge. This included elements that he took from Crowley's teaching and directly from the Golden Dawn material, with which Gardner was well familiar. He also borrowed from Leland's book and from the writings of other folklorists and anthropologists. His writings often blend poetic mysticism with antique language that seems like Victorian fakery of the "Ye Olde Tea Shoppe" variety.

In essence, the tradition that modern witches have inherited is a mixture of ancient pagan religion and magical practices. It has perhaps survived through secret oral traditions, but has certainly been overlaid with a variety of different influences. No-one is in a position to say how much of it dates back to original pagan cultures and how much is a recent invention. Even where one can see that certain concepts and details have been borrowed from the writings of nineteenth century occultists, that just begs the question of what their original sources were. Some witches claim that Crowley was himself a renegade initiate of a traditional coven.

In discussing these issues with present-day Canadian witches, I have come to realize that it matters little to most of them whether they are part of a tradition that has existed from time immemorial or one that was made up a few years ago. They believe that their religion is true to the spirit of the early pagan cultures, in that they respect the earth, the regenerative powers of nature and the divine female and male principles that mankind began to worship more than twelve thousand years ago. They are also convinced that their magical practices, whatever their origins, work in transforming their own lives and can serve as a powerful antidote to the materialism of modern times.

CHAPTER THREE

"Merry Meet, Merry Part, Merry Meet Again"

You have to be at least a little bit eccentric in order to be a witch. Although many modern witches live in suburban homes, work at ordinary jobs, travel on the subway and stand in line at the supermarket check-out counter, they are far from regimented in their beliefs.

Witches do not subscribe to what most people would see as a common sense scientific understanding of reality. They have rejected the authority of scriptures and the hierarchy of organized religion. They are generally uncomfortable with any kind of orthodoxy.

It is hardly surprising, therefore, to find a profusion of often conflicting points of view among witches. As I travelled across Canada, meeting a wide variety of pagans, I found that they took pride in the diversity of their opinions and beliefs. I was frequently told that there are almost as many definitions of what witchcraft is as there are witches.

This is true, to a certain extent, but fortunately it is an exaggeration. Otherwise one would be dealing with a completely chaotic phenomenon, and there would be no point in even using the word *witch.* All witches agree on some things, and there are many practices that are common to most members of the Craft.

Diversity of belief is itself an important characteristic of modern witchcraft. Unlike any organized religion, witchcraft is an oral tradition, handed down by word of mouth from one generation to another. It has no sacred texts, no written code of conduct and no central body that determines what witches should believe or how they should act. Although Gardner and others have gathered together some of the oral traditions and published them in books, these do not carry any stamp of authority. Most witches feel free to expand, adapt or disregard them, as they choose.

A religion that is founded on a sacred text, which is seen as the word of God, embodies a notion of universal objective truths. The concept of scientific objectivity can be seen as a product of this way of looking at the world. This way of seeing things has served an important function in Western civilization as it has tended to promote order and uniformity. It has helped to create the large organizations of the modern state and a science and technology that serve a mass society. It has also been used to suppress nonconformity, and, as environmentalists have recently come to realize, has failed to respect the diversity of natural life upon which our ecosystem is based.

Witches are in no position to claim that their beliefs have universal validity, and they have no wish to do so. They recognize that their original teachings have been changed and fragmented as they were passed on by word of mouth, that they have been adapted to fit with local circumstances or distorted by outside pressures. Their concept of the deity is not an absolute that is above and beyond nature, but a spirit that permeates all life. They see the earth, heavenly bodies, humanity and nature in all their diversity as manifestations of divinity.

They have no basis on which to reject other creeds or different forms of their own traditions, since they must regard these other beliefs as being equally valid expressions of a divinity that informs all things. Witches refer to their religion as a "path," a way of understanding life. They believe that other religions are alternate paths that ultimately lead to the same place. In keeping with their rejection of universal truths, witches centre their religious practice around small intimate groups. This style of worship tends to appeal to people who feel estranged by anonymity and uniformity of mass culture and long for the sense of community that they see as having existed in tribal societies.

Even the more conservative movements within modern witchcraft, such as the Gardnerians or Alexandrians, are referred to as "traditions" rather than organizations. Their basic unit is a coven, and all covens are autonomous. The traditions are maintained through a process of initiations and a hierarchical system of priests and priestesses. There are three degrees of witches, of which the third degree is the highest. The first degree is the rank of an ordinary member of a coven, who has been initiated into the craft after going through a period of apprenticeship. A second degree Wiccan priest or priestess can perform first degree initiations and run a coven under supervision. Only a third degree high priest or high priestess is considered qualified to run a coven alone. In order to achieve that grade he or she must have been initiated by another third degree Gardnerian or Alexandrian.

Many modern witches reject such hierarchical structures and run their covens on more egalitarian principles. There are also solitary witches who follow their own lights. Although a coven traditionally consisted of thirteen people, which corresponds to the number of moons in the year, the size of a modern coven depends more on how many people members of the group feel comfortable with and the amount of space available. Covens can range in size from three to twenty.

Traditionally a coven consisted of an equal number of men and women with the addition of one high priestess. Only the most traditional witches now concern themselves with having a sexual balance within the group. In fact some feminist covens exclude men altogether and there are also covens of gay men. While traditional covens stress the polarity of male and female and use this as a basis for some magical practices, gay groups either ignore this concept or stress the male and female aspects that exist within each person of either sex.

People who want to join a traditional Wiccan coven have to study the Craft for a year and a day before they are admitted. One of the things that they have to learn and understand is the traditional passwords of Wicca, which are, "Perfect Love and Perfect Trust." Modern witches do not necessarily bother with the specific time limit or follow the ritual of speaking the passwords during an initiation ceremony, but they generally accept the underlying principle that the coven is a close association of people who should know one another well and share a basic feeling of love and trust.

The concept of initiation is a common one among witches, and it is a way of marking the fact that someone has been accepted into the Craft, recognized as having a certain required level of dedication, commitment and understanding. Even among solitary witches there is a concept of self-initiation, by which someone makes a personal commitment to witchcraft.

During the times of persecution it was necessary for witches to be secretive about their practices. This concept of secrecy still persists in some traditional Wiccan groups. When witches are initiated in traditional covens, they swear a solemn oath, on their hopes of a future life, never to reveal the secrets of their art, except to a "proper person, properly prepared within the circle." The initiate is led into the circle bound and blindfolded, and then measured with a length of cord from head to heel and around the forehead, chest and hips. Knots are made in this cord to mark the different measurements and it is kept by the coven.

In the past, witches used to take some hair and nail clippings from the newly initiated member of the coven and keep them with the cord. If the oath was ever broken, the cord and the clippings would be "buried in a boggy place, with curses, so that as it rotted so the traitor would rot."

Whether to be secretive about their practices is now a topic of much debate among witches. Many people feel that there is no need for it anymore and it just contributes to public misunderstanding and fear of witchcraft. Others maintain that it is necessary in order to prevent the powerful magic knowledge contained in Craft traditions from falling into the wrong hands. The witches who believe in preserving traditional secrets often find their position undermined by those who are willing to make them public.

One practice that arose during the times when secrecy was a matter of life and death was that members of a coven would take on pseudonyms, known as "Craft names," which other witches would call them by, so that witches who were arrested and tortured would not be able to reveal the proper names of their confederates. The use of Craft names is still common in witchcraft, partly as a way of preserving the privacy of people who for professional or other reasons do not want to be publicly identified as witches, and also because the taking on of such a name when being initiated as a witch symbolizes a rite of passage, the assumption of a new spiritual identity. Many of the people I interviewed for this book asked that I identify them only by their Craft names.

In the elaborate initiation ceremony of traditional witchcraft, one important element in modern Wiccan symbolism has been adopted in various forms by other groups. This is a blessing known as the five-fold kiss. In the Gardnerian version of this, the high priestess or high priest, whichever is of the opposite sex to the initiate, kisses him or her on the feet, knees, genitals, breast and lips. The words that accompany the kisses are: "Blessed be thy feet that have brought thee in these ways. Blessed be thy knees that shall kneel at the sacred altar. Blessed be thy womb (or phallus) without which we would not be. Blessed be thy breasts formed in beauty (or breast formed in strength). Blessed be thy lips that shall utter the Sacred Names."

The words "blessed be" are used by almost all witches when they greet one another, say goodbye or close a letter.

Another traditional greeting, which is less commonly used in everyday parlance, but is nonetheless an important part of the Wiccan culture, is ''Merry meet, merry part and merry meet again.''

The ethical code of witchcraft is a very simple one, which reflects an absence of universal objective values in a tolerant and individualistic attitude. It consists of just eight words: ''Do what you will, if it harms none.''

There is a striking similarity between this and Crowley's dictum, ''Do what thou wilt shall be the whole of the law.'' But I think it more likely that Crowley got this concept from the witches than vice-versa, since the Wiccan version is present in every hereditary tradition of witchcraft that I have encountered. It is, anyway, a more socially responsible ethic than Crowley's, in that the freedom it advocates is tempered by a respect for that of others. It also implies, as many witches have pointed out to me, a respect for all nature in that its admonition of harming none includes both people and other living things.

It is perhaps worth pointing out, in passing, that my use of the expression ''living things'' derives from my own Christian background. To a witch, all things are living since there is no distinction between animate and inanimate nature. Witches believe that the divine spark of life permeates everything.

Witches also believe that their moral code is not one of licence, but of responsibility. It requires an individual to act in accordance with his or her true nature and to take account of the consequences of all acts. From a Judeo-Christian perspective it may by seen as licencious in that it does not accept the concept of sin, particularly as applied to sexuality. Sexual energies and fertility are central elements in witchcraft and they play a role in both its magical and religious aspects. In one traditional teaching that is often quoted by witches, the Goddess is supposed to have told her followers, ''All acts of love and pleasure are my rituals.''

The polarities of male and female principles embodied in the God and Goddess are an important aspect of magic in traditional witchcraft, and many less traditional groups also cultivate various forms of sexual or physical energy. This sexual element is usually at the level of the energy or electricity that flows between the two genders, and this is invoked in a symbolic way. Witches do believe that sexual activity can be used in magic by directing the powerful energies generated by orgasm into the astral plane for a specific magical purpose. But this is generally done by couples in privacy.

An exception to this is a traditional ritual known as the Great Rite, which can be performed in a circle on special occasions such as the initiation of a third degree high priest or priestess. In the Great Rite the two main participants represent the God and the Goddess and the ceremony culminates in their engaging in sexual intercourse. If this is done within the circle, the other members of the coven will either turn their backs or leave the room at the culmination of the ritual.

This ritual is usually performed in a tamer symbolic form that does not involve actual intercourse. In the symbolic version the man holds an athame, a ritual dagger, and plunges the blade into a chalice of wine held by the woman. The couple then kiss, and share the wine, which is usually then passed around to the other members of the coven or circle.

Witchcraft has evolved historically as a fusion of two elements. It is a pagan religion that is centred on the celebration of nature deities. It is also a craft, which embodies techniques for magically manipulating the natural forces that the deities represent. The idea of the magical practice as a craft is reflected in the fact that most witches refer to what they do as "work."

Some witches emphasize the magical aspects of Wicca, while others are more interested in worship and spiritual development. But both ingredients are always present to some degree. The principles of Wiccan magic are based on achieving a state of oneness with natural energies, while the religious ceremonies involve magical rituals in which people help bring fertility to the earth and participate in seasonal changes.

In their worship, witches draw upon the myths of many different pagan cultures, of which the most common are those of the ancient Greeks and Celts. There is a bewildering number of different deities, but it is a common belief among witches that these names represent different aspects of the same divine principles that permeate all things. These are what they refer to as the God and the Goddess. Most witches revere both these deities, but some tend to emphasize the Goddess in their worship and some feminist witches do not believe in the God.

These deities are emblems of the seasonal changes of nature, of birth, death and rebirth. They are ambiguous beings with many different faces, which embody both the light and dark sides of nature, and symbolize the great mysteries of life that are the basis for all religious consciousness. Like the Christian mysteries of the Trinity or the Resurrection of Jesus Christ, these are things that cannot be explained to the intellect, and must be intuitively grasped through contemplation.

Gardner wrote that the Goddess told her followers, "And thou who thinkest to seek for me, know that thy seeking and yearning shall avail thee not, unless thou knowest the mystery: that if that which thou seekest thou findest not within thee, then thou wilt never find it without thee. For behold, I have been with thee from the beginning; and I am that which is attained at the end of desire."

At the core of witches' understanding of the world is a belief in reincarnation, which is common in Eastern religions and in those of many primitive cultures, but is a characteristic that distinguishes witchcraft from the organized religions of Western civilization.

The God of the witches is seen as representing the sun, a life-giving deity who dies at the end of every year, and is then reborn. He is also represented as the spirit of the dark forests, the Horned God, a hunter who takes life in order to bring back food. He is Dionysius, a God of the vine, a symbol of natural abundance and ecstatic celebration. But he is also Hades, the God of the underworld and death.

The Goddess is sometimes known as Gaia, the earth-mother. But she is most often referred to as the Triple Goddess, who is worshipped under three aspects, as a maiden, a mother and a crone. The three faces of the Goddess are traditionally associated with spring, summer and early autumn, while her consort the Horned God rules the dark half of the year. The Triple Goddess is also linked to the waxing, full and waning phases of the moon, and therefore represents constant change.

The fact that the Goddess and God of the witches represent change and death is one of the reasons that witchcraft has always inspired deep fear in many people. When I first attended a witches' circle, I was quite horrified to see a man proudly displaying a large tattoo on his arm of the Grim Reaper, a hooded skeletal figure bearing a huge scythe, which symbolized death cutting down the bodies of living people. In medieval Christian culture this was a dreaded symbol of the cruel indifference of death. I could not understand why he should want to wear such an image, and considered it macabre that he should think it was a thing of beauty.

It was only after attending several Wiccan rituals and absorbing some of their myths that I came to understand how the image of death as a reaper can be seen as a comforting and joyful one that anticipates the rebirth of life in the spring. I had known at the outset that witches believed in reincarnation, but it took a period of gradual exposure and deepening understanding to emotionally grasp the concept that this implies an acceptance, and even love, of death.

Witches act out their myths in ritual and, in so doing, learn the mysteries of their religion through experience.

Ritual is present in all religion. In Christianity communion commemorates the Last Supper and also represents Christ's sacrifice of his body and blood as an atonement for the sins of mankind. In witchcraft, however, since there are no sacred texts or doctrines, ritual is the central focus of all worship as well as the way in which spiritual truths are understood.

In an oral tradition, rituals and the myths that they embody are many-sided and ever-changing. Most mythologies contain many different versions of the same stories. These stories are usually elaborated and adapted by successive generations. For witches, rituals involve a process of deepening understanding of old truths and discovery of new relationships between these and their own experiences.

A myth that plays a central role in many Wiccan traditions formed the basis for the rituals that were performed annually at Eleusis, a sacred shrine in ancient Greece. It was a celebration of agriculture and the rebirth of nature in the spring, and spread in various forms to other cultures in pagan Europe. It is just one of many old legends used in Wiccan ceremonies, and is not necessarily followed by all witches. But it is one of the most common, and it serves to illustrate the way that witches see the various aspects of their God and Goddess in relation to the mysteries of magic, fertility and reincarnation.

According to this myth, Persephone, the maiden Goddess, was wandering far from home gathering wild flowers when she ventured into the underworld, the domain of Hades, the God of death. Some Greek legends say that Hades abducted her, but most witches prefer versions in which she went there willingly, drawn by curiosity to explore the dark realm of death. Her mother Demeter, a fertility Goddess, spent ten days looking for her until she learned what had happened from Hecate the crone, a Goddess of wisdom. Demeter demanded that Zeus, king of the Gods, force Hades to return her daughter. In the meantime she refused to let the crops grow and the earth was barren.

Eventually Zeus persuaded Hades to let Persephone return to the earth for half the year on condition that she returned to him every winter, with the result that the earth was fertile during the summer and barren for the rest of the year.

The part of this story that tends to fascinate most witches is Persephone's relationship with Hades, who personified Death. In Gardner's version of the myth, Hades told Persephone that he loved her but she said that she could not love him, because he caused all that she took delight in to fade and die. He replied, "Lady, 'tis Age and Fate, against which I am helpless. Age causes all things to wither; but when men die at the end of time I give them rest and peace and strength so that they may return."

Persephone continued to reject Hades, however, and he told her that she must therefore receive the scourge of Death. This presumably meant that she would die, but it is always stated in this metaphorical way in the Wiccan versions of the myth. The scourge, a whip made of knotted rope, used in some witches' rituals symbolizes the scourge of death, which brings wisdom and rebirth. Persephone was scourged by Death and then came to love him and learned the magic that controls love, death and resurrection and the mystery that in order to be reborn one must love death.

Myths such as this one are performed in rituals at the witches' seasonal Sabbats. These eight festivals, which occur at roughly six-week intervals, are seen by witches as the spokes of the wheel of the year. When witches celebrate a Sabbat they believe they are symbolically participating in the cycle of nature by helping to turn the wheel and bring on the new season.

Halloween, often called Samhain (pronounced Sowen), is the most famous of the Sabbats. It is a festival of death that marks the coming of winter, the time when the country people of Northern and Western Europe would slaughter their excess cattle and salt the meat for storage. It was believed to be a time when the veil between the world of the form, the realm of everyday reality, and the invisible world inhabited by spirits was thin, and the spirits of the dead could visit with impunity. The fact that witches see this as a joyous festival has contributed to their bad image among the majority of the population, who tend to fear death and regard the witches' celebration of it as ghoulish.

On April 30, at the opposite side of the wheel of the year, witches celebrate May Eve, a fertility festival, to mark the beginning of half of the year that is ruled by the Goddess. This is also called Beltane, after a Celtic God of light and fire. Beltane is traditionally a fire festival when big bonfires used to be built and people would jump over them for good luck. As cattle were herded into their summer pastures they would be driven between two Beltane fires or over the ashes of one fire. It is also traditionally associated with games of courtship and dancing around the May Pole.

These are known as Great Sabbats, together with two other festivals that are traditional to Celtic culture: Candlemas, February 2, also known by its Celtic name Imbolg, which is also a light festival and celebrates the first stirrings of new life in the earth, and Lammas or Lughnasadh, August 1, which marks the beginning of the corn harvest.

The Spring and Autumn Equinoxes and the Winter and Summer Solstices are known as the Lesser Sabbats. They are also important occasions, but are less ancient in Western European culture than the Great Sabbats, which derive from the folk festivals of the agricultural year.

The Sabbats are occasions for worship and celebration rather than practical magic. A Sabbat gathering usually consists of the performance of a ritual, in which one of the myths of seasonal change and regeneration is acted out, followed by a feast in which the traditional ingredients are cake and wine or ale. These festivals are often occasions when members of several different covens and solitary witches get together to do a ritual and have a party.

The working sessions of covens, where the craft aspect of Wicca tends to take precedence over the celebratory worship of the deities, are called Esbats. They take place at least thirteen times a year on the night of the full moon, when magical energies are believed to be at their peak. Many covens and individuals also perform magical rituals on the night of the new moon, which is a time for initiating projects, building up energies to be released at the full moon, and clearing away energies that have been dissipating during the moon's waning phase.

Witches believe in the ancient theory of correspondence between what is within the human mind and what is outside in nature and the cosmos. They believe that a form of energy, sometimes called the "ether," permeates all life. This is the energy that people use to connect with one another on an emotional or psychic plane. The same energy is seen in the influence of the moon on the tides and the menstrual cycles of women. The strength of the sun's rays, the seasons of the year and the fertility of the earth are seen as manifestations of the same energy. Magic is a system for tapping into this energy and manipulating it in order to change one's own consciousness, or external events.

The unity of mankind with the natural world is represented in the primary sacred symbol of witchcraft, the pentagram. This is a five-pointed star, drawn as three interlocking triangles. It represents the five senses and the four elements fire, earth, air and water, with the addition of a fifth—the ether—which witches believe is also an element. Usually when witches draw a pentagram, they do so with one of the points of the star pointing upwards and two pointing downwards so that it has the form of a human body with arms outstretched and legs astride. Satanists also use the pentagram and usually draw it with two points pointing upwards to form the horns of a goat. However, this reversed form of the pentagram can be sometimes used by witches in certain traditions.

Witches often inscribe the pentagram within a circle to represent the unity between mankind—the pentagram—and the world—the circle. This is known as the pentacle. The pentacle, fashioned into a copper disk, is the most important of the magical tools of witchcraft. Witches often wear jewellery in the form of pentacles.

The tools of witchcraft, its magical rituals, dances and chants, the mystical systems like the Kabbala and astrology which it uses, and ultimately even the personification of male and female principles of life in the form of the God and the Goddess, are all methods by which witches try to put themselves in tune with the forces of nature. They are all concepts that assist in seeing the relationship between the unconscious mind, everyday reality and the forces of energy that create all life. Witches believe we are all part of a web constantly being woven out of the raw material of the cosmos. By understanding the nature of this web, they believe, it is possible to unravel and remake portions of the fabric of reality. According to one popular witches' chant, "We are the flow. We are the ebb. We are the weavers. We are the web."

"If you are wise, you can see where the threads are," one witch explained to me, "Then you can be one with them. But, if you are truly one with them, then you can have them flow with you. If you are one with the time stream, you can move time a little, move an event a little."

The purpose of an Esbat, or coven meeting, is usually to harness natural energies and direct them to some purpose, most often healing, blessing, protecting or some other positive social goal. Most witches accept that magic can be used for negative purposes, but see this as both contrary to the traditions of their Craft and dangerous. One of the laws of nature, in which almost all serious witches believe, is that magical energy grows like a flame and has a direct impact on the person who instigates it. According to what witches call "the three-fold law," whatever energy you create will eventually return to you with three times its original force. This applies to positive as well as negative energy.

There is a traditional belief that, as the secret teachings of Wicca were handed down orally from one generation to the next, every witch would write these teachings down in a personal journal that was called *A Book of Shadows.* This would only ever be seen by other witches and was destroyed after the death of the person who wrote it. It is unlikely that all witches kept a *Book of Shadows* until comparatively recently for the simple reason that few people could read and write. It is quite possible that this like many other so-called traditions originated with Gardner. Whatever its origins, many modern witches do keep a journal, if only because it is helpful to have a workbook containing a personal record of rituals and spells. One recent writer on witchcraft noted that many witches now use computers and keep a *Floppy Disk of Shadows.*

Almost all witches' rituals begin with the creation of a circle. This is the "magic circle" of popular legend. In some forms of ceremonial magic where demons are to be invoked, the circle is a protective barrier to keep the magician safe from the evil spirits that are conjured up. This is not usually its purpose in witchcraft. It is there, rather, as a boundary that keeps the positive energies raised concentrated in a specific area. It is also seen by some witches as a boundary that has been created between the everyday World of Form and the Invisible World, the spiritual plane on which magic is conducted. The circle is the witches' equivalent of a church or temple. The fact that it can be created anywhere and almost instantaneously distinguishes witchcraft from what are, in this respect, most aptly called established religions.

The circle may be drawn on the ground or simply outlined in the air above the ground with a hand or pointed sword—a procedure called "casting the circle." Sometimes a broom is used to sweep negative energy out of the circle. Salt and water is also sprinkled around the circle for the same ritual purpose.

Within the circle an altar is set up on which is usually placed a figurine or other symbols representing the Goddess and the God. Symbols of the four elements are arranged on the altar or around the circumference of the circle to correspond with the four cardinal directions with which each is associated. In the north, the earth is usually represented by a quartz crystal, which has long been valued by magicians as a material for focussing natural energy. Incense is often used to represent air and is placed in the east, while a candle might be placed in the south to denote fire, and a bowl of water in the west.

The ritual tools of witchcraft are generally arranged on or near the altar. The centrepiece of most altars is a copper pentacle on which magic symbols may be engraved. Other ritual objects are placed on the pentacle to be consecrated. The ritual knife or athame is used for casting a circle and directing the energy raised by witches within the circle. A magic wand is used as an instrument for directing energy. Since the athame is never used for non-ritual purposes, a second knife is usually available for chopping up the ingredients of herbal medicines or cutting cords used in magic.

The cord is a basic magical instrument used in spells that involve making knots to signify certain goals or forming webs out of lengths of cord held between members of the coven. In traditional covens the exact size of the circle is considered important and cords are used to ensure that the radius is the specified length. Some traditions also use cords to bind and take the measure of new initiates in an elaborate ceremony. These traditions also symbolically use a scourge in such ceremonies.

A cup containing wine (which is blessed and usually shared by the members of the coven) is another basic ritual object. The cauldron, traditionally used for brewing potions and herbal remedies, is also usually present and may be used to contain a fire.

In some traditions of witchcraft it is customary for people to perform rituals naked, called "skyclad." In other traditions, robes are worn. Many modern witches wear ordinary clothes in their circles. Traditional witches often wear necklaces, pendants and garters denoting their rank. Some other modern witches reject such ceremonial trappings, and may also be inclined to use fewer tools and less elaborate altar arrangements.

All these are regarded by many as simply window dressing or props, which encourage the unconscious mind to focus on a purpose and help the rational mind to clarify its intentions. As one traditional Wiccan high priest explained it to me, the unconscious mind has the intellect of a six-year-old and you have to play with it. The tools and rituals, he said, "are occupational therapy for the rational mind, so it doesn't keep looking over its shoulder."

At its simplest level, magic involves intensely visualizing a desired result, willing that it be achieved and projecting this intention across the ether, the invisible world, which is also commonly referred to as the astral plane. In order to accomplish this, witches raise psychic energy within the circle. They call upon the forces of the elements that reside in the four cardinal directions. Some would see this as invoking actual spiritual entities, while others would regard it as a symbolic way of summoning from their own psyche the energies that those spirits represent. They then try to build up this energy by dancing round the circle, chanting, holding hands so that the current of spiritual force flows between them. They visualize and try to form what they call a cone of power, which has its base around the circumference of the circle and rises to a peak above the altar in the centre.

Although I have never seen any incontrovertible proof that witches' magic works, I believe that the energy raised in a circle is something real and tangible. It is a current that you can feel moving through your body as you hold hands with the people on either side of you, swaying back and forth, vibrating with the rhythm of a chant or a dance. But I must admit that I have experienced the same kind of energy in the touch of a lover and frenzy of a crowd at a football game. I think that the charge of emotional intensity generated in these very different situations is similar to the energy raised in a witches' circle. The difference lies in the way that witches attempt to manipulate this energy to achieve magical results.

In a witches' circle, rituals are performed that can help to build energy, embody specific magical purposes, call upon the power that is symbolized in the deities, foster a sense of reverence and enhance the sense of community that exists in the group. These rituals may follow a set form or be more spontaneous, depending on the traditions of the group.

Before performing a magical act, members of a coven may have a discussion to consider its purpose and how this can best be achieved. Its object and consequences might be considered in divination by scrying (gazing into a crystal ball), or using runes, Tarot cards and other methods.

Word spells are often used, as these embody the energy of purpose at the same time as they make the intentions clear. It is customary to end any spell with the words "So mote it be," an old formula that means "Let this be so." Magical spells are also performed with the aid of cords, candles and poppets (handmade dolls). Once the spell has been formulated, and energies built up, the cone of power that has been created is released into the astral plane and the minds of the coven members concentrate on directing this energy to its projected purpose.

An important concept in witchcraft, as in all magical practice, is that of grounding. Magical energy is conceived of as being like electricity and the requirement that it be grounded is similar. Magicians believe that, once they have called energy from natural forces and used it, they must return it to the earth from which it came. Otherwise, they believe, there will be random energy flying around the astral plane that no longer has a purpose or a place to go and could harm the magician or others. Witches usually end their ceremonies by thanking the spirits for joining them and bidding them to return whence they came. They will then dissolve or ''banish'' the magic circle that they created for their rituals. One group whose rituals I have attended has a practice of singing the spirits home as they close their circle.

CHAPTER FOUR

Witchcraft on the West Coast: The Public Witches of Victoria

Victoria, British Columbia, is an ostensibly conservative city whose warm climate and picturesque setting have made it a haven for retired people. It seems a strange contradiction that this quiet cosy community also has the reputation of being a centre for witchcraft.

Jean Kozocari, a prominent Victoria witch, has estimated the local Wiccan population at 1,000, with a further 4,000 witches elsewhere in the southwestern portion of British Columbia. Public gatherings of witches in Victoria attract up to 200 participants, the city supports a monthly Wiccan magazine, and Canada's first and only pagan student religious club is located at the University of Victoria. A nation-wide network of pagan academics is organized in Victoria and witches from that city have also formed a group designed to improve public awareness and acceptance of the Craft.

It is hard to say why there are so many witches in this sedate city, but there are several possible explanations. Perhaps some witches have been attracted to Victoria by the same qualities that make it appealing as a retirement resort: its beautiful natural setting and the relative isolation. The Gulf Islands between Vancouver and Vancouver Island (on which Victoria is situated), provide a refuge for many people, including witches, who are seeking to follow alternate lifestyles and build intentional communities. One witch who grew up in Victoria described it to me as "a very spiritual place,'' and several others spoke in poetic terms about their feeling of a mystical connection with the wilderness.

When I went to Victoria, it was at the beginning of February and the rugged islands in the Gulf were shrouded in mist. It was easy to feel that one was entering a place of mystery, even though I viewed the islands from the deck of a very prosaic ferry where the smell of fresh sea air was mingled with an aroma of french fries from the cafeteria. I was arriving in time for Candlemas, the feast of the growing light, one of the four Great Sabbats of the year.

I had images in my mind of the ecstatic revels and strange rites of the historical witches' Sabbat, but I found the witches of Victoria gathered in an art gallery. They had come there for a poetry reading. Robin Skelton, a distinguished Canadian poet and academic who lives in Victoria and is also a witch, was giving his first local public reading in five years.

It was a polite, reserved, genteel gathering. Just three candles marked the significance of the night. It was an audience of university people, poetry-lovers and witches. There was nothing in the demeanour or dress of the witches that set them apart from anyone else, except perhaps for the rapt attention they gave to what for many was the first poetry reading they had ever attended.

As a highly respected academic and poet who can also give a very lucid and straightforward account of the traditional witchcraft that he practices, Skelton is a good spokesman for Wicca. So too is his mentor in witchcraft, Jean Kozocari. For both, witchcraft is a very simple and practical philosophy of life that does not in any way impair their ability to function as prominent members of society. When I interviewed them, I was given a sane and balanced view of witchcraft that is, I believe, worth describing in some detail.

Privately Skelton appears to be a shy man, with a quiet pleasant manner. But he has an impressive public presence. His high forehead is framed by a striking head of long grey hair and a bushy beard. He has a ring on almost every finger and on a chain around his neck he wears a metal pentacle, a witches' five pointed star within a circle. Dressed for the poetry reading in a tweed jacket, with the pentacle on his chest, he looked, at the same time, distinguished and untamed.

He read poems about cyclical changes in nature, growth, decay and rebirth. These were linked to everyday incidents and to the physical, emotional and spiritual changes in human life. The poems fused feelings and experiences with myth and history.

For the witches, this was a religious experience, close to the essence of what the Sabbat is intended to celebrate. In conversation with some of the younger witches after the reading, I was struck by the way in which they perceived a religious resonance in what I had felt as an aesthetic experience. I was reminded of the fact that in ancient Celtic traditions the poet or bard was a spiritual leader. Although the original religious significance of poetry has been lost for hundreds of years, poets have continued to use pagan gods and goddesses as images and symbols. There was nothing unusual in the fact that Skelton, as a poet, was invoking an Irish muse-goddess and fertility bringer. What was unusual was the fact that as a present-day witch, Skelton actually believes in the Goddess and worships her.

Skelton later explained to me that it was directly through poetry that he came to realize that he is a witch. He had been reading a book of Gaelic charms and spells when he heard that a friend's four-year-old daughter had fallen downstairs and was unconscious. It occurred to him that, as a poet, he was supposed to have magical powers. He made up a healing spell and the child woke up suffering only from a few bruises.

While he dismissed this at first as a coincidence, Skelton continued making spells and found that they nearly always worked. About 20 years after he first began making spells, he became friends with Jean Kozocari, a traditional witch, from whom he informally learned about witchcraft. She eventually initiated him into the Craft.

"I think I was a witch before I officially became one," he told me, voicing a sentiment that I heard in different forms from dozens of witches whom I interviewed. "It's a particular orientation towards life. It isn't just what you do. It's what you feel yourself to be. I had that attitude towards life from a very early age. I've always been a muse poet. I suppose you could call them visions, waking dreams of the Goddess."

We were sitting in the living room of his turn-of-the-century home, a large, high-ceilinged room, but warm, casual and comfortable. His witchcraft is a family practice. He usually performs rituals with his wife Sylvia, his two daughters and their male partners, and Kozocari. He holds a monthly meeting at his house, where someone gives a talk on an aspect of the craft: "We discuss it for an hour, then have wine and nibbles. There's no membership. It's a group of friends who come. Very, very casual — no bureaucracy, no secretary or president."

Skelton describes himself as "a Quaker among witches." He told me that the simplicity of the witches' creed was one of the things that most appealed to him about the Craft. He said his rituals are very short and simple: "I don't wave swords around, put feathers on the altar or anything."

Kozocari, Skelton's friend and informal teacher of Wiccan ways, later explained to me that precise and brief rituals were a tradition in her family. She said this practice was necessary during times of persecution, when they would not want to draw attention to themselves with elaborate ceremonies. She said they would want to quickly create a great deal of energy, focus it and then disperse it.

Magic and exorcism are things that Skelton approaches in a very casual, matter-of-fact way. He described himself as "not bad at exorcism," and talked about how he and Kozocari were occasionally called upon to help rid houses of unwanted spirits. He regards magic as work that witches have to do as a necessary part of their religion. But, he added, ''We should not lay claim to being the only people who can do this kind of thing. Sorcery is common to all religions. What is the difference between a miracle and an act of sorcery?''

''It's really very simple,'' he said, ''I suppose it's physiological as much as psychological. We do have an energy field. It makes sense to assume it can be directed by taking energy and focussing on that which you wish to alter. In healing, all I'm doing is reinforcing a person's will to health. Some people are in love with the fact that they are sick. You have to remove their sense of guilt.''

''It's not supernatural force. It's a hypernatural force. Everyone does it—women singing lullabys or when a kid is hurt and runs to mother who kisses it better. Most people are unaware they are doing it. We witches have learned to be aware and do things other people don't think of doing.''

Skelton said he uses magic for many things. He does spells to help people find jobs. He has only failed once, he said, when the person he did the spell for wasn't interested in going out to look for work. He said he does not lay curses. He admitted to occasionally doing a spell to get someone to go away. But, he said, it is difficult to do this if the person doesn't want to go, as there is a limit to how much you can impose your will.

As a university professor with obviously middle-class standing, Skelton recognizes that he is a special case, in that he is not as likely as others to be exposed to abuse because of his religion. He said he has noticed in recent years, however, that his colleagues are taking his beliefs more seriously. For example, a professor of military history ''no way inclined to mysticism'' asked him recently to do an exorcism for a friend who had a haunted house. ''Witchcraft is being accepted, perhaps with a decent amount of skepticism. It would not have happened ten or twenty years ago. If you wore a pentacle twenty years ago, people would have been surprised and shaken.''

Skelton described his daughter's recent wedding, which was celebrated with a Wiccan marriage ceremony known as a handfasting ritual. People dressed up in robes and about 25 witches—one of whom had brought with her a pet goat — performed a Wiccan ritual on the Skeltons' front lawn in the demure residential suburb of Oak Bay. "Nobody reported on it. Nobody paid any attention," he said. "I can't imagine that 25 years ago, when I first got here, if somebody did that in a front yard in Oak Bay, there wouldn't have been a brouhaha."

Jean Kozocari has been in the public eye as a witch for more than twenty years. A small, spritely woman, with a natural but refined manner, she told me how in the 1960s, when things like the Charles Manson murders were being blamed on witchcraft, "it was decided that a few of us should come out of the closet and make ourselves available, if asked and if we could do it without losing dignity."

Unlike some other public witches who court and enjoy the media exposure, Kozocari is somewhat reticent in her role. A woman who displays a core of traditional Upper Canada good breeding, which has been overlayed with her own casual playful manner, she spoke of witchcraft's "wonderful gallantry of etiquette. You are to be courteous, but you don't push yourself into the world."

Kozocari is a hereditary witch, who says that her family traced its written history to the 1430s, passing down the secrets of the Craft from father to daughter, mother to son, so the name would change every generation. "We survived," she said, recalling how witchcraft was a family secret during her childhood. "We never talked about it. It was like having a mad uncle in the attic. You knew it was there and never talked about it in front of strangers."

She said she was initiated into the Craft by her grandfather, whom she remembers working with the Iroquois in Ontario, correlating their beliefs with those of his family. She said he used to return home dusty and dirty, saying, "It's all the same."

She also received training in witchcraft from a Toronto stockbroker, who gave up his seat on the stock exchange after having a heart attack at the age of 38 and then re-established family Craft connections in Europe. She described him as "one of the most fascinating men I ever met in my life, an incredible instinct for the Craft. There is an old wives' tale about witchcraft that we are always told the time of our death, so we could get rid of anything embarrassing and put affairs in order. My teacher had a traffic accident. I was chosen to go in the middle of the night and go through a special door and take away anything that would embarrass (his family). The cupboard was bare. The story that I considered superstition proved to be true."

Witchcraft, to Kozocari, is something very ordinary, which has always been a part of her life. It is something that she does not feel she has to justify. She said that she tries to be as open as she can in talking about something that has an etherial quality. But, she said, she often finds her role as an unofficial spokeswoman for the Craft to be a difficult one as she sees witchcraft as something that cannot be packaged, written down or sold.

"When they do publicity for me, they always say I'm a white witch, and I hate it. But it's necessary. People think you're eccentric, an airhead but acceptable. There is no white, no black—just witches. Magic is magic. It depends what you do with it. Nothing is negative or positive. There's no right and wrong. Whatever works for you is absolutely right," she said.

This concept of magic as a neutral force that can be used for good or ill was emphasized by many of the witches I interviewed. There is generally much confusion over the notions of *black* and *white* witchcraft. In some circumstances they serve as useful labels, and witches themselves often use them. But it is important to understand that they refer to the good or evil purposes to which witchcraft can be put, rather than to the techniques that witches use and the powers they claim to wield.

You can take the same match to light the oven that you could use to burn the house down, Kozocari explained, but you don't call one kind of fire white and the other kind black. She said magic involves tapping into the energy that is all around us, focussing and directing it. This is the same energy that makes a plant grow out of the seed that is placed in the earth: "Witches are probably less superstitious than anyone else in the world. Magic is so absolutely normal. It's everything doing what it's supposed to do, working with the elements. I can't do Steven Spielberg. But magic works. Not always instantaneously. I've never done anything that didn't work. And I always got more than I asked."

Another witch in Toronto had told me that if you use the power of magic for bad purposes you will lose the power. I asked Kozocari whether she agreed with that. She replied: "I don't believe in a lot of retribution. All of us have to be allowed to make mistakes. I'm tired of goody-goody witches. If I think something needs doing, I do it and I take responsibility for what I do. Witches say they don't believe in being manipulative. That's what magic is all about. If you're not going to take responsibility, then what are you doing with this? I do what I know is right, following instincts, being responsible, making mistakes."

"Our instinct has become so civilized," she said, "We've cut ourselves off from instinctive ways."

People have forgotten how to adapt to the natural rhythms of nature, Kozocari said. "My calendar is split in half. The male part of the year begins on Halloween. Men in the tribe had to feed the tribe by hunting or war. It's the dark time, the strong, aggressive time, when I get organized and work better. The other half is gentler, the fertility period of the year. It is very dreamy and intuitive. Day-dreams and wishes come to the front."

"Our energy is so beautifully balanced. I have trouble with your calendar. The energy we create at one time takes us through to the next. We create energy to keep the wheel of the year turning. We were the first ecologists. We believe in the law of threefold return: what you have taken from the earth, you give back three times."

Kozocari sees the witch as a conduit, a channel for cosmic energy. She must be balanced and grounded, reaching her highest spiritual source but remain rooted in this world. "We're here in 1989. We can't opt out and live in the past. My broom is electric and it has a very long cord."

"One of the things I love about the Craft," she said, "is that the ancient, ancient rhythms and myths are constantly up to date because it has always been transmitted orally. It is the most modern and up to date religion, because it is always being reinvented."

The young witches in Victoria who listened in rapt attention to Skelton's Candlemas poetry reading, hold him and Kozocari in great respect. They regard them and a few other older witches as elders in their community, people whose knowledge and experience they can consult when problems arise. But the kind of witchcraft the young people practice is radically different from the traditional practices of their elders. They revere these traditions, but they are, indeed, reinventing them.

The younger witches of Victoria generally describe themselves as eclectic. Their basic beliefs are similar in many respects to those of Kozocari, but they draw from many different traditions and from their own personal experience to make new rituals. For many of them, feminism was a path to Wicca. Almost all of them say they were strongly influenced by the books of Starhawk, a radical feminist witch from San Francisco. The kind of enthusiasm that this feminist eclectic Wicca can inspire is illustrated in the following description, from the local Wiccan magazine *Hecate's Loom,* of a ritual led by Starhawk in Victoria in 1986:

> *Two hundred women gathered in the dark of night chanting as though they'd done it all their lives. We called out blessing and healing to others and danced around the now flaming cauldron, our voices ebbing and flowing as though perfectly*

> *orchestrated. We danced and chanted 'til somehow we became a single, giant spiral dance, twining in and out, raising with our voices and dance, a strength seldom realized. Our voices beautiful, our power impenetrable, we transcended time to return to when women gathered under the Moon as priestesses. As the cauldron's fire grew dimmer, we became an intimate group looking into each other's faces, pulling the energy in tighter in order to send it off to heal our loved ones and our planet. We then grounded this energy and ourselves by touching the earth and feeling the power sink deep into the earth. It was intense but not exhausting, though each person there undoubtedly had a different experience, we had shared a common bond—the power of women united.*

Idealistic about the potential impact of witchcraft on society, the young witches of Victoria are intent on giving the craft a higher public profile in the community. They have met with some resistance from some older, more traditional witches who believe that witchcraft is a private underground religion. They have also encountered some hostility from local people who believe that witchcraft is synonymous with satanism.

Fears about satanism and its supposed links with witchcraft are deep-seated in Victoria. In 1972, evangelical Christians accused a group of self-styled witches of practicing devil worship and attempting to perform a human sacrifice. This claim led to rumours that circulated in Victoria for sixteen years until the allegations eventually became the subject of a libel trial in 1988. Public fears were also fuelled by the publication in 1980 of a popular book, *Michelle Remembers,* documenting an alleged case of satanic ritual child abuse in Victoria.

This satanist scare has tended to colour local reactions to the city's flourishing and unusually public Wiccan community. The witches of Victoria have had to struggle to overcome negative public perceptions of their beliefs and practices. In doing this they have established good communications with churches and other community groups.

They have also worked hard at building Wiccan organizations to serve the needs of witches from different traditions. These efforts have made the Victoria witches leaders in the attempt to achieve public acceptance of Wicca in Canada.

A women's spirituality group, largely influenced by Starhawk, formed at the University of Victoria in 1985 and became the Holly and Oak Pagan Discussion Group, which operated as a subsidiary of the Alma Mater Society, the university's student union. This discussion group, which also held pagan rituals, soon became the centre of a heated controversy over the use of the university's inter-faith chapel. As a student religious club, members of the group felt they had a right to use the chapel, which was intended to be available to all religions. A booking was made for the fall equinox in 1986. But a few days before the Sabbat the group was told that the university chaplains had ordered that the booking be cancelled.

The chaplains were worried that witchcraft was associated with satanism in the minds of members of the community. They were themselves unsure of the distinction between witchcraft and black magic and they feared that church members would be outraged if the witches were allowed to use the chapel, and that a bitter confrontation would ensue.

The group held its Sabbat ritual elsewhere and invited the university chaplains to attend. Two chaplains who went to the ritual were favorably impressed with it. But the ban on the group's use of the chapel was not lifted. Meanwhile, the controversy had spread into the community. At Samhain, or Halloween, the group planned a public ritual in a local park, but the 40 participants were besieged by more than 150 curious or hostile spectators. "There were those there to learn and those there to burn," one of the witches who was present at that gathering told me.

Local pagans and witches were worried that the decision of the chaplains would serve to reinforce public prejudices by giving people the impression that the witches were indeed satanists. However, they understood that the chaplains were under considerable pressure from some sections of the local Christian community, and did not feel that they could allow the group access to the chapel until they were completely convinced that it would be appropriate to do so. The group met regularly with the chaplains for about six months. They held their Candlemas ritual on the lawn outside the chapel.

In March, 1987, the chaplains agreed to let the group use the chapel. This was seen as a significant victory for pagans everywhere in Canada, as it was one of the first forms of official recognition given to Wicca as a religious faith. In Victoria, where there is much public fear about satanism, the decision did a lot for the credibility of the witches.

Father Leo Robert, the Roman Catholic chaplain, who had originally opposed the pagans' use of the chapel and had struggled with the question for several months, became a defender of their right to religious freedom and tolerance. In a CBC television forum on witchcraft and satanism, Father Robert spoke so strongly in favour of showing tolerance towards witches that he was warned by one less charitable member of the audience that he would burn in hell. The witches also took heart from the fact that another panelist on the same program, a Vancouver evangelist not known for her liberal opinions, also noted that "Wicca people have quite good intentions."

Shannon, a member of the Holly and Oak Pagan Discussion Group and editor of *Hecate's Loom,* told me the chapel is "gorgeous as a ritual place. It does feel like one of our own places. We put a lot of energy into it, and a lot of love. We have good working relationships with chaplains. We have come a long way."

Her attitude was a marked contrast to that of Robin Skelton who told me that he has never been in the chapel. He said he would not feel comfortable performing a ritual in such an environment and prefers the human scale of a private home.

Although Skelton and Kozocari are public witches to the extent that they are open about their beliefs and prepared to explain them publicly, their practice of witchcraft is essentially a private one. They seek public acceptance insofar as they would like to see their religion tolerated by the community, but they do not want it to become institutionalized and do not see it as playing an active role in society.

In contrast to this attitude, I encountered an almost missionary zeal among many of the younger witches. They talked enthusiastically about how Wicca had transformed their lives and can have that kind of impact on others. They were actively engaged in building and strengthening networks and organizations.

Bryony, one of the leaders of the campaign for the right to use the university chapel, told me that she dedicated herself to the Goddess in 1985 and since then has been ''carried along with the flow of a river. I can change my course as to which side I go to. Things happen so naturally as if fated that they happen. If I work towards a goal and the Goddess means it to happen, it will happen. It's my decision whether I go with the river, swim against it, or leave it entirely.''

Bryony is an academically inclined woman with long curly blonde hair and a distracted, dreamy air, which belies her obvious organizing abilities. She has a background in psychology and computer technology, and now runs a pagan bookstore and cares for her young son. She hopes to resume her academic studies when her husband has completed graduate school. She said she came to Wicca through feminism and from doing historical research on pre-Christian religions, while playing Dungeons and Dragons, a game which involves creating characters from history, legend and fantasy.

Shannon and Bryony describe themselves as spiritual people, brought up in Christian homes, who became disillusioned with what they term patriarchal religion. Both women told me that they had been greatly influenced by ancient mythology and a love of nature.

Shannon, a small, energetic young woman with an open and self-assured manner, is a poet and an organizer. She writes poetry for the magazine she edits, and is organizing the Pagan Academic Network, a cross-Canada association of witches and pagans who are teaching or studying in universities and colleges. She said the discovery of Wicca brought a profound change in her life: "All of a sudden you're being responsible for how you live, how you consume and how you work. There's a certain illumination in that. People see it. The structurelessness of paganism and Wicca demand that you are responsible for your own decisions, responsible for how you live. No-one is telling you. You have to make a commitment for yourself every day. Do you support the objectivity bullshit and biological determinism, or write bravely and strongly? It makes a difference. People have to challenge their own views, risking your ass and your grade point average all the time."

Nearly all the witches I talked to in Victoria told me that magic worked for them. Most of the examples they gave were of healing magic, but they also use it in their everyday lives. Many of them told stories about spells that backfired. One woman said she suffered immediate retribution for an angry spell she made against a man who had broken into her car. Within hours of casting the spell, she said, her car was towed away and impounded for a parking violation. There were stories about spells that worked too well—loves and jobs found through magic that turned into obsessions. And there were spells that were not specific enough: Kozocari told a story about calling for a carpet for her basement and having a friend ask the next day if she could store a carpet in the basement, the only problem being that the carpet was a big one and Kozocari had forgotten to specify in her spell that her basement was divided up by pillars.

None of the examples they gave were spectacular enough to convince the skeptic. Most people encounter coincidences or ironies in life by which hopes and wishes are fulfilled or are answered in strange ways. Many people understand that by working on their inner selves, strengthening their will, and clarifying their wishes, they can realize their dreams, provided those dreams are realistic. In the same way people who cultivate desires can poison their own minds with their cravings.

What the witches call magic could also be described as prayer, therapy, meditation, creative energy or optimism. The important thing for them is that it works and helps them transform their lives.

"It works even when you don't want it to," said Shannon. "Calling things to you. Calling forth your own strength. Leaving behind your own guilt. Healing. The small miracles that witches can do for themselves. Changing ourselves as part of changing the universe. Magic is for knowing yourself, knowing your environment. It is not for pretty tools that cost lots of money. Tools are props. If the trained mind and heart is with you, it works. If you try to do magic when you lie all the time, it isn't going to work. It's going to do horrid things."

Shannon said she is ambivalent about publicly drawing attention to herself as a witch — something that many witches struggle with. "I'm sort of out of the broom closet and sort of not," she said, "I want to be a high school teacher, and here in Vanderzalmland that's scary. Society doesn't like to have radicals in any position that has voice. So essentially it doesn't want us in the kind of work we do. Witches end up in the caring professions and communication, where people want milquetoast and someone who is not going to rock the boat. People care what the teacher is telling their ten-year-olds about life, gender roles, civic responsibility, responsibility for the planet, appropriate modes of living and being. People get worried."

"The image of the wicked witch is still up there. People don't see the good things we do. Running and hiding is very nice, very safe, until they find you. I hide a bit and try to smash down the image of the wicked witch a bit, providing I can do it from a safe spot,'' Shannon said.

Some strong disagreements have surfaced in the Victoria pagan community over the issue of how public and how organized the witches should be. Bryony is one of the co-founders of a group called Witches Invoking Tolerance Caring and Healing (WITCH). This is primarily an anti-defamation group, aiming to promote public understanding of Wicca. It is also considering proposals for setting up a religious body to perform marriages, have apprenticeship programs and initiate or ordain clergy.

Some local witches were not happy with the public stance that WITCH was taking. They feared that courting public favour would cheapen what witches stand for, expose them to public ridicule, and attract shallow thrill-seekers to the Craft.

Fenris, a very private Victoria witch who felt compelled to come out of her seclusion in order to denounce policies of WITCH, told me in a letter, ''I am fed up with all the silliness and wasted energy. There is so much that needs to be done, and here are these energetic people fussing about whether or not we can advertise our religion without getting harassed for it! They forget, or simply don't realize, that the Old Religion has a time-honoured tradition of secrecy, not just because of the persecution times, but also because those meant for it will find it anyway. Yes, the celebrations were open in the old days before the Christians, but the real mysteries cannot be taught, only experienced and in silence one finds wisdom. The best teachers can only show you what you already know.''

Responding to a letter from Fenris in *Hecate's Loom*, one of Victoria's younger witches wrote, ''I live within society, and I want to be understood. We are part of the process to change attitudes, to assist in the evolution of human consciousness. Wicca cannot be easily packaged. Does that mean we should not rise to the challenge? In the past, our silence when others maligned or libelled us was taken to mean we didn't disagree with their assessments and so we tacitly allowed the Hollywood myth to grow. We set ourselves up for burning when we don't have outside support, when we become islands from society, when we see ourselves as separate from any of the creatures of this planet, including other humans.''

Shannon has declined to join WITCH because she is afraid of it becoming a hierarchical structure. She said that the proposed apprenticeship program and plans for formal initiations of high priestesses have created a crisis in the local Wiccan community, and that the more important issues are getting lost. ''I don't care if we can't perform marriages,'' she said. ''I do care about single mothers who can't afford groceries and risk losing their children because their child says 'goddess' in front of a social worker, or a woman losing her children because her husband has turned fundamentalist [Christian] on her.''

Skelton also sees a danger in the trend towards formal organization. One of the great strengths of the Craft is that it is essentially anarchistic and doesn't have a hierarchy, he told me. He said he is afraid of commercialism creeping into the religion and sees that happening at psychic fairs where people try to sell him crystals, photographs of auras and snake oil. ''It's odd for a witch to keep quoting the Bible, but one thinks of the money changers in the temple.''

''It is not a religion of the book and I don't think we ever should be,'' he said. ''I think it's going to spread because it seems to be doing so, with different groups, with different traditions in different places. I fear that somebody may try to unify the whole thing under an overarching system. I fear it as I fear a rigid orthodoxy.''

To Skelton, Wicca's potential for transforming society is no greater than other movements with which witches associate. Witches, he said, are concerned with ecology, sympathetic to feminism, against censorship, in favour of freedom of religion and freedom of speech. Wicca will not be a social force in itself, but the movements that witches support may be.

''A lot of witches are still in the closet. There are more of us around than are likely to admit it. As I see it, we may have a quiet, and perhaps pervasive, influence but I don't see it as being a social movement,'' Skelton said.

Kozocari is also a little worried the way younger witches are so ''gung-ho'' in their quest for public approval. ''I don't feel witchcraft is for everybody,'' she said, ''We have existed the way we are without a lot of public approval for a long time. I have a feeling that if Christianity would have remained in the catacombs it would have remained more as it started out to be.''

Although there are divisions and conflicts within pagan circles in Victoria, I did find that, unlike in most other areas in Canada, there were the makings of a genuine community of witches. Older traditional witches and more radical young feminists were co-operating, communicating and showing respect for one another. This was probably due to a combination of Kozocari's and Skelton's uniquely open and flexible form of traditional witchcraft, and the tolerant and soft-edged radicalism of the younger witches.

The young witches of Victoria are anxious to receive the sanction and acceptance of society. It remains to be seen whether their community can retain its cohesion and integrity once it achieves that public recognition.

CHAPTER FIVE

Witchcraft in Ontario: The Wiccan Church of Canada

"Witchcraft doesn't pay for broken windows," Gerald Gardner was warned in 1939, when he asked the witches of the New Forest why they practiced their religion in secret.

But a broken window did not deter Tamarra and Richard James from practicing their religion openly in Toronto and building up a business that has proven that witchcraft can pay. Their window was broken by a brick on the night they first held a public circle in their small store on Queen Street West in May 1979. Now they run a wholesale business called White Witch Products and own stores in Ottawa and Toronto.

The Wiccan Church of Canada, which they founded as a non-profit corporation in 1979, has grown to be the largest and best known public Wiccan group in the country. It has won a large measure of public acceptance for witchcraft in the Toronto area, by providing the media with a public face for the Craft and giving interested individuals a place where they can attend Wiccan rituals and classes. In obtaining permission to minister to members of its congregation in jails and hospitals, the WCC has proved to government agencies and Christian church representatives that witchcraft is a respectable religious faith.

The success of the James' businesses and the popularity of the Wiccan Church are indications of a burgeoning interest in witchcraft in Ontario. The witches of Ontario are, like witches everywhere, a diverse population. But Ontario witches, unlike those on the west coast, tend not to stray outside their own circles. Perhaps this is a reflection of the generally less friendly, more frantic and fragmented way of life that is found in Ontario. In the Toronto area, there is little intermingling and communication among the different Wiccan groups. Witches in Ottawa have made recent attempts to build bridges between different groups after years of sectarian hostility. However, one does not find anywhere in Ontario the kind of intergenerational, non-sectarian community of witches that exists in Victoria.

The Wiccan Church of Canada tends to dominate the public witchcraft scene in Ontario because it is the largest and most visible group.But the concept of a Wiccan church is an anathema and a contradiction to many traditional witches, who believe that the true essence of the Craft can only be maintained by remaining in small underground groups. The WCC is an established church in a movement that traditionally avoids all institutional structures.

Like any establishment, it occupies a middle-ground with which few people are entirely satisfied and which many love to hate. If you talk to any witch for long enough, almost anywhere in Canada, the conversation will sooner or later turn to the subject of the Wiccan Church. Some will tell you that they are embarrassed by its eccentricity, ashamed of its shallowness, annoyed by its stodginess or outraged by its arrogance. Others will say they are impressed with the breadth of its vision, the conscientiousness with which it educates people in the Craft and its levelheadedness in dealing with the public.

Conservative witches criticize the church for popularizing their traditions, while radical witches see it as hidebound and hierarchical. For the media and members of the public in the Toronto area, and particularly for the 1500 people who have gone through its doors in the past ten years, the Wiccan Church has been the first, and often the only, exposure to ancient pagan ways.

While the concept of forming a church of Wicca is not popular with traditional witches, Tamarra, the High Priestess of the church, justifies it by citing older traditions from pre-Christian times. The old pagan religions were public institutions with a priesthood that ministered to a laity. During the times of persecution, the religion was kept alive by a priesthood that went into hiding. They only taught the craft to people they knew and trusted, and then only after those people had made the commitment of joining a coven and pledging an oath of secrecy.

Without having a laity to serve, according to Tamarra, the priesthood became a sterile, incestuous elite. Now, she maintains, there is no need for that any more. Instead of just preserving the traditions of the Craft, the new priests and priestesses of Wicca can help it flower again by serving a large number of lay people, who want to worship the old Gods and Goddesses, but don't want to devote their lives to studying witchcraft.

The WCC has an active membership of about 400 people. It has an inner circle of about 14 priestesses or priests, who practice the Craft privately in covens, but also give classes and lead public rituals for the lay members. Having moved several times to accommodate its ever-increasing following, the church now occupies a drab three-storey building on Vaughan Road, a distinctly unfashionable area just outside Toronto's downtown core. The building houses the temple of the church, apartments where some members live and the Occult Shop, which is owned by Richard and Tamarra James.

The Wiccan tradition of not charging money for magic is honoured by the WCC in that no-one is charged for attending classes and circles, and the church operates as a non-profit corporation. There is obviously, however, a symbiotic relationship between the church and the James' businesses. People who attend classes and rituals are inevitably inspired to buy books, candles, jewellery, crystals, herbs and other items from the store.

From the street, the building does not present an inviting prospect. The entrance is marked only by a black pentagram painted on the wall with the words "Occult Shop" and an arrow pointing to a door between a shabby laundromat and a tattooing studio. The large store, which is located on the second floor, does a flourishing business in spite of its inauspicious location. It caters to members of the church and Toronto witches from other traditions. It also sells herbs and other religious supplies to some of the members of Toronto's West Indian community who practice Santeria. This is a religion that evolved in Caribbean and Latin American countries where ancient African pagan beliefs became intermingled with Christianity so that the Christian saints took on the characters and attributes of African Gods and Goddesses.

Although it is ostensibly an open public group, the WCC follows the Wiccan tradition of not advertising itself or proselytizing. Everyone is welcome to the church's Sunday evening circle, providing they are not under the influence of drugs or alcohol or exhibiting some other obviously antisocial tendencies. But little is done to encourage the merely curious or to reassure the faint-hearted.

I felt quite uneasy when I first walked into one of these Sunday gatherings. I had found my way up the stairs to the Occult Shop. It was closed and there was no sign to indicate where in the building the temple is located. I waited in the empty corridor for someone else to arrive. A young woman with purple hair came in, dressed in black. She returned my nervous smile with a blank stare, and I followed her through a metal fire door and into a room where about fifty people were waiting. Many of them were young people, but there were a few older men and women too. Some of the women were wearing long gowns and headbands, but what was disquietening for the neophyte was that several men were wearing ominous-looking black hooded cloaks. One of these, a thick-set man with a black beard, was holding a heavy wooden staff.

I was greeted with neither warmth nor hostility, but simply a casual indifference. My first impression was of a slightly sinister clique that did not welcome outsiders. This was a false impression, as I later realized. It was not a clique, but a collection of two or three different cliques and several other outsiders. They really were not a sinister group of people—just shy and extremely cool.

After an uncomfortable wait of about half an hour—WCC rituals are always spectacularly late getting started—the ice was broken by a man in a black cloak who was carrying a clip board.

''Can anyone take shorthand?'' he asked and received no reply. He tried again, ''Can anyone write very fast?''

As no-one else showed any interest in what he was saying, I ventured to say that I have had occasion to take notes at public gatherings. With no further questioning, I was thereby appointed scribe for the Norse ritual that was planned for that evening.

My lingering uneasiness about the nature of the ritual in which I was about to participate was somewhat assuaged by the heavy man with the thick staff. This man, I later learned, was the summoner, who calls people into the circle and stands guard to keep intruders out. He beat his staff on the floor and announced that the circle would begin in five minutes. This meant that it was time for everyone to take their shoes and socks off, and, for the surprisingly large proportion of the group who were heavy smokers, an opportunity for a last cigarette.

''Let those now come forward who would be ritually cleansed, who would be free of malice, and who would bear no ill towards any person,'' the summoner said, ''All must enter the circle without thoughts of retribution towards those who have wronged them. Let your entry into the circle divest you of all those grievous hurts and wrongs that the world has inflicted upon you. Only if you can dispense with these negative things can you acquire the positive benefits to be found within.''

Doubts and fears that were quelled by soothing words of the summoner's charge began to resurface as lights were extinguished and I was led to the ritual chamber nervously clutching the clipboard I had been given. Since I attended my first circle, the gathering place where people assembled beforehand has been changed so that it is now a room next door to the third floor temple area where the rituals are held. But at that time it was a second floor room, and that meant that to enter the circle it was customary for everyone to walk through darkened corridors and up a flight of stairs. I found myself shivering, not only from the sensation of bare feet on a cold floor, but also from the tension of moving from everyday reality into a world of shadows.

The temple was a large bare room, formerly used as warehousing space. The walls were completely black and on the floor a large white pentacle had been painted. The only illumination came from candles and bare factory windows through which some light filtered in from the moon and the city night. The group filed in solemnly and stood around the circle, repeating an eerie wordless chant. At the centre of the circle was a small altar bearing figurines of the God and Goddess, a large earthenware chalice, athame, a ritual knife and other ceremonial objects.

The air of magic and mystery began to dissipate as the ritual began. As the robed priest and priestess spoke the words for invoking the elemental powers, the guardians of the east, south, west and north, I became conscious of the theatrical element that is present in all liturgy. Perhaps because they were that night performing a Norse ceremony that they were not used to, there was some stumbling over the lines. As everyone turned to salute the spirits that were summoned from each of the four directions, I looked around the congregation, just as one would in an unfamiliar church of any denominations in order to know when one should stand, kneel or sit. I noticed that other people were doing the same thing.

In a sense, the Wiccan Church circles are like any conventional religious service. People follow ritual forms with as much feeling and reverence as they can muster. They sing songs with great gusto and some discord. Prayers are chanted in unison up to the point where half the congregation has forgotten the words and the chant becomes a little ragged.

If one was to compare the Wiccan circles with a church service, it would have to be a combination of the solemnity and ceremony of a Roman Catholic High Mass together with the ecstatic enthusiasm of a revivalist meeting. The Wiccan Church performs scripted rituals involving wine, incense and candles, as well as a series of objects whose use is foreign to Christian observances. The witches' circle also draws upon the personal energy of all the individuals in it, fusing this into an intense communal experience.

The words of the chants and rituals speak of earthly love and pleasures, gods and goddesses in natural forms, and the cycle of birth, death and rebirth in this world. People join hands or put arms around one another as they sing and chant, and they dance or sway rhythmically back and forth. Their worship is mingled with laughter and joy. A primitive energy emerges as the Toronto witches stamp their feet in time with their favourite chant: "Hoof and horn, hoof and horn: whatever dies will be reborn. Corn and grain, corn and grain: all that falls must rise again."

Ancient Greek myths are the most common source of the Wiccan Church rituals. But, like almost all witches, the WCC members believe that the God and the Goddess are universal principles that were known in different cultures by different names. Sometimes they will choose a ritual from a different mythology. At the first circle I attended, they performed the Braga, a Norse ceremony. The custom of drinking from the Braga Cup and making a solemn pledge originated at the funeral of an Icelandic king and the ritual was at first associated with weddings and funerals. But it is believed that it became an annual New Year ceremony.

The Braga was the kind of ritual one can easily imagine the Vikings inventing. It involved passing around cups of alcoholic beverage, quaffing heartily and bragging about how much conquering and pillaging they were going to do in the future.

Although it was in the form of a big party, it also had important religious significance. It was a way in which the Vikings would dedicate their lives to the Gods, and make everything they were hoping to accomplish in the year an offering to the deity. The Braga was also the beginning of a year-long competition in which the Vikings would all vie with one another to be the most successful in accomplishing the feats they had boasted of—the conquest of England was one such boast. At the next Braga, they would enter a good-humoured debate about whether they had fulfilled their pledges.

The Braga that was performed at the Wiccan Church was certainly less raucous and abandoned than one imagines the Viking ceremony would have been. However, it does illustrate one quite striking difference between a pagan ritual and a Christian church service. Although the Christian communion service does commemorate a feast, the Last Supper, it would be considered blasphemous by most Christians if members of a congregation were to laugh, joke and heartily swig the communion wine. For witches, laughter and play are just as much a form of worship as prayer. Wiccan traditions quote the Goddess as saying, "All acts of love and pleasure are my rituals."

In spite of the joviality and good humour that the Toronto witches brought to their Braga, the overwhelming impression was that most of them were very serious, almost earnest, about their religious beliefs. Many of the brags were about the things that people were planning to do in relation to their study of Wicca. The WCC holds weekly classes in the Craft in subjects that include the meaning of the Sabbats, the principles of magic, divination, robe making, the mythologies of different culture, pagan ethics and public relations. Each class has homework assignments, and members of the church have to complete a substantial number of classes before they are initiated as witches. As the cup was passed round the circle, one person after another boasted about plans for attending all the classes, completing all the homework, making robes, reading books, writing rituals, and researching Greek or Celtic mythology.

Many people talked about plans for their personal lives. They spoke of opening businesses, finding jobs, getting in shape, acquiring new skills, resolving problems in relationships—ordinary everyday concerns that one might hear in any group where people are open and comfortable enough to speak publicly of their personal goals. There were a few resolutions that hinted at more exotic pursuits, like a woman who talked about her pet snakes, and another who wanted to train her cat to sit on her shoulder like the witch's familiar in popular folklore. In spite of the Viking roots of the ceremony, there was little talk of aggressive pursuits, though two people did say they planned to improve their skill in Oriental martial arts and one person did brag about going hunting and returning with the biggest buck.

The boasts were mostly so serious and respectable that I found myself quite relieved when I heard something mischievous. That came from the daughter of one of the church members, the only child present, who resolved that she would "try to beat every boy in my class's face in, because they are slimy dirt bags."

Of course, that ambition is not exactly in keeping with the Wiccan ethic of not hurting others, as she no doubt well knew. I had been wondering about the morality of bringing up children in the Wiccan religion. I was questioning whether a child should be in a witches' circle, even though I realized it was an unfair question in that one never challenges the right of other parents to take their children to conventional religious services or classes. I was reassured to see that the girl was having fun at the ceremony and was feeling free to be a little rebellious.

I subsequently asked High Priestess Tamarra James about the role of children in the Wiccan Church. She told me that members do organize circles and an annual Yule celebration for their children, but will not encourage them to commit themselves to the Wiccan faith until they are old enough to make a decision and have had some exposure to other religious beliefs. Wiccans believe that each person has his or her own path to walk in life and must discover that alone. They pride themselves on never pressuring anyone else to adopt their beliefs.

"Because I believe in all the Gods I have no problem with there being a few more here and there. The important thing is tolerance," Tamarra told me.

One of the very basic lessons that I learned from attending the Braga was that, once one got beyond the initial impressions created by the dress and demeanour of many of those present, they were a diverse group of quite ordinary people. This is one of the messages that Tamarra tries to get across in her unofficial role as public relations spokesperson for her group and the Toronto pagan community in general.

A good-looking dark-haired woman, who once worked as a model and a hair-dressing instructor, Tamarra does not come across as threatening or spooky. Present and former members of the priesthood in the Wiccan church include a doctor, a policeman, a secretary in the armed forces, a computer technologist, office workers, nurses and business people. Many church members are students and they specialize in a wide range of disciplines from watchmaking to linguistics, from law to therapeutic massage.

In Ottawa many of the church members are federal civil servants. Some of them are forced to be secretive about their beliefs. One woman told me that she couldn't identify herself as a witch because she feared losing her job. She explained that the work she does requires security clearance, and one is considered a security risk if one belongs to a secret organization. The reason for this is that one might be subjected to blackmail. But in her case the only form that blackmail might take would be a threat to tell the security services about her affiliation.

By being open and above ground in their practice of witchcraft, Tamarra believes that church members can refute negative public images and misconceptions, ''just by who we are, and the various ways we are. We don't live together, have a diet we follow, dress the same or take any drugs.''

Even among those people in the Toronto pagan community who do not belong to the Wiccan Church, Tamarra is generally well respected for the depth of her knowledge and commitment to the Craft. Her own life story, as she tells it, is one of deepening appreciation for the richness of witchcraft, which she first espoused during a period of teenage rebellion. She said that the Craft she practices today is much more balanced than what she knew in the 1960s. Then, she said, she and her friends put a lot of emphasis on the Goddess in a knee-jerk reaction to patriarchal religion. They valued witchcraft to some extent for its shock value.

''It took me years to explain to my mother that the Craft was not what we looked and felt in those days,'' she said. ''A lot of us grew up, and discovered a richness and a depth with the Craft that we just scratched the surface of.''

Tamarra was born in Victoria, British Columbia, where her parents were prominent members of the community. Her mother was the city's first female alderman. She lived on a farm as a young child with her grandparents. She did not have much exposure to religion, until she moved back to the city and found that most of her friends were going to church. She began attending an Anglican church, learned the catechism, and prepared for her first communion.

''Maybe I was expecting too much,'' she said. ''I had a little white dress and went to the rail. I was excited. I was twelve. It was very ceremonious, but it didn't do anything for me.''

She compared this ceremony, which she found meaningless, with her own profound personal experience of her first menstruation. The church not only did not celebrate this rite of passage, but, she found, tended to denigrate it.

"When I had my period, my Mom was really neat. We went for dinner, had wine, and were women. Then at church I got all this stuff about women being evil. I couldn't correlate the two things. I stopped going."

At the age of 15, she began hanging around in a coffee house, reading all the witchcraft books she could find, most of which she now regards as "garbage." She used to carry them around with her in order to look witchy. She met people who introduced her to better books on the subject and eventually found out they were in the Craft. They invited her to a circle, which seemed like a "coming home" to her. She said it was a relevatory experience in the way that her first communion had failed to be.

In the mid-1970s, Tamarra married Richard, a television lighting technician, whose only experience with witchcraft had been with a group of "doper-magicians." They became involved with a group in California that held public rituals in the Sorcerer's Shop in Hollywood. Disturbed by the number of "very freaky people" who tended to spoil the services for the more serious students of Wicca, they started their own coven. After living in New York for six months and getting involved in an occult store and Wiccan circles there, they moved to Toronto and opened their own store in the spring of 1979.

Apart from the brick being thrown through the window and an attempt by one group of people to exorcise the store, Tamarra said they found they were generally well received by the community. "Mind you, we don't do anything spooky," she said, "I'll talk to anybody rationally. We don't do power trips and head games. I look like anybody else. I'm just not a highly threatening individual."

Occult stores play an important role in the pagan community. Besides being a place where witches can buy herbs, books, tools and other religious items, they serve as meeting places and information centres. They often provide people with their first contact with Wicca and other pagan or magical traditions. People with a serious interest in the Craft can usually find someone at an occult store who will help them with their studies and eventually put them in touch with covens or other Wiccan groups. Those with a more casual interest can become better informed about Wicca while browsing, consulting a Tarot card reader, or even obtaining materials and instructions for casting a simple spell.

Many occult stores actually create very bad public relations for Wicca, because they cultivate a spooky image and cater to the prurient. One often sees signs in such stores suggesting that shoplifters will be dealt with in devious magical ways. In the James' Ottawa store a sign, saying "Shoplifters will be frogged," can only be taken in fun. But such signs in other stores often display skeletons and ominous warnings like "You will be getting into more trouble than you bargained for." A dark decor, a predominance of black candles and crystal skulls, and ominously witchy looking store-keepers make such places appealing to many rebellious adolescents but uncomfortable and off-putting for others.

Many occult store owners do have some trouble with customers who are interested only in sex or black magic, and teenagers who visit the store for a giggle. Some deal with such situations better than others. Patricia Phillips, the owner of Otherworld, a small Toronto store, told me that she sometimes resorts to magic on such occasions: "A couple of groups of young boys were bulleting me with questions. They all started to feel a bit sick right then. I was upset and they had shocked me. Sometimes, when your emotions get a bit out of hand, things jump."

Inevitably there are stores, particularly those catering more to New Age consumers, that create a negative impression by overcharging their customers. Dohbran, who runs the James' Occult Shop in Ottawa, is worried that the public will ultimately become disillusioned with the occult as a result of its commercial exploitation. She said crystals she buys for $2 and sells at a modest mark-up are routinely sold in other stores for ten times their value. She told me that she is aware of people selling $7 talismans for more than $200, claiming that they have been imbued with magical properties.

''Sooner or later the buying public is going to wake up to the fact that it is being gouged by people who are offering enlightenment,'' she said.

While, at first, somewhat uneasy about selling the potions that the Jameses market as White Witch Products, Dohbran, who is not a member of the Wiccan Church, said she has come to regard these items as not only ethical but beneficial. She said people looking for magical solutions to their problems are being given some tangible objects that they can work with, together with instructions about how to use them in their lives.

The concept of empowering people to work on enriching their own lives is a central one for the Wiccan Church. Like any church, it provides personal as well as spiritual counselling. Magic is an element of the religion, as in all forms of Wicca, but is not strongly emphasized.

''I use magic as a last resort. It is part of the elitism, the mystique that causes people to be afraid of witchcraft,'' said Tamarra. ''Magic is prayer. We do it in different ways. Every faith has it. And even people who are not essentially religious have little rituals of magic.''

With its robes and incense, flaming cauldrons and elaborate rituals, there is certainly a mystique attached to the Wiccan Church circles. But their mysteries are quite similar to those that give religious people of all faiths cause to meditate: life and death, birth and change.

On the Sabbats the church performs mystery plays, dramatic recreations of old myths. One such play performed on the Sunday before the Yule Sabbat re-enacted the ritual slaying of the Holly King, the God of the old year, by the Oak King, the God of the new year. The body of the old God was placed under the Yule tree, and the witches danced joyously around the man who represented the corpse of the God, as they decorated the tree with fruit.

From some perspectives, this appears as a macabre ceremony, perhaps, but it is not necessarily any more so than Christian rituals representing the death of Jesus on the cross. In fact some witches maintain that the crucifixion of Christ was a recreation of this old pagan myth, and that the celebration of the birth of Christ at Christmas was timed to coincide with the victory of the Oak King, which symbolized the rebirth of the Sun.

The Yule Tree is certainly a pagan tradition, which predates Christianity. The Wiccan Church members also celebrate Yule by giving presents, and I heard at least one witch making the mistake of referring to them as Christmas presents. On the night of the winter solstice another mystery play was performed. This recalled a Greek myth in which Persephone, the daughter of the goddess Demeter, was forced to spend six months of the year in the underworld during which time the earth was barren. The Yule tree was decorated with flowers to anticipate Persephone's return and the fertility of summer. The feast that follows every Sabbat ritual is considered part of the ceremony and participants were encouraged to take their food into the temple and honour the God and Goddess with "laughter, wit and wine."

In the summer the Wiccan Church holds its circles in a nearby park. This provides an odd spectacle for a few curious onlookers, but inspires no-one to throw any more bricks.

The WCC has done a good public relations job for witchcraft in Ontario. It has, however, tended to generate hostility among other witches. Many of the witches from other traditions whom I have interviewed in Ontario have, for different and sometimes opposite reasons, expressed quite vehement objections to the style and substance of the WCC.

It seems strange that such an ostensibly inoffensive organization should inspire so much ill-will amongst a group of people who regard tolerance as a prime virtue. The reasons for this hostility lie partly in sectarian and political differences. It can also be attributed to personality conflicts and the unquestionable cliquishness of many WCC members who find a wide enough society within their own group that they do not need to socialize with outsiders. But the most basic cause of the conflict between the WCC and the other witches of Ontario is the problem that Victoria witches are also grappling with, though in a more amicable way. That is the dilemma of how to reconcile the unstructured, underground nature of traditional witchcraft with the desire of many modern witches for public acceptance and official sanction.

CHAPTER SIX

Conflicts among Witches

"Perfect love and perfect trust" are the traditional passwords for initiation into a coven. The phrase represents the kind of total understanding and acceptance that witches feel they must have in order to work together.

But the present-day Craft is beset with factional differences. There are many versions of witchcraft and the followers of each often engage in disputes over strongly held philosophical conflicts. This tendency towards infighting is notorious among witches and is sometimes referred to as "bitchcraft."

It is a problem that is not unique to witchcraft. Christianity has suffered over the years from a similar problem that has had much more dire consequences than the witches' squabbles, which seldom get beyond angry exchanges of letters in Wiccan journals.

Of course, with witches as with followers of organized religions, the majority are tolerant peaceful people, who are aggrieved by the bitterness of such disputes and see them as a betrayal of the basic tenets of their religion. Wicca is supposed to be a tolerant religion, which does not attempt to convert other people. Witches generally believe that different people have their own paths to walk in life and should be allowed to do so in peace. They do not claim to follow the one true faith and tend to take issue only with those Christians who confront them with Jesus Christ's pronouncement, "He who is not with me is against me."

But it is rare to find a witch who will not be inclined to make the odd joke about some other Wiccan groups or individuals. As the witches explained their own beliefs and practices in interviews with me, they almost all felt it necessary to distinguish themselves from others whom they found too superficial, too hierarchical, too sexist or too radical.

"So much could be learned between the various groups, if only they'd sit down and talk to each other," said one Ontario witch, "but people are more willing to play head games and ego trips and power trips and money trips."

The basic problem is that witches don't agree about what a witch is. Some will tell you that a witch is someone who has been properly initiated in a coven that can trace its lineage directly to Gerald Gardner. Others would agree with a Vancouver witch who told me that if a woman says, "I'm a witch," three times and means it, then she is one. Anyone who accepts either of these definitions would tend to see the other point of view as an insult to his or her own beliefs.

Between these two polarities, there are many different Wiccan groups, each of which has its own distinct character. All observe the same Sabbats and recognize a deity that manifests itself in nature. They all agree with the precept "Do what you will, if it harms none," though some prefer to couch it in archaic language. Most other issues are open to debate, and, when the debate involves questions of gender and politics, it can get quite heated.

There is no scripture and no dogma in witchcraft, no revealed truth or widely accepted body of belief that is sanctioned by some recognized authority. Covens are autonomous and there is no higher organizational structure. There are a few networks of Wiccan groups that have come together over a particular cause or common interest, but these cannot and do not claim to speak for all witches.

This lack of overall structure and the stress on an oral rather than a written tradition has its advantages in that it means that the religion is less likely to become hidebound and irrelevant to the needs of the individual believers. Each generation is able to adapt the tradition to its own times and every individual can follow the dictates of the God and the Goddess within. In times of persecution the autonomy of individual covens was a necessity, as it made it impossible for the church or state authorities to destroy the whole movement.

It also means that when disputes arise over Wiccan ethics or theology there is no final arbiter who can settle them and no accepted body of belief that can serve as a reference point for argument. One person will refer to an oral Wiccan tradition that was recorded in a book in the 1950s and another will reply that what her grandmother taught her was different. Some groups base their beliefs on those of ancient Greek, Egyptian or Celtic cultures, but others may challenge them on the grounds that their understanding of these ancient cultures is incomplete or that it is totally irrelevant to present day realities.

A controversy that filled several pages of three consecutive issues of *Harvest,* a Wiccan magazine published in Massachusetts, well illustrates the way in which sensitive present-day issues can become confused with a debate about ancient cultures. Dobhran, an Ottawa witch who runs an occult store and is very concerned about the public image of the Craft, was bothered by an article in *Harvest* advocating free love as a true pagan response to patriarchal morality. The article justified an aggressive approach to sexual liberation with reference to ancient Greek practices. Dobhran wrote a reasoned response stating that this attitude is dangerous in view of the AIDS virus, fails to appreciate the importance of love, intimacy and mutual respect in sexual relations, and is the kind of thing that gives witches a bad name. She said the ancient Greeks were not to be regarded as ethical models as they were sexist and militaristic, and sometimes indulged in human sacrifice.

This letter elicited an angry reply from the author of the article, who said Dobhran was defending Christian monogamy. The ancient Greeks that she was referring to were not as ancient as the ones cited in the article, the author said. She was referring to a degeneration of Greek paganism, which occurred after a patriarchal social system was imposed, the author added. When I last spoke with Dobhran, she was composing a lengthy and scholarly response, which she said was designed to show that it makes no sense to use historical arguments without examining the real present-day issues.

The question of what image the Craft is presenting to the general public was the central underlying theme of this debate, and other similar controversies that one finds in the many small journals and newsletters that are a feature of Wiccan culture. For some people, witchcraft is an expression of their rebellion against the mainstream society and culture, or a spiritual vehicle for social change. For others, it is a private religion and a way of life that can co-exist quite comfortably in any society that allows it to do so. The former want to use Wicca as a vehicle for changing society, while all the latter want is privacy.

These two groups are on a collision course. The radicals tend to see the traditionalists as failing to live out the principles of a religion based on respect for nature, which should oppose a society that exploits the earth. The traditionalists regard the radicals as people who have latched onto Wicca for their own political ends. Many traditional witches consider themselves to be feminists and environmentalists, but do not believe that the Craft is primarily a vehicle for political change. They feel particularly aggrieved at being accused of a lack of commitment to their ideals, when their position is simply one of not mixing religion with politics.

The same kind of controversy is also argued in theological terms since more radical feminists emphasize the Goddess, while traditionalist practices are based on the concept of balance between the Goddess and the God. The spontaneity and eclecticism of feminist Wicca is sometimes scorned by traditional witches as lacking in discipline and depth, while radicals look down on what they see as a sterile ''living-room Craft.''

Gardnerians and other traditional groups believe that the Craft is, and should be, an underground tradition in which secrecy is one of the sacred laws. Ironically, the Wiccan tradition that is most adamant about keeping the rituals of the Craft secret was founded by the person most responsible for letting these secrets out of the bag, directly by what he wrote in his published books and then through subsequent publication of other material he had collected. During his life as a practicing witch, Gerald Gardner compiled three personal Books of Shadows, one of which is now owned by Richard and Tamarra James. Although these manuscripts were supposedly secret, so many handwritten copies existed that inevitably most of the secrets found their way into print, often in slightly garbled forms. Two Irish witches, Janet and Stewart Farrar, eventually decided to include a complete version of Gardner's rituals in their book *A Witches Bible Compleat.*

Gardnerians' propensity to preserve secrets that have already been made public is often joked about by witches from more public traditions. One such joke is ''How many Gardnerians does it take to change a light bulb? It's a Craft secret.''

However, there is a sensible rationale for the attitude of Gardnerians and other traditionalists. It is, for one thing, a way of maintaining privacy and many Gardnerians are well-established professionals or otherwise conventional people, who do not want their colleagues or neighbours to know that they are witches. They also want to avoid casual public interest in such practices as ritual scourging and nakedness. In Gardnerian initiation ceremonies, the initiate is lightly beaten with a scourge, consisting of eight lengths of knotted cord attached to a wooden handle. The purpose of this is to induce a hypnotic effect by slowing down the circulation and to symbolize the concept that in order to learn one must be prepared to suffer. Some people have claimed that this is not a traditional element of witchcraft and was included by Gardner in his rituals because of his own sexual proclivities. Gardnerians and some other witches perform their rituals skyclad, though most Canadian witches do not.

A British Columbia witch with a Gardnerian background wrote in a letter, "People I know usually work robed. Skyclad is for use only among people who know and trust each other completely and all feel comfortable with it. No room here for coercion or voyeurism, although I know that happens in some groups. Working skyclad is very powerful in appropriate conditions. One of the nicest things about the homestead is that I have 40 acres, much of it treed, so I don't have to worry about invasions of privacy."

Many of the rituals of witchcraft have their origins in seasonal fertility rites, and sexual interaction plays an important part in Wiccan circles. This does not usually involve more than kissing, hugging, courting games and the symbolic representation of sexual intercourse by plunging a dagger into a chalice of wine. The Great Rite — a ceremony that culminates in a couple making love—is not often performed, but it is generally accepted as a legitimate element in the practices of witchcraft. As one might expect among adherents of a religion that incorporates sexual intercourse into its most sacred ceremonies, witches often have an uninhibited approach to sexuality in their everyday lives.

Present-day witches are often forced to be defensive concerning their beliefs about sex and nakedness because of what they see as an unhealthy and prurient attitude to these things among other members of the public. Many witches have told me that they are almost as sick of answering questions about nudity and sexual mores as they are of explaining that they are not satanists and do not practice black magic.

Among witches who are open and public about their religious beliefs, there is some debate over whether they should flaunt their sexually liberated attitudes or present a more sober conservative public face. Some witches maintain that it is necessary to be discreet about this issue, simply because they believe that sex is natural and holy, and that is something that most people in our culture are not able to understand and respect. Others criticize the more discreet attitude as buying into the Judeo-Christian morality and trying to present a false image of witches as "goody-goodies."

Witches are a very diverse group of people, and they include those who lead monogamous life-styles as well as those who are sexually active in various different ways. Among non-monogamous witches, as with other sexually active people today, there is a lot of concern about AIDS and other sexually transmitted diseases. "Is it still the Great Rite, if you have to use a condom?" asked one correspondent in a Wiccan newsletter. The same newsletter later announced that someone had come up with the idea of a "Condom consecration ritual."

It makes sense for many witches who regard Wicca as a profound body of mystical teachings and forms of worship to stay out of this kind of public debate about matters that they consider peripheral to their faith. The easiest way to avoid getting involved in controversy and confrontation is to stay private and underground. Many have been discouraged from being more open about their beliefs because of what they see as the superficiality of some of the more public groups. One witch told me that in her opinion the Wiccan Church of Canada almost single-handedly drove all the other Wiccan groups underground, when it was first established in Toronto in the late 1970s, by adopting promotional gimmicks such as a spell to aid the Toronto Argonauts in a Grey Cup game.

"People read books, buy capes and candles, call themselves witches and proceed to act and speak in ways ranging from pernicious to just plain silly. This kind of thing has done more harm to the Craft than the persecution of the Middle Ages," members of Isis Urania, a traditional Toronto coven, stated in a pamphlet called *Wicca, the*

Ancient Way, published privately in 1981. A member of this group explained to me that they published the pamphlet, which provided a general introduction to Wiccan beliefs, to counteract negative images of the craft that they felt were being propagated by more public witches in Ontario.

The purpose of secrecy is not just to avoid public exposure. Traditional Wiccan groups believe that they possess a complex and powerful system of teachings, ritual and magic which could be misused if it fell into the wrong hands. They fear that their teachings could be distorted, their rituals trivialized and their magic directed to evil purposes.

Witches believe in the power of their own magic, and feel that this power is something that they have to take responsibility for. They do not have a concept of sin and they believe that, in order to act wisely and use magical powers well, one has to have a clear understanding of the nature of the universe and one's role in it. To impart fragments of their magical knowledge to people who are not dedicated to learning the laws of nature would, in the view of most witches, be like giving matches to a young child.

This may seem like a patronizing view. But most of us are like children with regard to the sophistication of our understanding of magic. People tend not to take it seriously. They are not fully aware of its positive uses and negative effects, and are therefore apt to play with it.

The magical teachings of Wicca are embodied within a complex system of practical knowledge and religious beliefs that traditional witches believe can only be passed on to a suitably dedicated student within the closed confines of a coven. They believe that their teachings could be dangerous, if imparted in any other way.

Witches are cautious about who they take into their covens. Although they do not now have to worry about someone turning them in to the inquisitors, they do have to consider whether the person seeking initiation as a witch is what they consider to be a proper person, ideally someone who is open, courageous and curious, as well as kind and honourable. It also has to be someone who members of a coven feel that they would like to work with in an intense and intimate setting.

What most traditional witches see as central to their Craft is not the script of the rituals that one can find written in books, nor the more theatrical or titillating aspects of these rituals that appeal to the public imagination. For them the true secret of the Craft is the magic and spiritual intensity that evolves from the experience of performing these rituals with a dedicated and intimate group of fellow practitioners. This is the secret that they cannot share, because it can only be learned through experience.

"The Craft is rich with unspeakable secrets and mysteries well guarded by the fact that they cannot be expressed in words to those who are unready, for they will not be able to understand," the authors of *Wicca, the Ancient Way* state.

A great disadvantage of the unstructured nature of Wicca is that it makes it more difficult to achieve public recognition and acceptance. Many witches say that they do not want this anyway. But some would like to have their religion legally recognized as a legitimate faith, so that their organizations could receive charitable donations and their clergy could perform marriages. The difficulty that is encountered is that once people in authority have been convinced that Wicca is not a subversive or unethical movement they begin to ask questions like "Who ordains the clergy?", "What central body are they answerable to?" and "Who is in a position to say which people are legitimate Wiccan priests and priestesses?"

Wiccan individuals or groups sometimes present themselves as representatives or leaders of the Craft, in order to satisfy the requirements of bureaucratic bodies. They often encounter criticism from other witches, who distrust their motives, do not like the way they present themselves and do not accept them as leaders. Such situations tend to confuse government bureaucrats and leaders of other religions, who will then decide not to deal with Wiccans until they present some semblance of unity.

Toronto witch Charles Arnold fell foul of this kind of conflict and is afraid that his failure may have set back the cause he was fighting for. Arnold, who has practiced witchcraft for about ten years, works as a secretary at Humber College of Applied Arts and Technology. He is an energetic and ambitious man, who has been trying for years to promote unity among pagan groups in the Toronto area. He is enthusiastic, but also irascible and opinionated, and in assuming the role of peacemaker has often tended to inflame smouldering conflicts. He readily admits that a lively magazine called *Rags to Witches* that he edited for about three years succeeded in alienating almost everyone in the Wiccan community at some time or another.

Arnold made a public name for himself with his well-publicized effort to win the right to paid holidays from Humber College in order to celebrate the Wiccan Sabbats Beltane and Samhain. He did this through a labour arbitration hearing in which he succeeded in proving that Wicca is a legitimate religion, that he is a genuine follower of it, and that the Sabbats are religious holidays. When a ruling was made in his favour it was generally regarded as a significant victory for the Craft in that a quasi-judicial body had concluded that Wicca does have the status of a religious faith.

Inspired by this success, Arnold went on to apply to the Ontario Ministry of Consumer and Commercial Relations to be licenced to perform marriages. This move did not sit well with some other people in local Wiccan circles, who resented the celebrity he had achieved and questioned his credentials as a high priest. The ministry turned down the application after receiving letters opposing it and following the appearance of a Toronto *Star* story in which two people criticized the plans.

The *Star* story quoted a woman who complained that Arnold had asked her to attend classes in the nude. Arnold denied this allegation, saying he conducted rituals naked, but never classes. The newspaper story did not state that the woman was the owner of an occult store that was engaged in a business dispute with Arnold. The other person quoted was a witch Arnold had attacked in his newsletter, claiming that the man was in fact a born-again Christian. This man was quoted as saying that Wiccan weddings or handfastings are only supposed to last for one year and a day. This may be true of some traditions, but others believe that a witches' marriage can last not only until death but through future reincarnations.

Ideally, if witchcraft were to receive a certain amount of official recognition and sanction, it would be not as one entity but as several different denominations of the same religion, just as Christianity is accepted today. We take it for granted that each Christian church has its own ministers, its own charitable foundations and conducts its own marriages. It is inconceivable that a situation would arise where the only Christian minister qualified to perform legal marriages would be a Roman Catholic or a Southern Baptist. One might perhaps understand the conflict that Arnold's campaign caused if one could imagine being in a non-Christian society in which a sizeable and diversified Christian community was afforded no official sanction, where a Lutheran pastor applied for the right to perform marriages.

As long as some witches want this kind of public recognition, they will have to get it through individuals or groups that they can accept as their representatives. They will have to find some way to prevent such an effort from being undermined by the other witches who do not believe the Craft should obtain legal status, either because it is a secret underground tradition or because it is seen as an instrument of revolutionary change. This involves a lot of dialogue and careful planning, and some groups are working hard at that. Arnold may have encountered fewer problems had he done more ground-work and made peace with his enemies.

Besides politics and sectarian differences, there is another dimension to this problem. That is the legitimate fear that the increasing popularity of witchcraft may result in the religion being cheapened and commercially exploited. Many affluent middle-class people are now exploring different non-traditional spiritual alternatives in what is commonly referred to as the new age movement. Many entrepreneurs have seized upon the opportunity to exploit this trend. Crystals, Tarot cards and runes, traditional tools of the Craft, have become high-turnover items in occult and new age stores. The new age movement has generated a demand for classes and workshops in witchcraft. Some groups even offer correspondence courses in witchcraft. Witches can make a lot of money by giving readings at Psychic Fairs.

In the Gardnerian tradition there is a law that states, "Never accept money for the use of the art, for money ever smeareth the taker." Most witches adhere to the principle that one should not work magic for money or charge people for participating in Craft rituals. Most witches agree that it does not make any sense to say that there is anything wrong with Wiccan business people selling Craft-related goods and services, including Tarot readings, especially as this is one of the few ways that witches can safely and openly make a living. But some believe it is wrong to charge a fee for teaching about the Craft, and this is an issue that has caused some friction.

Charles Arnold makes no bones about charging for his classes. He maintains that the principle of not charging for knowledge of the Gods worked in ancient tribal societies where the religious leaders were supported by the community. He says it is now natural that someone who spends years learning about the Craft and devotes several hours to preparing lessons to expect some remuneration in exchange. He also believes that charging students for classes gives them an incentive to learn.

Arnold told me that his ambition is to make a million dollars, but that he had modest expectations for the classes in dowsing, crystal work and other Wiccan techniques that he was offering to people in Toronto's new age movement. He said he would be charging $59 for 12 hours of classes, hoped to get at least five students in each class and trusted that their cheques would not bounce. Why was he gearing these sessions to the new age market? ''Know anybody in the Craft that's got money? New age people are willing to pay for classes,'' he replied.

While Arnold appears to be a conscientious teacher with a fairly good knowledge of Wicca, his situation illustrates the potential for abuse. He told me about someone else who was charging for classes whom he believes to be a charlatan. Having met that person, I am inclined to agree. The problem here is not that some people offer to teach things they do not know enough about. There will always be such people, in all walks of life. The problem is that when someone becomes established in the public eye as a leader of Wicca, there is an opportunity to exploit that position for personal gain.

This situation is not peculiar to Wicca, but what is different is that witchcraft has no generally agreed upon standard for the training and initiation of its clergy. For example, the teacher who I believe is probably a charlatan told me that he is a Magus, a high priest in a tradition that is too secret for him to name.

When I first began talking to witches and reading their magazines, I was shocked by what seemed to be a lot of petty bickering over who was and who was not properly initiated by whom. I have come to realize that it is only through this kind of argument that witches of different traditions and backgrounds can establish for themselves which people are to be trusted as spokespeople.

Most traditional Wiccan groups strictly adhere to a hierarchical system, which involves three degrees of witches. One has to study the craft for a year and a day before being initiated into a coven as a first degree, rank and file witch. After a further period of study and work within the coven, usually at least a year, he or she can then be initiated as a second degree witch, a high priest or high priestess. The second degree witch can initiate others to the Craft and may lead a coven, under the supervision of a third degree, which is the highest rank in the Craft.

Members of these underground traditional groups often look askance at some of the public witches, who they feel do not have their depth of understanding and commitment to the Craft. Some non-traditional witches reject the three degrees as an unnecessary hierarchical power structure, while others have developed their own equivalents. One of the goals of WITCH in Victoria, which represents a network of mainly eclectic feminist witches, is to establish an apprenticeship program for Wiccan clergy. Although members of this group distrust hierarchy and institutionalization, there is a perceived need to set standards, both for their own benefit and for the sake of obtaining legal recognition.

Unlike the Roman Catholic church, Wicca has no excommunication. Someone who fails to live up to Wiccan ethics or causes trouble may be banished from a coven, but an initiation as a witch cannot be revoked. In occult stores or Wiccan magazines, one occasionally sees little notices stating that a certain person is no longer accepted as a member of a certain group or that an endorsement of a particular group has been withdrawn.

It is an unfortunate fact of life that people judge smaller non-traditional groups by the behaviour of a few members, while an established religion is not measured by the character of its rogues and apostates, even if they happen to be prominent television evangelists. That is why witches are constantly chagrined by the extroverted behaviour of the flaky few who are attached to the mystique of witchcraft.

''What are we doing this for?'' asked one Gardnerian witch. ''People seem to have forgotten that the purpose behind the whole thing was the worship of the Gods. It got lost in fancy robes and jewellery and 'My coven burns more incense than your coven.' All the real good people are dropping out and going underground, to the detriment of the pagan movement."

Perhaps making a virtue of necessity, members of the Isis Urania coven maintain that people whom they call "make-believe witches" serve as guardians of the secrets of the Craft by frightening away the merely curious. "They linger on the fringe of society wearing the costumes and masks of what they wish they could be. Their loudness and their shortcomings disgust and repel those critical or hostile to the ideals of the Craft."

Since anyone can claim to be a witch or a pagan, there are inevitably some groups and individuals who use paganism as an excuse or a cover for activity that runs contrary to all Wiccan traditions. One such group are White Supremacists who adopt Norse or Celtic mythology as a justification for racial hatred. Some right-wing political activists in Western Canada have taken to calling themselves Odinists, after the Norse god Odin, who was the master of magic, science and the arts—and a god of war. It is salutary for witches, who often maintain that their ancient earth-centred mythologies can transform society, to remember that magic and Norse mythology also formed a basis for Nazi ideology.

Another right-wing racist pagan group operates in Toronto under the name The Reformed Celtic Church. This group attacks blacks, North American native people, Jews and Freemasons, all of which it sees as threats to their attempts to preserve the purity of the Celtic race and culture. A few years ago the group offered a knighthood and life-time privileges in the Reformed Celtic Church to anyone who would take retaliatory action against a number of named individuals whom the church considered a threat. That this group has nothing in common with the rest of the Toronto pagan community was underlined by the fact that the names of people listed as threats included the city's most prominent witches.

There is no question that groups such as these have no place in the spectrum of Wiccan traditions, since they fail to observe one of the few universally accepted Craft tenets — "Do what you will, if it harms none." But what sense are we to make of the huge range of beliefs that can legitimately be considered as Wiccan? That is a question that many witches struggle with.

Charles Arnold told me he isn't sure what the Craft is or where it is heading. "There are so many different directions we're being pulled. There are still a few vultures hanging around, people taking advantage for money and power. There are people trying to break down every tradition, trying to throw men out, or saying you have to be gay. There are people who say crystals are more important than pentagrams. There's Aztec, Hindu, Eskimo Wicca. It's something different for everyone. I know what it is for me. The power is there no matter what."

Like the early Christians or the Protestant churches after the Reformation, Wiccans are presently exploring many different political and religious directions, sometimes fighting and sometimes marveling at their own diversity. Viewed from the outside, one can see in Wicca, as in organized religions, a common thread, a set of fundamental attitudes that makes witchcraft a distinct religious philosophy. All witches believe that the earth is sacred. Almost all believe that the female principle in the self and the universe is at least as important as, if not more than, the male. Witches all agree that the psychic energy within the individual is one with the force that governs all life. Magic may be seen as taking the form of political action or influencing the human psyche on the astral plane, but all witches agree that it can transform reality.

The hostility and confusion with which outsiders often respond to their religion, together with the desire of many witches to achieve some degree of public acceptance, has led many Wiccans to work hard at building bridges and mending fences. Witches from different traditions in many parts of Canada are coming together in networks and informal groups to try to increase their mutual understanding and improve their public image.

An example of this is the Wiccan community in Ottawa, which was rife with feuding until very recently. People from several different traditions who were not on speaking terms before have begun to gather for a regular monthly event that they call a Meet and Greet, where political differences are left at the door. The name for these sessions is taken from a traditional Wiccan greeting: ''Merry meet, merry part and merry meet again.''

CHAPTER SEVEN

Radical Witchcraft

When I set out in search of witches, I expected to encounter some bizarre people in exotic situations. The images that now stick in my mind, however, are mostly of simple domestic scenes.

I think of a father nursing a baby with a bottle in a downtown Toronto apartment while talking about rediscovering the divinity of the earth. I remember a suburban living room in Victoria, B.C., where a man sat working at a computer, a small boy kept grabbing at my pen and notebook, and a young woman talked distractedly about the Goddess as she tried to defrost a chicken that she had forgotten to take out of her freezer.

Modern witchcraft has come to be epitomized for me in memories like one of a group of people sipping brandy and using tarot cards to unravel emotional problems, or two women discussing psychology, science and the practical applications of magic while drinking tea in front of a log fire.

What I have learned from these and dozens of other Canadian witches is that pagan beliefs and magical practices strike a deep resonance in many present-day lives. These old ideas are often being reinterpreted, however, and fused with modern concepts to create different ways of looking at the world. The new versions of witchcraft that are being created apply myth and magic to therapy, personal growth and political action. At the same time, there are some modern witches who prefer to adhere to more traditional ways.

Witchcraft presents a set of powerful images that have a wide and varied appeal. Some people are drawn to the mystique of magic and the romance of ritual, while others are seeking the simplicity of an earlier way of life. Modern witches may be seeking an alternative vision of nature and mankind, an escape from conventional moral codes, a spirituality based on self-expression and sensuality, or a combination of any of these things.

The very name of witchcraft is shocking to most people, and is therefore a potent symbol of defiance and rebellion. Many women identify with the witches of history as victims of patriarchal persecution, and are now reclaiming that title as an emblem of female wisdom and power.

The people who call themselves witches in Canada today do so for many different reasons and hold a variety of beliefs. If modern witchcraft is a movement, it is one that is coming together from different directions, sometimes heading in opposite ways, but often merging on a wide middle ground.

When I first tried to map out these diverging paths, I perceived two basic forms of modern witchcraft: traditional and radical. I subsequently found that most of the witches I encountered actually fell somewhere between the two categories. However, the categories are helpful as they do show the two basic polarities around which the world of witchcraft now revolves.

Traditional witches adhere to what they believe to be the ancient practices of the Craft, while radical witches feel free to create new versions of witchcraft. The traditional witches are people who grew up with or discovered the Craft and adopted it as a way of life. Radical witches are feminists, ecologists and political activists who found witchcraft in a quest for a spiritual dimension to their political beliefs.

The first group includes hereditary witches who follow traditions passed down to them either by their own relatives or those of friends who have introduced them to the Craft. Their beliefs can be widely divergent and are often sensitively guarded like precious family heirlooms. It also includes those who follow the more recently formulated versions of witchcraft that are contained in Gardnerian, Alexandrian and other similar traditions. These usually place a great emphasis on the polarity of the God and Goddess, the interdependence of male and female principles in magical workings. They often avoid publicly identifying themselves as witches and place a great stress on the validity of their initiations. To them, someone who becomes a witch is "a proper person, properly prepared." This is a person who has been studying the craft for at least a year and has shown the courage and curiosity deemed necessary for exploration of the unseen world, together with an attitude of reverence for life.

Radical witches identify with symbols of witchcraft, but reinterpret them in new ways. They often draw more on their own energy and experience than on traditional beliefs and practices. They take the position that it makes no difference whether their Craft is inherited, rediscovered or made up, as long as it works for them. Many of them believe that the so-called traditions of witchcraft were mostly invented in the 1950s, and refer to their own practices as "traditions" even though some of them were made up in recent years. They tend to see Wicca less as a recreation of the Old Religion than as a new spiritual movement.

Most of these new witches are feminists or eco-feminists, people who combine the principles of ecology with feminism. Some feminist groups exclude men, and others are willing to accept non-sexist men but tend to attract mainly women. There are also groups of gay men, who call themselves Radical Faeries. As one might expect, radical groups put a great deal of stress on political activity around environmental or feminist issues. They believe that politics is a form of magic. According to some more radical definitions, witches are people who choose to identify themselves as such.

The majority of modern witches, who fall somewhere between these two poles, describe themselves as eclectic, and combine various aspects of traditional and non-traditional Wicca. The terms radical and traditional are not necessarily exclusive of each other. A large number of traditional witches are also feminists and ecological activists, and there are many who adapt their traditions to include new practices. Alternatively, many people who find witchcraft through feminism and ecological concerns acquire a deep knowledge of and respect for its traditional beliefs.

There are also many people who use witchcraft or its trappings primarily as a means of self-expression. They revel in its secrets and ritual regalia, and are less interested either in its traditional spiritual values or present-day social significance than in its supposed spookiness and shock value.

Witches in southern Ontario have long smarted under the adverse publicity attracted in the 1970s by a group of self-styled white witches called the Order of the Black Rabbit. The leader of this group courted the press, showing off his robes and ritual tools and hinting at arcane secrets. He once told the Hamilton *Spectator* that it is hard to find virgins in modern times to put on the altar in black masses. The group dissolved after a member was charged with bigamy, following an incident in which he introduced police to his two wives while they were investigating suspicions regarding a human skeleton that he kept at his house.

More recently witches in Hamilton were chagrined by a newspaper article that profiled an amiable but feckless group of witches who proudly showed off their Wiccan tattoos and jewellery but forgot to take some of the essential ritual tools to a disorganized Sabbat gathering arranged especially for the benefit of journalists.

"I used to think it was better to be regarded as silly than sinister. But now I'm not so sure," said one Hamilton witch after reading this article.

It is impossible to come up with any reliable estimate of the number of witches in Canada today, because witchcraft is still largely an underground movement, with few organized groups and no membership rolls. Witches are not even always aware of other people from different traditions who may be practicing the Craft in their own area. A witch from northern British Columbia told me, "This area is quite rural, and I suspect there are far more pagans than meet the eye, but we have no way to contact one another. The gatherings that we do hold are not secret, but due to the secluded locations of people's homesteads, it amounts to the same thing!"

In a 1981 census, 2295 Canadians stated that their religion was pagan, about a third of these being from Ontario and another third from British Columbia. A sociologist who has studied witchcraft in Canada concluded that this census represented an underestimate due to people's reluctance to report a stigmatized religious preference. The current resurgence of interest in witchcraft, particularly feminist and other non-traditional forms of Wicca, has gained momentum since the census, in which the majority of people who reported themselves to be pagans were men.

There are now undoubtedly far more female than male witches, even though many traditional covens stress balance between the sexes. Some witches in Ottawa see this as a problem and appealed in a newsletter for single male Wiccan priests to move there. Other female covens are equally anxious to keep men out. On the west coast most of the witches in non-traditional Wiccan groups are women, although they do not necessarily exclude men.

In 1988, sociologist Kate Sandilands did a study of witchcraft and neo-paganism in Canada. She provides much insight into the make-up of the Wiccan population today. She did not try to estimate its total number and the survey that she conducted tended to be oriented to politically active witches and other pagans who were listed in a resource directory compiled by the radical group Pagans for Peace.

In spite of the radical bias of the group she surveyed, Sandilands found that 42 percent of them fit into the category of traditionalists, in which she included eclectics who place an emphasis on traditional ways. As might be expected, these were generally older people, more likely to be married and more conventional in their lifestyles. A majority of all the pagans surveyed were urban dwellers and well-educated, with 75 percent having at least some post-secondary education. More of the radicals surveyed were from western Canada, while most of the traditionalists were from central and eastern provinces. The radicals were often students or unemployed, but the majority of traditionalists worked in business or service-related fields. I was surprised to learn in conversation with Sandilands that she found the most common occupations among traditional witches were in computer technology.

My experience in talking with witches from various traditions and different regions of Canada led me to believe that radical witchcraft is certainly more prevalent in the west. This is hardly surprising as there appear to be more overt radicals of all descriptions in British Colombia than elsewhere in Canada. I think that the reason for this lies in the natural tendency for people who want to explore alternate life-styles to choose warm and pleasant places in which to do so.

Traditional witches tend to be more underground, but can be found in most regions. In central and eastern provinces, witches who are public about their beliefs are more likely to be eclectics who lean towards traditional practices.

The majority of Canadian witches appear to live in the major cities in Ontario, on Vancouver Island and the lower mainland area of British Columbia. There are Wiccan groups in Montreal, but they keep a very low profile because they feel that the climate of a culture still permeated with Roman Catholic influences is inclined to be hostile to their beliefs. When I asked one Montreal witch why he did not want to be public about his beliefs, he replied, "Why play with fire, especially if you happen to work in a government office."

In the prairie provinces, witches are scattered and also inclined to be afraid to identify themselves. In Edmonton, a small pagan community is centred around the Ordo Templis Orientis, a secret organization devoted primarily to ritual magic. There are also a few witches in the Maritimes and those whom I contacted were traditionalist or eclectic in their basic beliefs, while politically active on environmental issues.

Many of the witches whom I met were well-read, intellectually inclined people, often with a particular interest in science-fiction and fantasy literature. Their interest in mythology and the occult was often complemented by knowledge of psychology and recent scientific theories that reject old experimental and analytical methods and explain natural phenomena in terms of a complex series of relationships. They were inclined to be pragmatic in their descriptions of magic, explaining it in terms of natural forces rather than mysterious powers.

"All of it is metaphor," one eclectic witch told me. "The symbols only serve to remind you of a law that keeps the universe together."

The same woman, an artist from Vancouver, said magic might be mainly a form of positive thinking and described it as "using your will in a humble sort of way to create a change in the universe." She told me that she uses Tarot cards, "not because I want to find out who I'm going to marry or any of that stuff but as a tool for something deep inside me to communicate something I don't know."

I found that many witches had experienced strong religious feelings in childhood, but had found that the religion they grew up with did not suit their own spiritual leanings. One witch from Nova Scotia said he had been in a seminary before gravitating towards witchcraft, and two others had studied theology at university. One witch, who used to be taken to a spiritualist church as a child, told me, "I felt uncomfortable praying to something I didn't know about and believe in, and being forced to sing strange little songs. We witches sing strange little songs, but we are not forced."

Some witches are hostile to organized religion, mainly as a result of abrasive campaigns against witchcraft mounted by some fundamentalist Christians. Others maintain a respect for the religions they grew up with. A witch from New Brunswick told me that she keeps a statue of the Virgin Mary on an altar in her home as a sign of recognition that all religions worship the same life forces.

One of the traditional rules of witchcraft is that it does not advertise itself or seek to make converts. People who become witches do so because they have discovered the religion for themselves. Many people talked to me about discovering in Wicca a set of beliefs that corresponded to the way they had always felt or thought. They would explain that they now realized that they had always been witches, but had not come to realize that until later in life.

Modern traditional witches are people who have taken the Craft as they found it, and usually devoted many years to learning what they believe to be a complex and profound way of understanding the world and developing spiritual powers.

Gardnerians tend to be the most private and conservative witches. Often they are older people who entered the Craft in Britain in the 1950s and have since moved to Canada. Gardnerian Wicca is quite prevalent in British Columbia, where there is a sizeable population of older retired British people, but its followers have very little to do with other more open Wiccan groups. One 50-year-old Gardnerian in Vancouver told me that his associates in the Craft regard him as "a young 'n." I have met several younger people in Ontario who were introduced to Wicca through Gardnerian covens and still have much respect for the tradition. But most of these people now have a more eclectic approach to witchcraft.

One witch compared Gardnerian Wicca to colonial diplomacy. He said, "They are trying to maintain cohesive world-wide tradition. There is a tendency to suppress independent thinking. They drill you in their way of thought."

Alexandrians are more free-thinking and flexible in their approach. But they differ more in style and emphasis than in fundamental beliefs. Both these traditions drew quite heavily upon the techniques of ceremonial magic that were developed in Britain in the late nineteenth century and are often criticized by other witches for being too formal in their approach. Those who follow these and other similar traditions say, however, that the forms and rituals are simply ways of obtaining a deeper understanding of one's relationship with the forces of nature. They are often similar to eclectic witches in explaining it all as basically metaphorical, but believe that it is valuable to preserve the complexity of the original symbolism.

"If you take away too much, it all dissolves into, 'Hello clouds. Hello sky. Hello fuzzy bunnies,' " said Cerridwen, High Priestess of a traditional coven in Hamilton, Ontario. She told me that the difference between the outer forms and the inner experience of Wicca is "like the difference between reading about making love and doing it. It sounds dead boring, though exotic, when you describe it, but being there is really different."

An intensely spiritual woman who has been in the Craft for about 20 years, Cerridwen was able to provide me with some insight into the wide range and complexity of traditional Wiccan beliefs. She belongs to the Isis Urania tradition, a group of nine covens founded by a hereditary witch in Vancouver. Hereditary traditions tend to differ a lot from one another depending on how well they were handed down from generation to generation and what particular historical or geographic considerations affected the way a particular family or group of families practiced the Craft. Cerridwen's tradition is similar to Gardnerian and Alexandrian Wicca in many respects, especially in the way it combines the ancient folk magic of country people with more sophisticated systems of mystical thought.

Cerridwen described Wicca as "The most important thing in my life, in the same way as the ground is what I need to walk on—background and foreground at the same time. Being a witch is who I am as well as what I do."

Like dozens of witches I have met, Cerridwen discovered Wicca after being deeply involved with Christianity. She had been doing a master's degree in theology and was a devout practicing Roman Catholic, but found that the social teachings of the church were becoming increasingly incompatible for her. She began seeking for another spiritual path that would suit her better. "I need ritual like I need air," she explained.

At that time, she was also being troubled by psychic experiences that she could not understand. She began to study the Tarot as a way of channelling and making sense of these experiences.

Cerridwen said her studies did not make her psychic experiences go away but gave her a way to deal with them. Her study of Tarot led to an interest in magic, and eventually meeting up with some witches, whom she found to be "sweet but usually very silly people, who were difficult to take seriously."

She practiced witchcraft on her own, with the help of the many books that were beginning to surface on the subject in the late 1960s, until she met the members of a hereditary coven in Toronto. She said they were "kind, intelligent and real people, who really loved the God and Goddess and knew what they were doing."

The teachings of traditional Wicca are embodied in the rituals, but their inner meanings are explained to a student of the Craft by a high priest or high priestess over years of training. The student has an intimate relationship with the teacher, who he or she is encouraged to regard as a personification of the God or Goddess.

"The teaching structure is magically designed to help students understand themselves and how they fit into the universe," said Cerridwen. "It's a very trusting loving relationship. That doesn't mean that people don't act like assholes sometimes, but that's part of the universe too."

Khaled, a high priest of Quicksilver, an Alexandrian coven in Ottawa, described how one of the most critical things that an initiate has to learn in early Craft training is how to distinguish between true intuition and wishful thinking or delusion. Real intuition relates to reality and the information it gives you is true, he said, whereas wishful thinking is a fantasy. The images that come into your mind are all hallucinations, but some have something real behind them, others don't. When you are receiving telepathic messages or talking to the spirits, you have to take a radar pulse off something inside yourself in order to make sure that what you are doing is appropriate to your nature and situation. Khaled explained, "It's the same process as assessing the politics of a group you are involved with."

Khaled, a self-employed professional, who has been in the Craft for 18 years, described himself as "discreetly public." He said he can afford to be so, as he does not feel he will lose many clients as a result of public exposure. He said he was once fired from a job at a children's hospital when it became known that he was a witch.

The hierarchical relationship between the high priest or high priestess and the student is seen by traditional witches as natural and necessary. The high priestess is regarded as the final arbitrator of all issues facing the coven. She is referred to as "the first among equals." If members of the coven who have reached a sufficient level of understanding of the Craft disagree with her on some fundamental point, they are free to leave and start their own coven.

But feminist and eclectic witches often see the hierarchical structure, and the emphasis on male and female polarities in the traditional Craft, as petty, authoritarian and sexist. Traditional witches deny the charge of sexism, saying that they are feminists and are merely recognizing the biological fact that all life springs from the interplay of male and female. They say that the hierarchical relationship between student and teacher is necessary for the transmission of a coherent and complicated body of knowledge.

Maggie, a British Columbia woman who has been initiated in the Gardnerian and Alexandrian traditions and now practices a more eclectic form of witchcraft, told me in a letter: "The true Wicca I know, without exception, are very ethical and disciplined people, and traditional Craft itself has built-in safeguards (which don't always work!) against the misuse of knowledge. That's one of the reasons why I think the traditions are important, although I am aware that many people believe you should just do your own thing. So you should, as long as your thing is disciplined and you work only for the good of all and according to the free will of all."

Some peace and environmental activists have been attracted to witchcraft because they felt that they needed a spiritual dimension to what they were doing. Wiccan beliefs fit well with the new scientific and spiritual concept of Gaia, which sees the earth as one living organism. Sam Wagar, the founder of Pagans for Peace, a network of radical witches and pagans, said that witchcraft helps radicals, who have become disillusioned by attending hundreds of demonstrations that do not seem to have much impact. Witchcraft, he said, helps to reconnect people with basic principles of respect for the earth and at the same time places a value on symbolic ritual action, making it easier for people to act even when they do not think they will be successful.

Religious inspiration for political action is, of course, nothing new, and various Christian groups have been doing dedicated work for decades attempting to promote social justice in many parts of the world. Witches often forget this as they judge Christianity by their negative experience of its more conservative extremes.

World hunger has always been a prime focus for charities run by organized religions. When Geneva Hagan, a British Columbia pagan, became deeply concerned about the same issue, she felt uncomfortable working within the framework of a Christian group and decided to form a pagan charity called CERES (Convocation of Earth Religions to End Starvation). This group is now working on small projects in Mexico, Nicaragua and Kenya.

Hagan's description of why she became concerned about world hunger provides an interesting response to the common conception that mysticism is a form of escape from the problems of the real world. In 1976, she said, when psychedelic drugs were still in vogue, she had a devastating experience of merging with the global consciousness: "Hunger and war were no longer happening 'over there' while I remained a safe and well-fed bystander. These calamities were happening to the life of this planet that I Am, to the collective body of my own species, where the experience of my Self has its roots."

Many people, who are working towards the emergence of a society that respects women and the natural world, have begun to believe that this kind of change will not be possible without a fundamental change in religious and cultural attitudes. They believe that the suppression of women and destruction of the environment are inherent to a religious system that excludes the female principle from its deity and does not consider the earth to be sacred. They have concluded that a new set of spiritual beliefs is needed, as well as political action, in order to save the earth and restore women to their rightful place in society.

"Because women's spirituality has been basically written off the face of the earth for the last several thousand years, the only way of having any sense of history is to go back to the ancient roots," said Pashta Marymoon, a feminist witch from Ottawa. "We are trying to understand from those roots things that we intuitively know. As we begin to understand ourselves as separate from the patriarchal culture, we see those things reflected in the ancient traditions. Then we have to make a faith structure out of them that works for the modern-day world."

Marymoon's Craft name reflects her own unique spiritual path. She is at the same time a lesbian feminist witch, a Quaker and a Christian. Unlike many feminist and traditional witches, who have little time for Christianity, she values the teachings of Jesus Christ and tries to re-integrate Christian spiritual values, which she sees as having become fragmented from an earlier more holistic way of seeing the world. She also respects the egalitarian spirit of Quakerism. A graduate student of theology, Marymoon is the mother of a married daughter and a teenaged son. She and her partner Faith were the first Canadian lesbian couple ever to be married at a Quaker meeting.

As feminist witches re-invent the Craft, one of the first things that many feel has to be thrown out is the God. As Marymoon put it, some separatist lesbians ''not only don't want to have anything to do with men in their lives, but certainly aren't interested in any cosmic guy hanging around.''

Other feminist witches do value the God as well as the Goddess, seeing both as polarities within what was once an unbroken unity of life. Marymoon told me that this is the way she feels at a deeper level, but that it is difficult to relate this inner belief to an everyday reality in which, she says, ''I find it increasingly difficult to tolerate men, period.''

Many women struggle with this kind of conflict, as do some men who find it hard to accept and fit in with the cultural models of masculinity. It is easier to love God, while not liking men, if one follows a religion in which the male deity is seen as being separate from mankind and everything else he created. In Wiccan beliefs, however, people are incarnations or manifestations of the Goddess and the God. Ideally all witches would feel both divine aspects present in themselves, as all people contain both male and female elements. In practice however many female witches tend to relate primarily to the Goddess and seldom mention the God.

Starhawk describes the appeal of ancient pagan forms to people in contemporary society as being ''linked to a growing realization among many strata of people that the dead world of mechanism, the world of domination, cannot sustain our inner lives, nor our lives in community with each other, nor the life of the planet. The rebirth of earth religion is a part of a broad movement that challenges domination—that seeks to connect with the root, the heart, the source of life by changing our present relationships."

Starhawk's writings and teachings have been a major influence on almost every Canadian feminist witch that I have met. Starhawk is a psychotherapist, peace activist, screenwriter and author of three books on witchcraft. She is probably the first and only known witch ever to teach at a Roman Catholic educational institute and her participation in workshops organized by the renegade Dominican priest Matthew Fox have created waves of controversy within the church.

She travels to Canada frequently to give workshops and lectures. I attended one such event at the University of Toronto. Her presentation attracted about 200 people, mostly women, representing what appeared to be a wide cross-section of society. I was particularly impressed with the way in which Starhawk, a pleasant cheerful woman with a low-key manner, was able to inspire this large and disparate group of people to engage in a spontaneous, hectic and somewhat chaotic ritual. People played with streamers, chanted and joined together in a dance that spun a frenzied spiral around the sedate gothic university hall.

Ritual in Starhawk's view is a way of creating bonds and building community, a means of overcoming the estrangement and sense of powerlessness she sees as endemic in our culture. A ritual, she says, is a meeting-ground "where people can share deep feelings, positive and negative—a place where they can sing or scream, howl ecstatically or furiously, play, or keep a solemn silence. A pagan ritual incorporates touch, sensuality and humour. Anything we truly revere is also something that we can ridicule respectfully. The elements of laughter and play keep us from getting stuck on one level of power or developing an inflated sense of self-importance.''

Starhawk sees witchcraft as a means by which ''we can reclaim our power to shape ourselves and the world around us.'' Magic is, to her, a means of causing change in accordance with will, and political acts of protest or resistance are therefore acts of magic.

Members of Pagans for Peace and feminist Wiccan groups on the west coast apply this principle, both in magical rites that are directed towards political ends and in direct political action. The value of magic in political protests is not necessarily dependant on any supernatural effects. Rituals can provide groups with a means of reinforcing their feelings of commitment and solidarity. They can communicate an emotionally powerful message with more impact than political speeches or slogans.

In a protest against logging on the west coast of Vancouver Island in the summer of 1988, a group of demonstrators blocked a road with sticks that they had previously carved, painted, decorated with shells, leaves and feathers, and charged with magical energy. These may not have been more effective than any other road-block, but the persistence with which the demonstrators kept replacing the sticks after the logging crew removed them apparently had some impact, as the logging company eventually decided to suspend its operations in that location. When some of these protestors were subsequently on trial for disobeying court injuctions, they took a large, round, smooth stone to court with them and laid their hands on it at the beginning of each day's proceedings. According to a witch who was involved with this group, one of the court officials eventually joined them in this ritual and expressed admiration for the protestors' sincerity and dedication to their cause.

Feminist witches regard their circles as being more egalitarian than traditional covens. Women who do not have much knowledge of Wiccan teachings and practices are nevertheless encouraged to share their own experiences in life and interpret the traditions in the light of this experience. The concept is that every woman has something to contribute and has psychic energies to share, which come out of her experience of being a woman.

Instead of following a set pattern of ritual, eclectic or feminist witches create ritual together, out of their own common experiences and their understanding of ancient myths. It does not matter to them whether the forms they follow are an authentic recreation of the worship of old pagan cultures. What is important is that their rituals should be powerful and meaningful for them.

These rituals usually incorporate basic elements of traditional Wicca, such as the circle, the four cardinal directions, invocation of the Goddess, and raising of a cone of power. They may or may not use traditional tools or props, like athame, chalice, pentacle, wand, incense, candles, cauldron and cords. But the rituals will often involve a form of spontaneous play-acting in which women help one another to work on their personal concerns.

A ritual for overcoming guilt might involve each woman making a doll or mask to represent her own monster of self-deprecation. An anger ritual can involve women screaming and howling their anger, telling one another they have a right to be angry and then rephrasing their angry feelings in positive terms. By massaging and praising one another's bodies, women can create a ritual that will enhance their own sensuality and self-esteem.

Self-mocking humour can also play an important role in such rituals, as in one described to me, in which women would state their own shortcomings in terms of an exaggerated denial, repeating things like, "I never put myself down, not me." The denials would be repeated with more and more vehemence and eventually be turned into positive statements in which each woman takes responsibility for her own faults.

For many women today, espousing the title of witch can be an act of reclaiming a heritage lost in over a thousand years of patriarchal society. It can also be a gesture of defiance. Woman's International Terrorist Conspiracy from Hell was the name that one of the earliest U.S. feminist witch groups gave itself in 1968, a far cry from the present day Victoria, B.C. organization that uses the letters WITCH to spell out Wiccans Invoking Tolerance, Compassion and Harmony. The earlier U.S. group suggested in one of its manifestos that "you are a witch by saying out loud 'I am a witch' three times and thinking about that."

This simplistic formula resembles a children's game or nursery rhyme. Feminist witches do, in fact, often base rituals on children's games. Such games are seen as part of the conditioning process by which people's attitudes are moulded. Just as children learn through the repetition of words and patterns of behaviour, adults can use the same methods in an attempt to unlearn negative programming. Words have the power of creating, revealing or reinforcing the thoughts and feelings that they name. Witches see this as a form of magic.

A Vancouver witch and anarchist told me it was in this way that she first declared herself to be a witch. She said she was inspired by the idea of being able to access self-granted spiritual powers. She said her beliefs involve "the freedom to invent our lives as we go, the freedom to ultimately be our own judges about what is of value, what is holy and what is obscene."

Many present-day feminists see the history of the witch-hunts as a lesson in how a male-dominated society needs to suppress female power and wisdom. The pagan priestesses, midwives and healers who were killed in the witchhunts are perceived as saints and martyrs of feminism. The way in which the definition of witch was popularly transformed from wise woman to seductress or hag is seen as an example of this culture's systematic denial of female values.

A song that is circulated by feminist groups for use in day care centres and kindergartens attempts to restore the historical image of witches to its rightful place:

Who were the witches, where did they come from?
Maybe your great, great, great grandma was one,
Witches were very wise women they say,
And there's a little witch in every woman today.

Witches knew all about flowers and weeds,
How to use all their roots and their leaves and their seeds.
When people grew weary from hard workin' days,
They made them feel better in so many ways.

When women had babies, the witches were there
To hold them and help them and give them care.
Witches knew stories of how life began,
Don't you wish you could be one, well maybe you can!

Some people thought that witches were bad,
Some people were scared of the power they had.
Power to help and to heal and to care
Isn't something to fear, it's a pleasure to share.

In Wicca, a woman can identify with the Goddess and feel that her own body and spirit are sacred. Many Wiccan women have told me that they found this to be a very liberating concept after growing up with religious notions that tended to make them feel that their body was dirty and their natural instincts sinful.

"I have the feeling that women need to value themselves," Barbara Smith told me. Smith, a half-Indian, Wiccan writer and teacher, goes by the name, Cornwoman. "I see men's challenge to learn brotherhood, to take care of and nurture other people. Women's challenge is to learn to love themselves, to learn to be comfortable and love their body in all its aspects."

Blood ceremonies associated with menstruation are one way in which Wiccan rituals can help women feel more comfortable with themselves physically. The idea for these ceremonies comes from native traditions. But Cornwoman, who grew up in a Native North American culture, said much of the lore of the menstrual hut and the women's Moon Lodge has been forgotten in native communities.

Women are made to feel unclean, she said, when they have a period, because they are not allowed to touch ceremonial items. Many native elders were sexist, she said, and had the attitude that "a man needs a good woman to tie all the tobacco ties and make sure the feast is on time."

According to Cornwoman, the subtle influence of the Christian church caused a shift in Indian culture from a female-oriented or partnership type of spirituality to one that was male-dominated. She said it was because of Christian influences that women were required to wear full-length nightgowns in the sweat lodge, whereas they went bare breasted before. The Indians began to refer to the Creator as a male, even though most of the old myths refer to women as the origins of life.

"These are Christian influenced myths that most medicine men feed into because it suits them," she said, "There's very little acknowledgment of the earth. Only as a very passive thing—a nicey, nice mummy always there for her kids, all nurturing and many breasted."

Cornwoman said she was inspired to explore Wicca after attending a blood ceremony led by Starhawk, which showed "a real honouring of basic womanness."

Now Cornwoman, who is of mixed race, practices a hybrid of Wiccan and native traditions. Blood ceremonies are important, she said, because most women either find their period "very painful and yuk" or say "I'm Superwoman. I feel nothing. I'm just as good as any man any day of the month."

"What women need to do is balance and centre. They should acknowledge that the body does go through changes at different times in a monthly cycle, that the reason they get bitchy is the body is telling them to take a break and do inner work, go to the menstruation hut figuratively or actually, pray, meditate, and become renewed. Then, after the bleeding time, go back to their families and communities revived and refreshed, take the inner knowledge that they have found and use it in their communities."

The Crone aspect of the Goddess, representing the wisdom, power and repose, has become an important symbol for many older women. A group of women in northern British Columbia invented a Croning Ritual to celebrate reaching menopause. The woman who is becoming a Crone goes through a weathered old gate on a homestead owned by one of the group while her friends chant and sing, and congratulate her for reaching the other side. Maggie, who invented the ritual, told me in a letter, "Now my men friends want cronings too, which is fine, since Cronos is also Saturn—'the old goat.' "

On one of the islands off Vancouver Island, a community of older lesbian women have all taken on the surname Crone. They publish a magazine called *Web of Crones,* which treats issues of interest to older lesbian and Wiccan women. "Every gathering makes us stronger. Everything we learn fits somewhere. What we bring to one another is matched by what we receive from each other," one woman wrote in connection with an annual gathering on Hornby Island, which attracts Crones from across North America.

The Crone is also the woman who lays out the dead. She is Goddess of the waning moon, the dark Lady of the Night. She represents fear and anger, the destructive forces of nature and the shadows within the human psyche. These are things that witches believe must also be respected and revered.

According to Cornwoman, the natives on the west coast have a legend about a wild woman of the woods, whom they call Zuniqua. She manifests the dark aspect of the Goddess. She is a giantess of whom the children are afraid. She is free and independent, and takes lovers when she wants to. Cornwoman said that she has seen a mask of Zuniqua with a crescent moon above her head, a symbol of the witches' Goddess.

Feminist witches believe that by recognizing the dark side of the Goddess in themselves they can, as one woman put it, "Enter pain and come out the other side."

Women are often taught not to show anger and to suppress grief. But witches believe that one should accept negative emotions and recognize them for what they are. By being honest with oneself in that way, they maintain, one can begin to understand what caused the pain or anger and transform it into positive energy. Otherwise the emotions will remain buried, they say, inaccessible and out of control.

The magic that witches perform obviously works in that it does seem to effect a transformation of their own lives. Some of them are affected with the same fervour about their beliefs as one sees in born-again Christians. They talk enthusiastically about how things fell into place for them after they began to worship the Goddess. The religion encourages them to trust their instincts, respect their own bodies and feel connected with the natural world. It also gives them a sense of their own power as women and witches, a belief in their ability to make an impact on society. Sometimes, however, the new-found faith will lead them to become intoxicated with their own rhetoric and offer clichéd sentiments as magical solutions to complex social problems.

The value of this newer form of witchcraft and the impact it has on people's lives was crystallized for me in a meeting at a Buddhist Vegetarian restaurant in Vancouver's Chinatown, with three witches who were on their way to a Greenpeace meeting. They were three women from very different backgrounds, who had come together through attending a "witchcamp" run by Starhawk. One was an ecologist, who had recently discovered witchcraft, another had been a witch for a long time before getting involved in environmental politics, and the third was an intellectual who had found in witchcraft a philosophy that put her in touch with her own body and the earth.

"For me witchcraft and particularly camp has been really liberating for my body," said Pearl, a rather austere, quiet woman who taught science in high school. "I've been living in my head a student and a teacher for years. I saw my body as just the thing that walks around carrying my brain.''

Lyndsey was a refined blonde-haired English woman who worked as an executive assistant in a brokerage firm. She said she had practiced as a solitary witch for years, until she came across Starhawk and began to get politically active. Lyndsey was an eclectic witch, who was also studying the Craft in a traditional coven. She said, ''I can relate to the archetypes of Wicca very personally. I can pick and choose.''

Dianne was an artist who has exhibited her work at galleries across Canada. As an ecologist and a feminist, she said, she tried to reflect her values in her work, and discovering witchcraft had brought a spiritual dimension to this. She said, ''My life is so incredibly rich right now, and I think about how much despair was in my life. I have a sense of knowing myself that comes from connectedness on that larger scale.''

''The kinds of beliefs I had as a teenager, as a product of the '60s, have come full circle again. I didn't turn my back on those ideals. But I got bogged down with the practicalities of staying alive,'' said Dianne. ''When I met Starhawk, other friends who were with me were weirded out by the fact that she's a witch. I knew I belonged there. I knew I'd always been a witch.''

All three women talked about the need for witches who respect the earth to make a contribution towards creating a clean environment and a sustainable society. They spoke about simple personal practices like diet, recycling and avoiding the use of environmentally harmful chemicals. They were also active in ecological groups like Greenpeace and were working on *Witchwords,* a Vancouver Wiccan magazine, which puts an emphasis on bringing together spiritual beliefs and political activity.

In feminist Wicca, non-hierarchical structures are devised to ensure that each woman in the group has an opportunity to speak and participate fully in rituals. One such device is the North American Indian practice of passing a feather around the circle and having each person speak as she holds the feather, thus ensuring that the more reticent and less aggressive members of the group have an equal say. One disadvantage of this is that it tends to be a slow process and energies can get dissipated.

Lyndsey expressed some frustration with this, and told me that one advantage of the traditional Wicca that she is studying is that she can make swift progress in learning the set ritual forms and symbolism, so that they become second nature to her. She said this gave her a respect for the power of the teachings that had been handed down through the traditional Craft. This is valuable, she said, but so too is the spontaneity and sense of personal power that is achieved in feminist Wicca.

''It's okay to rediscover the wheel over and over again, because if you discover it for yourself you really know it,'' Pearl said.

Like most feminist witches I have met, all three of these women talked about witchcraft having given them a new sense of connectedness with the world and a belief that, when they follow their instincts, their lives flow with a natural current.

''I'm feeling myself more and more strongly every day,'' said Dianne. ''If you are following your bliss, doors open for you.''

Pearl said, ''I know fate moves in patterns. I used to be fighting it, not knowing which pattern I fit into. Now I ask for a signal, and a signal comes. It doesn't even have to come from natural things like clouds and earthforms. It could come from billboards.''

The signals that Pearl and Lyndsey received from the universe were encouraging them to leave the security of their middle-class lifestyle. Pearl said that getting in touch with her body had put her in touch with the earth, and the next logical stage in that progression was to leave teaching, move to one of the Gulf islands and take up organic gardening.

Lyndsey seemed more than a little afraid of the changes in her attitude that were making her work in the city more difficult to tolerate. She said she found the aggressive male environment of her brokerage firm, with its dedication to short-term profits, was becoming increasingly difficult to stand. She also found that the more aware she became of her own body the more difficult it was to put up with the pollution of the city and the unhealthy indoor environment of her office building. But, she said, "I've never been without a conventional job."

Lyndsey's fears illustrate an inherent problem that besets the radical element in Wicca. It is one that is common to all radical movements. The problem is that it is easier to transform oneself than the society around one. As a result, many radicals find themselves increasingly isolated from the mainstream society, and the more isolated they become the less influence they have. They create close bonds with one another while severing their connections with outsiders. As they become more critical of society, their message often becomes more strident and less effective.

Radical forms of witchcraft have the capacity to help individuals and heal some social ills, but they also have great potential for self-destruction. The rituals and practices that help foster a sense of community among radical witches, and make them more committed to addressing social and environmental problems, can also tend to make group members dependent on one another and isolated from the rest of the world.

More traditional witches, together with other people who involve themselves deeply in mystical or magical disciplines, are faced with a similar danger under a different guise. They can also lose touch with the mainstream, not for political reasons, but because of a preoccupation with psychic dimensions of experience that are not generally recognized in our society. A few of the witches appeared to be isolated, unstable people who had become obsessed with supposedly magical influences on their lives. I met at least two such individuals who maintained that they were engaged in "magical wars" with other witches who were trying to harm them.

It is partly for this reason that witches place a great emphasis on the concept of *grounding*. As a magical technique, grounding involves a state of mind in which one regards oneself as a conduit for energies that reside in the earth or the deeper levels of consciousness and must ultimately be returned to the depths from which they have been raised. But grounding also represents an attitude to life in which a consciousness of magical or psychic dimensions is rooted in an awareness of everyday reality.

Most of the witches I met were at least trying to keep their political and ecological values grounded in a pragmatic approach to the society in which they live. They also seemed to succeed in maintaining some balance between mundane reality and the invisible world of magic and psychic forces. While it may appear that modern witches often have their heads in the clouds, they are attempting to keep their feet on the ground.

CHAPTER EIGHT

Other Forms of Paganism: Shamans, Druids and Elves

Many people are drawn to witchcraft today out of a yearning to reconnect with the roots of human spirituality, to restore a more balanced view of our place in the world, and to re-establish a magical relationship with the forces of nature. These desires are also leading other people to explore different forms of pagan magical belief.

People who practice these other kinds of modern paganism generally regard the earth as sacred and engage in magical techniques for aligning themselves with the spiritual plane. Though they do not call themselves witches or draw upon the traditions of witchcraft, in many cases the sources for these beliefs are the same as those of witchcraft: the shamanic practices of primitive cultures and ancient European myths. Some present-day shamans look to North American native culture as a model for their spiritual practices, while other pagans seek to re-create ancient world-views through scholarship or intuition.

Shamanism is a name now given to what is believed to be the earliest form of magic and religion known to mankind, but it is now widely known, particularly in new age circles, as a method for healing and spiritual discovery. The word *shaman* comes from the tribes of northern Siberia, but the practice has been found in primitive tribes and indigenous traditions all over the world. In Canada, shamanism was practiced by the Inuit and there are some aspects of shamanism in traditional native culture, as practiced today, particularly on the west coast and in the prairies.

Shamans, in primitive cultures, were able to break through the veil of everyday consciousness and enter unseen worlds. Animal masks and other props would be used to symbolize the spiritual connection between mankind and the rest of nature, as shamans put themselves into a trance by means of fasting, dancing, chanting, drumming or drugs. With the help of an animal guide they made what was seen as a dangerous spiritual journey, in which they would often have to wrestle information from gods or demons. If they were successful, they would return with a cure for an illness, an explanation for a crop failure, or the solution to some other problem about which they had been consulted. This would usually be communicated in symbolic form, often in a very theatrical healing ritual.

Shamanism was popularized in the 1970s by Carlos Castaneda's fictional accounts of a Mexican Indian sorcerer, and has become something of a fad in new age circles in recent years. One of the most prominent American exponents of modern shamanism, Michael Harner, noted in his book *The Way of the Shaman* that the word is now used by anthropologists to refer to people from a variety of cultures who used to be known by such terms as *witch, witch-doctor, medicine man* and *sorcerer.* He went on to write, "One of the advantages of using the term is that it lacks the prejudicial overtones and conflicting meanings associated with the more familiar labels."

One might conclude, perhaps unfairly, that present-day shamanism is a form of sanitized witchcraft performed by people who do not like to call themselves witches. Many of the people who now practice shamanism certainly do not consider themselves witches and would not normally adopt the label *pagan.* However, shamanism's roots are in pagan cultures. One aspect of shamanism, the practice of taking on animal characteristics, is used as a magical technique by many people who do call themselves witches and pagans. Other people who adopt it are motivated by the same basic desire to rediscover an ancient spiritual connection with nature that has been lost in our civilization.

Most of the people who seek out the primitive power of shamanic wisdom do not have to venture into the wilderness. Instead they venture into the sterile, enervating environment of hotel meeting rooms, convention centres and lecture halls where the new age shamans conduct their workshops and seminars. The only equipment they need is a cheque book. In my experience, modern shamans do make one concession to their 12,000-year-old heritage: they do not accept Visa or MasterCard.

It was in one such hotel meeting room that I had my first exposure to modern shamanism. It was a workshop conducted by Ed Kenney, a therapist from Thunder Bay, Ontario, who teaches and practices the techniques of shamanism, but divorces them from the original belief systems in which they evolved. One person described Kenney's method to me as the "McDonalds or Burger King approach to shamanism."

This "Universal Shamanism" is described by Kenney as "an ancient power available to anyone today." It does not involve holding any particular religious faith, although it does assume the kind of harmony with the natural world that is characteristic of native and pagan beliefs. According to Kenney, "By the nature of its direct connectedness to all things, one is able to see clearly, to speak lovingly, to touch from the heart, and to be in harmony within our modern-day lifestyle at all times, everywhere."

The tools that Kenney uses to help people enter a shamanic reality are the Ojibwa drum and rattle. These serve to keep out external sounds and the sonic drive of the drumming contributes to a trance-like state.

Kenney was drying his drum with an electric hairdryer when I arrived. Dressed in a 1960s-style embroidered shirt, he had a relaxed and casual manner. He impressed me as being a rather intense man, with a balding head, bulging forehead and a thick black beard. He explained that drum skins absorb moisture and have to be dried out.

Since modern shamans do not usually practice near an open fire, the hair-dryer appears to be another important tool of their trade.

"We are one family," Kenney told the group of about thirty people. "This is a way to get connected very quickly, as if you have known one another for thousands of years."

"We have," said a woman, who later told me she was a hereditary witch of Latvian descent.

The group meditated to the sound of the drum and rattle, which almost succeeded in drowning out the noise of the subway that rumbled under the hotel. It was the second day of the workshop, and in the first day the group had learned how to journey into the lower world in order to find "power animals," spirits who act as guides and protectors on shamanic journeys.

A shamanic journey is a passage into a state of waking dream. Our culture links dreams with fantasy and imagination. It sees them as having less validity than the world of everyday reality. Someone who fails to make that distinction is usually considered to be insane. Shamans believe that what one sees in a trance or waking dream is just as real as ordinary experience. The difference between shamans and people with psychiatric disorders is that shamans know how to distinguish between the two different levels of reality.

The lower world is one of these other levels of reality. One encounters a confusing array of creatures and it is necessary to attach oneself to the spirit of an animal who is friendly and protective. This is one of the things that people in some native traditions do in a "vision quest," an initiatory rite involving solitude and fasting. In Kenney's brand of shamanism, one has another person make a shamanic journey on one's behalf to find an animal spirit, which will present itself as willing to undertake the role. The shamanic trance in this case is induced through meditation and monotonous drumming.

One mentally enters the lower world through a hole in the ground. This could be a groundhog hole, a crack in a rock, a well, or even a hole at a golf course, Kenney explained.

A woman volunteered to do a journey to find a power animal for me. We lay side by side, with the drum beating. Within what seemed like less than a minute, the woman, a homemaker from London, Ontario, began excitedly breathing into my chest. She pushed me into an upright position and held onto my shoulders. It was explained to me that what she was doing was breathing the power animal into my chest and pushing it into my back.

She told me she had wanted to find me a cat, but had first seen a bald eagle. She continued to look for a cat and saw cougars and other felines. But the eagle told her, ''Take me, or I'll take you up in my talons.'' She said that, after she had breathed the eagle into me, she felt that she was riding on my back, soaring high and looking down on the world.

Kenney told me that his clients include teachers, business people, lawyers, chiropractors, nuns and priests. Shamanism is primarily used for healing, he said, and is particularly effective for helping schizophrenics. But it can also be applied to financial decision making and various other activities. Power animals can help you buy a home, plan a business venture, improve your performance in sports, and produce more creative art work, he explained.

Members of the group talked about problems they had in the restaurant with a rude waiter the day before. They discussed whether to send their power animals down to deal with him. ''Not to give him a hard time,'' Kenney said, ''That would be malpractice in shamanism.''

Kenney went on to talk about how power animals can be useful in everyday life. He gave an example of a woman who sent hers ahead to deal with the traffic lights when she was in a hurry.

Everyone in the group had apparently been successful in entering the spirit world and had colourful visions except for one man. This was a student in a university native studies program. He told me that everyone else in his program thought that he was nuts to want to come to this workshop because they do not believe that you can divorce shamanism from native cultures. He said he came because he wanted to experience things for himself, but found he was unable to get into it. Perhaps it was because he was unable to turn off his conscious mind, he said.

I did not make it into the spirit world either, but I did what I suspect a few others might have been doing. I faked it. In doing so, I applied one of the lessons that I had learned about shamanism in the course of my research. A good shaman or professional psychic of any kind makes it a practice to study people. Even if they do believe they have the gift to see beyond the veil of reality, most psychics are aware that this gift may sometimes desert them. As their reputation and livelihood depends on satisfying their clients, it is wise to take out a little insurance and observe ordinary details that might be of help when doing a psychic reading or a shamanic diagnosis.

I do not doubt the power of shamanism to heal people within the context of a primitive culture. I can also see the value that it has for twentieth century urban people in putting them in touch with their instinctive and unconscious selves. But I was not convinced by the bright and beautiful visions that this group of people achieved almost instantaneously in the course of a two-day workshop. I suspect that if any of them had really found their way into the lower world they would have been terrified.

I did encounter shamanism again, however, but in a different context, not divorced from its spiritual roots as in Kenney's universal shamanism, but as a part of an integrated set of beliefs. This was among groups of white people who are dedicated to learning and re-creating for themselves the native culture of North American Indians.

Many white people who have become disillusioned with competitive, materialistic and exploitative aspects of Western society have been drawn to native culture because of its emphasis on nature. Disillusioned urban white people have found a new sense of balance and connectedness in the native teachings of the medicine wheel. This is a rich and subtle system of correspondences between natural elements, plants, animals and human attributes. These white people have felt attuned to profoundly peaceful and relaxing native ceremonies like the Sweat Lodge, a sauna with a spiritual dimension, and the Pipe Ceremony, in which sacred tobacco is smoked in a circle as a form of prayer to the Creator. They have experienced a sense of liberation in the drumming, chanting and dancing that is also an integral part of traditional native culture.

All over Canada, particularly in urban areas, there has been a burgeoning in recent years of native-style medicine societies, lodges and circles exclusively comprised of white people. These groups are sometimes led by Metis, or others claiming some native ancestry, but seldom by full-blooded native people. Some of the members of these groups live and breath their particular version of native spirituality. They are more earnest about it and more idealistic than almost any native person, and in that respect, amongst others, they are missing the spirit of the original culture.

The west-coast Wiccan elder, Cornwoman, gave me an example of the kind of misunderstanding that occurs when white people adopt native ways and superimpose them on their own cultural assumptions. She said a group in the United States is exploiting people by charging $2,000 for vision quests in Death Valley. A vision quest is traditionally an initiation in which a person spends several days fasting alone in quest of a shamanic vision.

The group that offers these experiences does not have to provide food or board in its $2,000 fee, but it is not just that aspect that bothered Cornwoman. The hostile environment of Death Valley was an inappropriate location for a vision quest, she said, and the fact that it was chosen betrayed a lack of understanding of native culture.

White people see the vision quest as a test of their strength against nature but for natives it serves a completely different purpose. In traditional Indian communities people grew up in continual close proximity to other people. For them, the test of the vision quest is to experience being alone and finding oneself in that experience. The location for the quest is immaterial and need be no more than about 50 yards away from their house, Cornwoman said. White people, who are used to being alone, turn it into a rugged test of endurance, and in doing so completely change the meaning and purpose of the ritual.

''No Indian would be dumb enough to do a vision quest in Death Valley,'' said Cornwoman.

Many native people refer to the white people who adopt their traditional ways as the great tribe of ''Wanna'be'' Indians. Some are understandably bitter about what appears to them as a final insult from the white race, who have taken their land, destroyed their culture and are now appropriating their religion.

I saw this response in the look of pained disbelief on the face of a lone native person who found himself among a group of about 70 white people at a gathering of the White Buffalo Society Rainbow Circle in a Toronto college auditorium. The meeting was billed as a seminar on shamanism led by Cherokee medicine woman Pa'ris'ha. About a dozen white people with feathers in the hair, many wearing buckskins and beads, beat on drums, shook rattles, and made whooping and yelping sounds like the Indians in the old Hollywood westerns. I had noticed the real native person present and wondered what his reaction would be. I watched as he looked around in obvious discomfort and amazement. He shook his head and left. I do not know whether he was given a refund on the $50 fee that was charged for the two hour seminar.

Pa'ris'ha is a very energetic heavy-set woman with grey frizzy hair. She looks white, but she talks Indian. She refers to herself as ''the one they call Pa'ris'ha.'' While relating an anecdote concerning the Christmas season, she spoke of ''this that you call winter,'' and ''the tree that you call pine.'' Again, I thought of movie Indians, and was relieved to find that once Pa'ris'ha got further into her presentation she spoke normal English, as does any Indian who is not hamming for the tourists or a movie audience.

She explained that, in spite of her looks, she is sixty percent Indian. I gave up on trying to calculate what combination of ancestors one must have in order to be of that precise racial mix. She said she grew up on a reserve in the United States and always had to contend with the prejudice that her white skin inspired. She said many people think she is just another white woman trying to play Indian. She said, "Every time I was tested within medicine circles, I had to go a longer distance because of my white face. It has taught me how to sit outside, and look in, and measure myself only with my own yardstick."

Wearing feathers, she said, is not a way of "playing Indian" but of using costume as a prop that helps a person shake free their "vibrational energy." Pa'ris'ha said her teachings are "handed down directly by the purest Native American bloodline that exists in this generation."

Pa'ris'ha's disciples are mostly middle-class professional people, and they radiate the innocent glow and pure enthusiasm of cult followers. At one meeting, which I attended, they gave testimonials about how their lives had been changed by her teachings. Each testimonial was accompanied by yelps and rattles from the other members, in the manner of an old fashioned Christian revivalist gathering. They regard Pa'ris'ha as a prophet, who has announced the beginning of a new age of White Buffalo Medicine, which will bring world peace and brotherhood.

Most of Pa'ris'ha's seminar on shamanism involved a series of exercises in which the audience paired off and practiced seeing into one another's mind and embracing one another's aura, the field of psychic energy that is believed to surround the human body. I did not see any auras, but I must confess that I enjoyed the holding hands, touching foreheads, and dancing around that was involved in the attempt to do that. It struck me that this non-sexual, but nonetheless sensual, anonymous intimacy is part of the appeal of sessions like this in a repressed and impersonal urban environment.

I was reminded of the craze for Mesmerism in Europe in the eighteenth century. Franz Mesmer was the Swiss physician who believed that the human body contains a health-giving magnetic flow that could be improved by one person laying his hands on the thighs of another. The theory may not have been very sound, but many people did indeed find this form of therapy beneficial to their mental health.

Simply joining hands in a circle and chanting or praying together, a practice common to Native North American and European pagan traditions, is a way of fostering and expressing a sense of community and interconnectedness that many people lack in their everyday lives. At the end of Pa'ris'ha's seminar, her followers touched their hearts with their hands and raised their arms in unison as they sang ecstatically about their spirits ascending from the earth to become a part of all that is and has ever been.

Community and a sense of connectedness with the world is something that has also been partially destroyed in native culture. I could understand the response of the Indian who looked disgusted by the feathers and the ecstatic dancing of these middle-class white people, in the light of what white society has done to native culture.

Tourists who drive through a Canadian Indian reserve in search of the exotic are invariably disappointed and sometimes ashamed. They usually see poor, often dispirited people hitch-hiking or driving run-down cars. Along roads lined with makeshift shacks and prefabricated homes, the only buildings that show signs of affluence and pride are often the Christian churches. Once powerful indigenous nations, whose traditional culture respects the earth, are now forced to live in some of the most marginal, least productive areas, and live off meagre hand-outs from the people who invaded their land.

Old cultural and spiritual traditions have survived among Canada's native people. But, except in remote areas, it is only a minority who wholeheartedly adhere to them and they are no longer a cohesive force. They cannot be so in the way they once were, because the native religions embody a way of life, a set of relationships between nature and human communities, that has been destroyed by white society.

Many young native people are now returning to their old religion, however, and deriving strength from it. While white people are recreating Indian religion for themselves, it is also undergoing a revival among native people. I had an opportunity to experience the difference between these two revivals when I attended a pipe ceremony at a Toronto residence for native men, soon after I had gone to a similar ceremony conducted by a group of white people.

The native ceremony was very simple and moving. Many of the participants were people who had been experiencing difficulties with alcohol and coping with urban life. It was led by a man who said he used to be "a skid-row bum" and had lost an arm during a period of alcoholism.

Herb Nabigon told the group that his native religion helped him get his life back together again. He said he did four-day fasts every year for four years before Ojibwa elders gave him the privilege of carrying a ceremonial pipe and becoming a spiritual teacher. He spoke about the sacred fire that burns within each person and in the centre of the earth, and the need to overcome negative emotions like anger and jealousy that can extinguish that flame. Drawing simple examples from everyday life he spoke of the value of respect for the self, other people and the earth.

During the ceremony an eagle feather was passed around the circle of about forty people. Each person spoke as he held the feather about what the traditional teachings meant in his own life. Many of the group of about forty people said that they had not attended a native ceremony since they were children. One man said he did not even know that there were any medicine people on the reserve that he came from. Another man sadly told the circle that he used to have a feather like the one he was holding, but had lost it one night when he was drunk. Others spoke about the importance of keeping the sacred flame alive.

Nabigon filled the pipe quite casually and passed it around, asking each person to rotate the pipe so that it would point in each of the four directions, smoke from it and touch the ground with it as a mark of respect. With the exception of the pipe carrier himself, there was probably no-one present who knew nearly as much about traditional native teachings as the white people who have learned Indian culture. But this ceremony was more powerful and more natural than those of the white people. As each man held the pipe, he did so with the reverence and intensity that comes from a recognition that it was something that belonged to his own earliest memories and came from thousands of years of his own native culture.

The other ceremony that I attended was held by the members of the Dream Star Lodge, a shamanic lodge of ceremonial medicine. They meet for a pipe ceremony on the night of every full moon in a house in Toronto's east end. When I arrived, they were demoisturizing their drums, but, unlike Ed Kenney, they did this in a traditional way before a log fire. The logs were the kind that you buy in a supermarket wrapped in paper, but the drums were decorated with authentic-looking Indian designs.

"Did everybody see the moon," the lodge chief, Oriah Mountain Dreamer, asked a group of about 15 people sitting in a circle on her living room floor. The room was lit only by the fire, a few candles and a purple electric quartz crystal lamp. At the centre of the circle were some feathers, crystals and a vase of flowers. Someone asked where the flowers came from.

"Loblaws, strangely enough," replied Oriah, a tall slim elegant blonde-haired woman.

The members of the lodge all have ceremonial names like Gentle Laughing Wolf, Crystal Fingers, Otter-Holds-The-Earth and Trembling Leaves. They follow the teachings of Harley Swiftdeer, a shaman of Irish and Cherokee descent, who, I am told, smokes Turkish cigarettes and lives in Los Angeles. One of the group, who suffers from asthma, told me that Swiftdeer will not enter her house unless she lifts her smoking ban, but that he is able to use his shamanic powers to protect her from his second-hand smoke.

They are a very earnest group of people. They explained to me that having a sense of humour and not taking themselves too seriously is one of their teachings. But they seemed to lack the spontaneous sense of fun that one usually finds in traditional native culture. They spoke a lot about cleansing their *chakras,* shifting their centres and walking their paths with heart. *Chakra* is a Hindu term for a point of energy within the human body and has nothing to do with North American Indian religion, but the "Wann-a'be Indians" have no qualms about mixing different spiritual traditions. They also like using native words and they frequently say "ho," apparently an Indian expression signifying approval of some thought or sentiment.

At the pipe ceremony several members of the group reverently produced carved crystal skulls from little felt bags and placed these in front of them as an aid to meditation. When a visitor picked one of these up to look at it, he was warned to be careful as it was very expensive. On a table in the next room some of these skulls were exhibited for sale at $400 each.

Quartz crystals are an important element in most native medicine. They are believed to be a living rock, and come from the "veins of the earth." Traditionally Indians gathered crystals and other small objects of personal significance to them and carried them around in pouches called "medicine bundles," which served as spiritual aids or charms.

While the members of the White Buffalo Society seemed to emphasize the more exotic elements of Indian culture, the dancing, chanting, feathers and colourful dress, the Dream Lodge people appeared quieter, more serious. They too enjoyed a good Cherokee chant, but they were also all engaged in a very thorough study of the teachings of the medicine wheel and the meaning of different native ceremonies. The medicine wheel relates the four directions of the compass with the four elements and a series of other attributes of the natural, human and spiritual worlds. It counterbalances positive and negative aspects of life, and provides a set of practical guides for living in good health and harmony.

Most of the lodge members are women. I realized as I talked to them about their beliefs that many of them had found these teachings to be a helpful guide in their efforts to escape the negative programming and harmful experiences that are often an unfortunate consequence of growing up female in a patriarchal culture. Many of the lessons that they drew from native teachings involved overcoming dependencies and expectations that they had been brought up with and replacing these with self-acceptance and self-awareness. The native beliefs helped them to have the confidence to walk their own paths in life.

The desire to connect with and understand a spiritual world seems to be an ancient and all-pervasive impulse but it is hard to ignore the influences of several thousand years of social development. I believe it is easier for white people to connect with the ancient ways of their own culture than that of the North American Indians.

However much white people respect and try to emulate native ways, they are always delving into a culture that is basically foreign to their upbringing and temperament. They speak words that sound like a parody of bad translations of an indigenous language. They may understand the native ceremonies and customs, but they cannot fit easily and naturally into them. They seem more pious, more naive and more sanctimonious than Indians who grew up with these ceremonies and perform them casually and gracefully.

Indian traditions embody a sane and balanced view of life, in which mankind co-operates with nature and derives wisdom and power from contact with the spirit world. For many urban white people who have lost faith in the values of their own culture, this seems like a very precious thing. They are willing to pay a lot of money for it, but, somehow, it still eludes them.

In a similar quest for a spiritual connection with nature and an escape from the values of the dominant culture, some other Canadians are exploring different forms of paganism. Some of those I encountered were engaged in a scholarly attempt to understand and reconstruct ancient European pagan beliefs, while others were apparently inspired more by their own intuitive perceptions or visions of nature spirits. Some considered themselves part of a new pagan movement, while others were fiercely independent and reluctant to even attach the label *pagan* to their beliefs. What they all shared was a desire to revive the kind of magical relationship between nature and mankind that existed in earlier cultures but has been denied by modern science and organized religion.

One common trait I encountered among present-day pagans was a willingness to expose themselves to ridicule by espousing beliefs that may be rational within their own framework, but would seem quite bizarre to most people. I found an interesting example of this in the writings of Dorothy Maclean, a Canadian who was one of the founders of the Findhorn Community, which was fabled for growing a garden on hard, barren soil on the north-east coast of Scotland. The garden became famous throughout the world as an example of what can be done through co-operation with nature, as it supposedly produced exceptionally large vegetables where little could be expected to grow. In books written by members of the community, she and her colleagues have explained how they planned and planted the garden under the guidance of nature spirits, who appeared to them while they were meditating.

When I read Maclean's account of her communication with the spirit of a Monterrey Cypress tree in 1967, I was at first amused by the earnestness with which she described something so apparently ludicrous. But then I was impressed with the sanity of the message that she was relating. She wrote that the spirit told her, "Man is now becoming controller of the world forests and is beginning to realize how much these are needed by the planet. But he covers acres with one quick-growing species, selecting trees for economic reasons with no awareness at all of the planet's needs. This shows utter ignorance of the purpose of trees and their channelling of diverse forces. The world needs us on a large scale. Perhaps if man were in tune with the infinite, as we are, and were contributing his share, the forces would be in balance. But at present the planet needs more than ever just what is being denied it—the very forces which come through the large and stately trees."

In *The Findhorn Garden*, published by the Findhorn community in 1975, Maclean described how her contact with nature spirits arose organically from her childhood in Canada. She lived in a beautiful old house next to a wood with her two brothers and delightful loving parents. They had gardens of vegetables and flowers but she was not so much attracted to cultivated plants. She said she loved wandering in wild places. God, she wrote, was to her "an indwelling presence, the core of what I am and what everything is. God is life itself, speaking through all life."

This inner guidance told her to tune in to the nature spirits of clouds, of rain and of vegetables. These spirits which she called *devas*, using the Hindu word for "good spirit," were she discovered part of a hierarchy of beings, from the earthiest gnome to the highest archangel. The devas are the architects of plant forms, while gnomes and fairies are the craftsmen who build up the forms from the energy and plan channelled to them by the deva. She said these formless beings can make themselves visible and take on a shape intelligible to humans.

According to Maclean, the devas and nature spirits imparted practical information about how best to plant and care for each species, as well as providing insight into the true divine nature of the plants. She explained that she was not a gardener and could not impart any horticultural lore other than what was channelled through her by the devas.

It is hard to categorize these beliefs in the context of neo-paganism since they clearly represent a form of intuitive, direct communication with the spirits of nature, and contain little religious mythology. The belief in elemental powers is common to many pagan cosmologies. Witches believe that the elementals are the purest spiritual forms of the four elements, the raw energy from which all life is formed. The devas and archangels belong to Hindu and Christian religious systems, but there they appear in different roles. Fairies and gnomes play a major part in much pagan myth and folklore.

The only other information I can supply about the religious practices of the Findhorn community is that when I visited there a few years ago it was at the time of the summer solstice. My friend and I were met at the door by a small bearded man with penetrating eyes and a somewhat quizzical expression. He told us that we were welcome to wander through the garden but that all the members of the community were busy with a solstice celebration. The plants and vegetables were indeed impressive, but not as spectacularly large as I had expected. The land did not appear as barren or as exposed to the elements as is fabled. Although it was in a northerly location, it was in an agricultural area where others had presumably succeeded in growing some plants without the guidance of the spirits.

Irrespective of the validity of the claims made about the Findhorn garden, Maclean's account of her communication with the spirits does provide an insight into a kind of intuitive nature worship that represents one pole of the spectrum of contemporary pagan beliefs. I found a very different approach to paganism in Ottawa where I visited a scholarly Druid who uses painstaking research into an ancient world-view as a way of stepping outside the values of contemporary culture.

Seán Ó Tuathail has immersed himself in Irish Druidism for the past ten years and publishes a quarterly journal of ancient Irish culture called *Cainteanna Na Luise*. He is a published poet and scholar who is conversant with eight different languages and has written articles on zoology for journals in Canada, Britain and the United States.

Ó Tuathail, who cultivates a crusty curmudgeonly manner, does not like the label *neo-pagan* because he fears being associated with what he describes as "pop paganism." He speaks scathingly of people who wear robes and pentacles for fashion, and impose a veneer of paganism over a fundamentally Christian morality, worshipping a Mother Goddess who is really "Jehovah in drag."

Being a present-day Druid is a very serious matter for Ó Tuathail and one that involves an almost total absorption in a world-view that has been submerged by more than 1400 years of Christian culture. The Irish Druids were the last survivors of the priestly caste in a Celtic culture that once dominated Europe. They were gradually forced by the Romans to flee to the northern and western fringes of the continent, surviving in Ireland until about 560 A.D., when they were supplanted by a Christian clergy.

The Druids were philosophers, poets and mystics. They worshipped Celtic gods and goddesses, a disparate and rather unruly band of deities who seemed to spend much of their time fighting. These gods personified various human qualities and skills, with each god having several different attributes.

The appeal of Irish Druidism for Ó Tuathail lies in what he terms "its flamboyant complexity." He is not, in fact, Irish. He uses his grandmother's family name as a pen name. He said he likes the Druids' respect for animals and trees, their fiesty individualism and the fact that they did not worship omnipotent gods. He was also drawn to their spirit of "joyful pessimism," which is epitomized in such expressions as "the situation is hopeless, but not serious," or "isn't life terrible, thank goodness."

I got the impression that he was speaking from his own experience when he told me that finding an alternate spiritual reality can save the life or sanity of someone who feels trapped in a society that does not satisfy his needs and aspirations. He told me that he has always lived in a state of dissonance with the dominant culture, coping with a disfiguring birth defect, and developing an intense love of learning and nature.

He grew up in Wisconsin, strongly disliking the ethos of the United States, and immigrated to Canada on the day after he legally came of age. While his own personal interests as a teenager and young adult included philosophy, psychology and a variety of non-Christian religions, he described his parents as upper middle class Sunday Christians with no intellectual or cultural interests.

In Canada, he has worked at a variety of jobs and has obtained two Canada Council grants for his poetry. While doing zoological research, he kept a series of exotic animals, including cobras. He now lives in Ottawa with his black cat, Tixtlilt, an Aztec word meaning "Little Black Face," the name of a God of Good Health.

Ó Tuathail does not like to be categorized. He told me that he is "gay," but added, "if 'gay' is a life-style, then I'm 'homosexual.' "

He has practiced magic for a long time and says that he knows that it works. Shamanism was one of the spiritual disciplines that he explored before he discovered the Irish Druids, but he mocks the currently popular new age brand of shamanism: "Easy love spells in ten lessons. You too can be your own shaman. Instant everything."

His own idea of shamans is starkly different from the popular form. "They're weirdos," he said. "They (real shamans) had epileptic fits. They went through horrendous initiations, fasting, nearly starving to death. Some of them went blind or were lame. They were shunned by people on a daily basis."

Druidism first attracted him in 1979 and five years later he began to publish *Cainteanna Na Luise*. This is a quirky publication, which reflects the world view that it describes. It is uncompromisingly scholarly but also whimsical and chaotic, so that learned dissertations on early Irish epic poetry are interrupted with humourous anecdotes. Normal laws of syntax and spelling are disregarded. Uniformity of spelling and the logical structures of modern English grammar belong to the mind-set of our culture, Ó Tuathail says, and in order to get into an Irish pagan way of seeing things one has to escape these rules.

Ó Tuathail describes the journal as a personal expression: "The Irish have always thought talking has value, whether anyone is listening or not."

He said he was inspired to start the journal because he had seen too much "trash," too many incorrect images of Druids. His pet peeve is a group of self-styled Druids who perform rites at many neo-pagan summer festivals dressed in white cloaks. The Druids wore almost every colour under the sun but never dressed in white, he said.

The group to which he was referring was actually founded as a joke in the 1970s by a group of U.S. college students who were required by the regulations of their school to attend some kind of religious services. They formed the New Reformed Druids of America and invented rituals for fun. Since then the group began to take itself seriously and made attempts to discover what Druid rituals really were.

Ó Tuathail's purpose in studying the ancient Druids is, like that of other neo-pagans, to adapt it to present day life. But Ó Tuathail believes that in order to do that one must get as close as one can to the original culture. If, for example, he wants to understand what the Druid attitudes might have been to airplanes or cars, he researches what they had to say about chariots.

On a deeper level, Ó Tuathail's Druidism involves a different kind of relationship with the deity to that of either traditional Christianity or most neo-pagan beliefs. The Celtic Gods did not have to be worshipped. They were respected and revered but they sometimes fought with humans and did not always win. If people decided to defy the Gods, they were not met with heavenly vengeance but merely a withholding of supernatural aid.

The magic that Ó Tuathail practices is influenced by his linguistic research. In the Irish language, he explained, one does not say "I am happy," but "happiness is upon me." If one is doing a Druidic spell, one therefore has to be aware of the emotional viewpoint from which one is calling happiness to come down on someone rather than trying to influence the individual to be happy.

One of the many aspects of Druid culture that Ó Tuathail admires is their love of and respect for trees. The Druids associated different kinds of trees with the months of the year, the letters of the alphabet and the names of Gods. Certain trees were held to be sacred and even long after Christianity was established it remained illegal to cut them down. The rowan tree was a tree of life to the Druids and had magical and oracular powers. It could be used to compel demons to answer difficult questions. Its berries were the food of the gods, and its wood was used for making magic wands. Ó Tuathail always bows and salutes a rowan tree when he meets one.

In following the Druid custom of talking to trees, and believing as they do that trees talk back, Ó Tuathail recognizes that he might be considered eccentric. He lowered his voice as he explained this belief to me, and joked about men in white jackets coming to get him. In order to communicate with trees, he explained to readers of his journal, one has to stand receptively in front of them, feel the message they emanate and translate it into words. One has to avoid projecting one's own expectations or just imagining that they are talking. One must also be careful what one says to a tree, it seems, as they are often haughty and can easily feel snubbed. Then, of course, one can never be sure that they are telling the truth.

Visiting Ireland and doing rituals in the sacred Druid places is another aspect of Ó Tuathail's attempt to connect with ancient Celtic culture. He feels free there to make his ritual salute to every rowan tree he meets and perform rites at wells or stone circles without anyone paying much attention. Irish Catholicism absorbed Druidism, incorporating pagan gods as saints, ritual objects as relics, magical sites as shrines. Even after 1400 years some of these old beliefs have survived. Ó Tuathail was perhaps not exaggerating much when he claimed that the majority of present-day country people in Ireland still believe in magic and the little folk, or will say ''Give them a bit of milk, even if they don't exist.''

Ó Tuathail does not believe, as do many other pagans, that his beliefs can reshape the world. He believes, like many traditional witches, that pagan individuals and the movements that they join, together with other people who share their attitudes on ecology and peace, may have an impact. But he views his spiritual beliefs as simply a personal expression, a way of seeing the world that helps him feel more comfortable in it.

It is somehow typical of Ó Tuathail's attitude and beliefs that, when he talked with trees, they did not have any great truths to communicate. They apparently talked about being offended by not being treated with enough respect, and asked Ó Tuathail if he admired their delicate arrangements of berries and leaves. They disclosed no secrets of the universe and did not appear to have told any anecdotes or memories from the past few hundred years.

Another glimpse of the proliferation of current neopagan beliefs can be found through a western Manitoba couple who also talk to trees, and sing to them in order to encourage them to grow.

Like Seán Ó Tuathail, Aran and Sky Silmeryn publish a little magazine. But it is as different from the dense single-spaced type of *Cainteanna Na Luise* as one could possibly imagine. *Magic Feelings* is a bi-annual collection of poems, stories, richly ornamented ethereal drawings and articles about elven lore.

The Silmeryns describe themselves as elves. ''It is often so, that those who don't understand being elven, will mock our dreams and aspirations,'' they wrote in one issue of the magazine, ''They say they 'cannot see our pointed ears' — nonetheless, WE can FEEL them there. Yes, we have starlight in our eyes, but it doesn't blind us. Rather, it illuminates the world-picture, and enables us to pierce the veil of human illusion and deception. Hold to what you believe in! Speak only truth and speak it with wisdom. High Powers guard and guide you!''

Elves are a generic name for fairies and other nature spirits. The elven lore that the Silmeryns live by comes from a variety of sources, besides their own intuition. The most clearly identified of these are the fantasy writings of J.R.R. Tolkien, author of *The Hobbit* and *Lord of the Rings.* The Silmeryns frequently quote from Tolkien and they use a language called Eldarin, which he invented.

Even though it includes fiction in its sources, the elven way does have its roots in European folklore and pagan beliefs. Tolkien was a highly regarded linguistic scholar, who had a wide knowledge of Norse and Celtic myth. He used this knowledge in writing his fantasies. The Silmeryns own writings also draw upon such sources as the Druid tree calendar, and ancient Irish epics. In one article in *Magic Feelings,* Sky tried to show through analysis of Druid myths that Lug, the Druid god of light, was an elf.

In folklore, the magic of the elves and fairies was one of enchantment and mystery. It was not something that was worked at through occult study and the use of formulas and tools, as was the human magic of witches and magicians. It was a miraculous gift of unknown origin. It was a magic that was associated with sacred places, plants and trees. The most common way for people to fall foul of the fairies and be harmed by their spells was to cut down one of their sacred trees.

Elves have always been prominent in European folklore, and until a few centuries ago most people believed in them almost as much as they believed in Christ and the Devil. In popular imagination today, elves and fairies evoke different images, the elf being dumpier and grumpier than the fairy. But originally the words *elf* and *fairy* were used interchangeably to denote a variety of nature spirits. These were supposed to have existed since the beginning of time as guardians of the natural world. They varied in size from giants to tiny creatures smaller than blades of grass, but most often they appeared in human size. It was believed that they only made themselves visible when they wished to do so or in special magical locations, and then only to sensitive people. The Irish believed that these spirits, which they called leprechauns, would disappear at the blink of an eye, but would stay as long as one gazed steadily at them.

Elves were often associated with witches and may have historically been actual descendants of Stone Age tribes whose pagan beliefs formed the basis for witchcraft. In popular legend they rode across the sky on Halloween night, joining with the witches in wanton revels. Some people believed that they were the ghosts of pagans who could not find their way to heaven but were not bad enough for hell.

Like witches, they were sometimes feared, but also loved and respected by country people. They were believed to snatch babies from their cradles and kidnap mortal youths and maidens in order to mate with them. Some people, perhaps, used this myth as an excuse for more mundane misdemeanours. Elves or fairies often gave people gifts, magic bags of food, grain or money, that would always remain full.

At one seventeenth century witch trial, a man who was accused of witchcraft because he possessed a curative white powder explained that he got it from fairies. He invited the jury to go with him to see for themselves. The members of the jury showed no desire to risk an encounter with elves and he was acquitted.

A fear of elves evidently lives on in the prairie provinces. The Silmeryns told me that they were forced to leave their previous home in Torkton, Saskatchewan, because they were labelled and persecuted as "satanists," by people who either did not know them at all or were mere acquaintances.

Their magazine is a labour of love, "part of an offering to the Mother" for which they accept no payment, they explained to me in a letter. I had told them I wanted to find out more about elves. "There is a scattering of elves in Canada," they replied. "They are not really an organized group."

"As for elven lifestyle—well, at present we still reside in society, though we are currently looking for land to purchase to dwell upon. Do not think, though, that we are all talk of good things and no action. We strive to live as lightly as possible in a town," they wrote.

Living lightly involves a spartan existence. They do not use a refrigerator or many other electrical appliances because of pollution and energy wastes. Their love of music has led them to make one exception to this rule by having a tape deck. They do drive a car as they need one to look for land, but they intend to give that up once they settle in the wilds. They raise as much of their own food as they can, gathering herbs for teas and medicines. Most of their garbage is recycled or used for compost.

The Silmeryns celebrate the eight pagan festivals, and also have their own elven rites and gatherings. Whenever possible, these are held outside in natural surroundings. "We venerate both the Lord and the Lady," they told me. "Recognizing the divinity in ourselves and in all life, and recognizing the male and female principles that we, like everything in the universe, embody."

"Ever shine the stars," they wrote in closing their letter, and on the envelope was a printed sticker that read, "Pointed ears are a sign of intelligence."

According to the Silmeryns, "There are probably as many views on what 'being elven' is as there are elves." As I did not run into any other Canadian elves, I have had to rely on their views. Unfortunately, they did not, either in their correspondence or their magazines, ever get around to saying exactly what their conception of an elf is.

Their emphasis is on what an elf does. Elves, they say, plant trees, establish sanctuaries and care for the earth. Their magazines contain practical advice on saving energy, recycling and gardening. Elven ethics involve never lying, cheating, stealing or playing "head games," being responsible for oneself and respecting all living beings. They treat others with courtesy and gentleness, and are willing to give of themselves when needed. As an elf, "one obeys the Law, and its name is Love," they say. "One looks for the good in everything."

"One listens to one's heart," write the Silmeryns. They seem to be people who are living out a dream. Like the Findhorn people, their guidance seems to come from their own inner voices and what they perceive as the spirit of the natural world around them.

"With my perceptions, I will continue to shape my reality," Sky wrote. "Not alone! This reality is shared by all those who love and seek to care of the earth, and who wish to live in harmony with it."

Some people today are trying to revive old religions through scholarship, while others are using intuition to recreate ancient beliefs. It is hard to know what our ancient ancestors really believed. But the dream of connecting with a long lost world is one that lends purpose and meaning to some present-day lives.

My encounters with present-day shamans, Druids and elves left me wondering whether it ultimately makes any difference whether a belief system is painstakingly reconstructed from ancient text, copied from an indigenous culture or conjured up either from one's own imagination or someone else's. Ultimately what matters is whether it works for the individuals who follow it, and provides them with a code to live by.

CHAPTER NINE

Lion Serpent Sun

On November 20, 1984, an estimated three hundred thousand viewers, tuned in to the Christian television talk show "100 Huntley Street," were shocked and uplifted to hear the harrowing tale of a couple who found Jesus Christ after escaping the clutches of a murderous satanic cult in Victoria, B.C.

Canadian evangelist David Mainse showed the television audience in 43 communities across Canada and the United States a photograph of the man who, he said, tried to sacrifice the lives of a transient couple in a satanic ritual in 1972. The photograph depicted a bearded man with long black hair holding a sword and kneeling on a floor decorated with a circle containing an intricate pattern of angels and devilish bats. This was the ritual room of the Church of Satan in Victoria, the viewers were told, the very room where Len Olson, now a Pentecostal minister, and his wife Sheila almost stepped into hell.

Witchcraft still inspires fear in some people today and conjures up images of devil worship and human sacrifice that obsessed popular imagination in the sixteenth and seventeenth centuries. Many people suspect a link between witchcraft and the sinister practices of satanism. Such fears and suspicions were the focus of a libel case in 1988, which could be characterized as a modern Canadian witch-trial.

Two years after his first accusation, Mainse asked his audience for their prayers and financial donations to help in a battle with the Prince of Darkness. The man whom he and Olson had characterized as a devil's disciple was suing them for libel, and, according to Mainse, "That is very much something that Satan is promoting."

The alleged satanist, Mark Fedoruk, who has since changed his name to Lion Serpent Sun, maintained that he was in fact a follower of Wicca in 1972. He said the story of human sacrifice that Olson told on television was simply a drug-induced fantasy. Olson had been smoking a particularly strong form of marijuana from Thailand on the night of October 14, 1972, he said. Sun's lawyer, Robert Moore-Stewart, said Olson, who had been using the story as his ticket to evangelical religious circles for the past twelve years, had "literalized and scripturalized a bad trip."

The case came to trial in June, 1988, and Victoria's Courtroom A was filled to capacity for what promised to be the strangest and one of the most sensational libel hearings in Canadian legal history. The ranks of the regular court followers—retired people seeking more lively entertainment than that provided by Victoria's stately parks and decorous tea-rooms—were swelled by a large contingent of fundamentalist Christians, who sat as far away as possible from the witches and occultists accompanying Sun.

The six-week trial provided the media with titillating details of naked rituals, harrowing accounts of Olson's lurid allegations and humourous stories about Sun's version of the same incidents. In considering the issue of whether or not Sun was a satanist, as Olson and Mainse had claimed, the hearing delved into medieval witch-hunts and arcane realms of occult mysticism. It provided the public with a fascinating glimpse of witchcraft as it was practiced in the hippie sub-culture of the early 1970s. The trial stirred up long-standing conflicts, fears and prejudices in Victoria, where rumours about satanism have been rampant for many years. There was a widely propagated legend in the city that Victoria is one of the world's greatest centres for satanism. This belief persisted among many local people, although there have been no confirmed reports of occult-related crime in the city, and no-one there has ever publicly identified anyone, other than Sun, as a satanist. Sun maintained at the trial that Olson's story was the crux of this myth.

The libel hearing was welcomed by some members of both the Christian and occult communities as an opportunity to publicly explore this issue. Many witches, however, were worried that the trial would expose their beliefs to public vilification and ridicule. They were particularly uneasy about the case, because Sun, who claimed to have been a follower of Wicca in the past, was not accepted as such by many of the witches. He now describes himself as a bishop in the Holy Catholic Gnostic Church.

The Gnostics historically were a heretical Christian sect who believed that the supreme God exists outside the universe and that the world was the evil creation of a lesser deity, who jealously withheld knowledge from humanity. The Gnostics believed that knowledge was the way to achieve identity with the true God. The serpent in the Garden of Eden represented for them a compassionate female aspect of God who imparted knowledge and the hope of salvation to humanity. They interpreted the teachings of Jesus Christ in the light of this belief and saw understanding of positive and negative aspects of the world as one of the keys to wisdom. Present-day Gnostics generally believe that one must accept the light and dark sides of the self in order to achieve balance and pursue an understanding of the ultimate divinity.

Clearly the basis for Gnosticism, the belief that God exists outside of an evil world created by a lesser being, is very different to that of witchcraft, which reveres the natural world and sees the Goddess and God as inseparable from it. While the magic rituals that Sun performed in the early 1970s had many Wiccan elements, they also included invocations of gods and demons that had nothing to do with pagan beliefs. One witch told me she was bothered, not only by the fact that Sun's pantheon of Gods included Satan, but that it also included Jesus Christ.

In 1972, Sun was running a bookstore in downtown Victoria, called Diddling Metaphysical Books, a name culled from an Edgar Allan Poe short story. The store had a back room where a group of young people met regularly to perform magical rituals and smoke marijuana. Sun was described in a 1972 newspaper article as having clear blue eyes, long hair, a beard "and an appearance some would describe as Christ-like."

Now thirty-nine years old, his dark hair shorter and his beard trimmed very small, his blue eyes look piercingly from a thin face drawn tight with tension. Like his face, his manner is a study in light and shadow. He is warm and genial, but suspicious; witty but intense. He told me that he had been warned to curb his sense of humour while testifying in the trial. But he was a little perturbed to find himself described in one newspaper story as "a grim hatchet-faced man." He said, "I didn't think I was that serious."

Sun said that he always has been very spiritually inclined. He always believed when he was growing up that he would be a priest, though he did not realize then what kind of priest he would end up being. Sun told me how he used to bury toys, when he was a child, as a gift to all the dead children. Adults found this spooky, he said, adding that his mother was also perturbed by his early interest in reading about witchcraft and demonology. He said he first became intrigued with magic when he read Grimms' fairy tales at the age of six.

One of the members of the group that gravitated around Sun in the early 1970s described him as "a holy man." She said she was drawn to him after seeing him on television and being aware of "an aura around his eyes: it was the light shining from his eyes."

At that time, Sun was giving public lectures to student groups on witchcraft and the occult. An account in a student newspaper of one such lecture at the University of

Manitoba shows that the witchcraft that he believed in was somewhat different from the pagan witchcraft practiced by most Wiccans: ''Fedoruk explained that his cult believes in both Christ and the devil as being parts of an inseparable duality: 'All religions are the same in this respect — they come down to dualities. You can't have good without bad, night without day, Yin without Yang.' ''

For that lecture he wore clerical garb with an inverted cross around his neck. The inverted cross is currently used by satanists as a symbol of their rejection of Christianity. When one of the students asked him about the inverted cross, he told his audience, ''I can't see anything more negative than a man nailed to a cross.'' When people wear the cross as a positive symbol, he said, ''it indicates to me that they'd do it again.''

The group that met to perform magical rites in Sun's bookstore was described by former members as an eclectic one, which drew upon Eastern mysticism, witchcraft, gnosticism and other occult sources. One former group member, now a commercial artist, said he joined because the group showed ''extreme reverance for the spiritual nature of our lives.'' He said they also had very good parties, with alcohol and marijuana always available.

Gary Gage-Cole, one of the founders of the group, said it placed a lot of stress on etiquette. ''We had a saying, 'Etiquette before magic.' We liked to be around people who liked to be around people. We enjoyed the challenge of new ideas, the idea of being adult.''

It was to this circle that Len and Sheila Olson gravitated when they arrived in Victoria in 1972. Len was, according to Sheila, anti-Christian at that time. The couple had come to Canada from England and led a migratory lifestyle, which eventually took them to Dawson Creek, B.C. Sheila said they moved from there to Victoria with their three young children to get away from some personal problems they had encountered: 'It was in the business community . . . They were into wife-swapping and I was raped.''

The couple was given an introduction to Sun through their friend, Gerry Edwards, in Vancouver. Edwards was a member of the Church of Satan. This is a California-based group founded in 1966 by former lion tamer and police photographer Anton LaVey. The Church of Satan believes in self-indulgence, treating man as just another animal, showing kindness to those who deserve it, wreaking vengeance on enemies, respecting the strong and despising the weak. LaVey maintains that these values are more in keeping with the twentieth century than Christianity. His church uses magic, which it calls psychodrama, as a way of liberating man's true nature. Satanists often call themselves witches, but despise ''white witchcraft'' as much as they do Christianity.

Sun was a member of the Church of Satan for one year. He said he joined in order to get a subscription to the church's magazine, *Cloven Hoof*. When the Olsons met Sun, Sheila said, he told them that he and his friends were practicing Wicca, and they should not talk about Satanism. Len said Sun told him, ''Satan is another name for God and it is one and the same. It could be good or evil, depending on your own desires.''

The Olsons attended the rituals in the back room of the bookstore. According to Sun's ex-wife Judy, it was Len Olson who supplied most of the marijuana for these gatherings. Sheila maintained that the group was preoccuppied with evil. She said members would talk about ''whacking a few chickens' heads off'' and graveyard rituals, and would then say that they were only kidding.

The couple decided that they wanted to be initiated into the group. The initiation ritual, held in October, 1972, was obviously a disturbing experience for them. The circle on the floor of the ritual room, painted with the pattern of angels and bats, was surrounded by Hebrew letters standing for the names of God and symbols of fire, water, wind and earth. The names of Satan, Beelzebub, Lucifer and other fallen angels, balanced by the names of biblical persons, were written in a mystery script called Theban. A stained-glass window in the room depicted Baphomet, a mythical being with a winged androgynous body, a goat's head and cloven hooves. This image is similar to that of the devil as depicted in some tarot card decks.

Members of the group performed their rituals skyclad. The initiation involved a symbolic scourging with a macramed lash, and a five-fold kiss from the high priest or priestess (Lion or Judy Sun) on the feet, knees, genitals, breasts and lips. The rite also involved the high priest or priestess lying on top of the initiate, who was on the floor with a cloth drawn up between his or her legs.

Sheila Olson said the nude initiation ceremony, "terrified me . . . It made me think about discussions at the different meetings we went to — about the Sharon Tate murders and Charles Manson and his harem in the desert. We'd talked about animal sacrifices and orgies . . . Whenever Len and I said 'None of that,' they said 'Just kidding.'"

Nevertheless, the couple attended another ritual on October 14. This was to be an enactment of the myth of the Descent of the Goddess into the Underworld. Gary Gage-Cole played the part of Hades, God of the Underworld, and Judy Sun played Persephone, daughter of Zeus. She was required to strip off garments and jewelry to enter Hades's world and all present did the same. She was then 'symbolically bound and scourged."

After the ritual some of the members of the group left and about six others, including the Olsons, sat around the circle drinking mead, eating salmon sandwiches and smoking the Thai marijuana from a hookah pipe. The Olsons claimed in court that they had sworn off marijuana after being rattled by the initiation ceremony and did not smoke any that night. But everyone else testified that Olson smoked heavily. One group member said he had never seen anyone smoke as much pot as Olson did that night.

As Olson described it on the 100 Huntley Street program, "I looked in these faces and the people we thought we knew in this coven, these witchcraft people, I looked in their faces and they disappeared. And I saw these demons. I'd never seen demons before in my life, and I saw these demons. I saw these faces, and their whole bodies and faces were transformed. And I realized that I was almost in hell.''

According to Gage-Cole, ''Things started going crazy. Leonard was saying to Sheila, 'They're going to kill us. They're going to kill us.' Lion tried to calm them by bringing in a statue of Christ in the pose known as the Sacred Heart. This is an image of Christ with his heart exposed. Len was saying 'They're all demons.' Lion was saying 'Look, Len, Jesus is here.'''

This did not alleviate Olson's fears. In his view, the statue was brought in because ''they were symbolically killing Christ, by killing us.''

At this point, according to Gage-Cole, Sun decided to shut down the circle. The group believed that in order to do that they had to disperse the energy that they had summoned with their rituals. They did that by holding up their athames.

''Bringing daggers into the circle with Leonard in the state he was in was a mistake,'' Gage-Cole said. ''He started yelling, 'They're going to kill us.' So then we went ahead and dispersed the energy with our fingers, instead of the daggers, pointed over the top of the circle.''

Olson said he began to think of Jesus for the first time in his life and sang a hymn. He said the pure sound of a flute came out of his vocal chords. The knives were raised to their throats, Olson said, but the gentle voice of Jesus spoke in his ear and told him to step out of the circle. He said Sheila, who had fallen under the influence of the demonic group, tried to pull him back, saying, ''Len, it's okay to die. Come back into the circle.''

According to the Olsons, Len at this point commanded the group to drop their swords and they did so. Then they said they bolted out of the store. Gage-Cole testified, ''Len bolted out of the room as soon as we broke the energy. Sheila was still in the room. She was being apologetic.'' He said he put on his robe and went into the front room of the bookshop, where he saw Sheila Olsen getting dressed. He said Leonard Olsen was fumbling with the lock and had to be helped to open the door.

The Olsons said that the experience prompted them to seek out Jesus Christ and that they subsequently went to the Glad Tidings Church and became born-again Christians. Sheila explained, "I said we had to see a minister because that night I realized the devil was real. And if the devil was real, then God had to be real."

They said they also reported the incident to police. In what was a crucial piece of evidence at the trial, a retired police officer testified that Olson's original complaint was not of attempted murder, but that Sun and two other men tried to have sexual relationships with his wife while she was in the circle.

Olson subsequently became a Pentecostal minister and director of Teen Challenge, a Vancouver outreach centre for teenagers. During the next twelve years, he often repeated the story of how he and his wife were nearly sacrificed to the devil.

Sun testified that he began having business problems when Olsen started distributing a pamphlet called "Set Free" telling the tale of his narrow escape from a satanist cult. He said fundamentalist Christians harassed people outside his bookstore every day and inserted pamphlets in his books. Some had megaphones, he said, and shouted things like "Thou shalt not suffer a witch to live."

Sun said he told Olson at that time, "I want to remind you I used to be a biker and it's not beneath me to give you a punch in the nose." He said Olsen covered his ears with his hands and chanted repeatedly, "Jesus loves me. Jesus loves you."

When later questioned about his biker connections, Sun said he was never a formal member, but had friends who were members of a gang in Kamloops, where he lived before moving to Victoria in his late teens. His friends belonged to the Devil's Escorts, which became Satan's Angels and then Hell's Angels. He said he rode with them and after he moved to Victoria rode with another outlaw biker group called the Pharaohs.

In 1977, the newspaper *The Victorian* quoted Olson in a story which began: "Satanic witches, who summon the presence of the devil and make human and animal sacrifices for their beliefs number almost 1000 in the capital city, says a former Victoria resident who claims he and his wife barely escaped the witches' clutches with their lives."

Olson was quoted as saying, "They're still in Victoria. Everytime I make a trip to Victoria, I see at least a dozen of the witches. Many of them are prominent business people and a substantial number are newspaper people. During the daytime they can't be picked out from anyone else. . . . Their peddler—or the man who tries to bring in new members—is a long-haired hippy-type character who carries a bible under one arm. His method of enticing new members is to try and sell the white or good witch routine. There are no white witches. It's just a front. And for the most part they're after young girls."

Public concern about satanism in Victoria was also generated by the publication in 1980 of *Michelle Remembers,* a popular book written by local psychiatrist Lawrence Pazder and patient Michelle Smith. While undergoing therapy, Smith recalled that she was abused by devil worshippers when she was a child. The book detailed a series of brutal physical tortures that she said she suffered. She went on to describe the devil himself appearing before her. As her therapy progressed, she remembered more than a hundred lines of verse, which she said were spoken by the devil and described his plans for spreading evil in the world.

Pazder, who is a Roman Catholic, believed his patient's story, and local Catholic clergymen took it seriously enough to bring it to the attention of senior church officials in Rome. The doctor and patient, who have since had their previous marriages annulled and married one another, are now widely considered to be experts on satanic ritual child abuse.

In the book, Pazder stated, without naming his sources, that there is a lot of psychiatric literature about satanic cults, that they are a world-wide organization, older than the Christian church and "one of the areas where they're known to be active is the Pacific Northwest."

Apart from Smith's own memories, the only documentation presented in the book to support the contention that satanists were active in the Victoria area was the 1977 article in *The Victorian* quoting Olson.

Olson's allegations were repeated in 1982 in the Vancouver *Province,* which ran a story about how "Victoria's witches and Satanists, people leading shadowy double lives, frustrate police forces, social workers and Christian churches, who are constantly beset with rumors about their devilish activities, but never seem able to pin them down with hard evidence."

The following year at Halloween, a Victoria hospital hired additional security guards because of a warning that a satanic cult group might kidnap babies for use in their rituals. A story in the Victoria *Star* stated that hospital officials did not, however, believe in the threat, which originated from the concern of a fundamentalist preacher that unbaptized children would be taken by the devil.

The persistent rumours and concerns about satanic cults and occult-related crime in Victoria surfaced again recently. A CBC television reporter who investigated these concerns said he talked to police and coroners and was not able to find even a suspected case of satanic or occult crime.

After the "100 Huntley Street" broadcast, Sun said he was attacked in downtown Victoria, lost a tooth and had his nose broken. He said that on another occasion he was jumped on by a man calling him a high priest of the Church of Satan. Since 1984, he has been hospitalized three times for anxiety. He said he suffers severe headaches every day and fears for the safety of his daughter. He also said that his work giving lectures and appearing on television explaining metaphysics has dried up since Olsen's story spread. He has been on welfare since 1982, done occasional teaching, haircutting and landscaping work.

"I am feeling very persecuted. There's been devil-bashing going on. Of course there's people profiting from it — David and Leonard. They're asking for prayers and pledges," Sun said. "To me these men [Mainse and Olsen] are anti-Christs. I feel, if Jesus came back today, they would be the first ones out there with the hammers and the nails because maybe He might have tattoos or He might be a She and black."

"I feel like I'm the one on trial," said Sun. In a sense he was, but that was because of the nature of the libel action that he had launched. He was alleging that Mainse and Olson libelled him by calling him a satanist and saying that he had attempted to kill the Olsons in 1972. Their defense was that these statements were true or, at least, fair comment. So the evidence in the trial examined the 1972 incident and addressed the question of whether or not Sun was a satanist at that time. As the court probed this man's personal religious ideas and practices, often comparing them with satanic and heretical beliefs from the past, it did indeed take on something of the character of an inquisitional witch trial.

Perhaps the most bizarre piece of evidence in the whole hearing came from one of the expert witnesses. Sun had called expert testimony from Victoria witches Jean Kozocari and Robin Skelton, who told the court that most of his group's rituals and symbolism appeared consistent with Wicca, though Skelton conceded that some were a little eccentric. Then the defense called Carl Rashke, a professor of religious studies at the University of Denver. Rashke shocked the court with a theory that resembled the denouement of an occult horror movie.

The professor linked the alleged attempted human sacrifice on October 14, 1972, with the arrest 666 years earlier of members of a group of noblemen who confessed under torture to worshipping a devil whom they called Baphomet. He told the court that a human sacrifice might have been planned by Sun's group to celebrate the dawning of a new satanic age. He said a satanic age is 666 years long, corresponding to the number of the Beast in the biblical Book of Revelations. Members of the Order of The Knights Templars were arrested in France on October 13, 1307, he said, 666 years and a day before Sun's ritual on October 14, 1972.

The Templars, who built up a trading empire during the Crusades, became the most powerful commercial force of their time in Europe and were also strong critics of the religious orthodoxy of the church. The French king, who had fallen heavily in their debt, persuaded the Pope to prosecute them for sodomy and heresy. When they were found guilty, the king was able to confiscate all their property.

No-one knows what the reality was behind the devilish practices that they confessed to under torture. It is possible that the Baphomet figure that they said they worshipped was really the Moslem prophet Mohammed, conjured into a devilish form by the Inquisitors. Some of the Templars were executed but there is a mystery about the fate of the majority of the members of the order. More than 400 years later, in the eighteenth and nineteenth century, various occult groups and masonic orders claimed that they possessed the secret knowledge of the Templars that had been preserved through the intervening generations.

Gary Gage-Cole and Judy Sun, Lion's ex-wife, now belong to a secret occult order that was indirectly influenced by the Knights Templars. This is the Ordo Templi Orientis (O.T.O.), which means the Order of Eastern Temples. It was founded in Germany early in this century, but its dominant influence was the English magician and mystic Aleister Crowley.

Gage-Cole testified at the trial that many of the rituals used by Sun's circle in the early 1970s were copied from Crowley's works. He said the group did not adopt all the teachings of Crowley, who made references in some of his works to blood rituals and human sacrifice.

Sun produced for the court his group's *Book of Shadows*. He said he had agonized over doing this as he had sworn to keep it secret. Stamped on the leather cover of the book was an inverted pentacle bearing a goat's head, identical to the symbol that appears on Anton LaVey's *Satanic Bible*. Sun said he did not believe the symbol represented Satan. He said he also had the symbol emblazoned on his wedding ring, and it was there "to remind me constantly not to turn things upside down and not to use scapegoats."

One passage from the *Book of Shadows* stated that nothing is absolutely evil and a time will come when the Archangel of Evil will have his "angelic nature" restored to him. Professor Rashke interpreted this as a prediction of a new age when Lucifer will rule the earth.

A lawyer representing Mainse put it to Sun that the ritual on October 14 was a sacrifice to mark the beginning of a new age and that Crowley wrote that the planet should be bathed in blood at the beginning of a new age. Sun replied, "I'm quite shocked by what you're saying."

The jury gave its verdict after 15 hours of deliberation over two days. It found that it was not true that Sun attempted or intended human sacrifice. But it also made the finding that it was substantially true that Sun was a satanist in 1972. The jury awarded Sun $10,000 damages and costs.

Mainse and Olson decided to appeal the decision. Mainse wrote in a 100 Huntley Street newsletter: "Dr. Raschke, professor of Religious Studies at the University of Denver, said, 'This is the first time in North America that anyone has been stated by a court of law to be a satanist.' We have received an education such as no other forum could have provided in satanism, witchcraft and the whole new age religion. This research will form the basis for several weeks of teaching on these things in the months to come, should Jesus tarry further in His return."

"Furthermore, I believe God is leading us to appeal to a three-judge panel of the Supreme Court of B.C. on certain points of law in order to seek a protection for the right of broadcasters in the public interest, so that others both secular and religious will not be afraid to allow people to say what they sincerely believe needs to be said to warn and protect others,'' wrote Mainse, asking his supporters to donate money to a defence fund.

In October, 1988, British Columbia Supreme Court Judge William Davies ruled that a jury cannot award costs and that the costs would be equally divided between the two parties. Since the costs were greater than the $10,000 award, Sun's victory is a hollow one.

In a recent television panel discussion on witchcraft, Sun complained that he was the victim of a modern-day witch-hunt. He said, ''I was burned by the state.''

CHAPTER TEN

Satanism and Black Magic

In a small town in south-western Ontario, there is a culvert called Hell. It is where a group of up to forty teenagers go to burn bibles, consult ouija boards and worship the devil. Soon the piece of wasteland where the culvert lies will probably be developed as a subdivision, and the kids will find a new spot to socialize, take drugs and practice their makeshift rites.

Social workers say this is mostly an adolescent rebellion against the rigid Christian values of a rural community, a source of entertainment in a town where there is little recreation for kids who have neither the means nor the desire to play hockey. But the ouija board told one girl to kill her parents and another is inclined towards self-mutilation.

All over Canada there have been reports of animal sacrifice, suicide and even murder in the name of Satan. There are also allegations of children being sadistically sexually abused in satanic rituals.

After a period of initial disbelief and denial, police and members of the public have begun to realize that we have a new social problem in our midst. Occult crime has become a hot topic in police training programs, social workers are attending workshops on satanism, ex-satanists are becoming regular guests on daytime television shows and the public is reading more and more stories about satanic crime in the newspapers.

Much confusion surrounds this issue, however. Police often get erroneous and misleading information in their training manuals. Social workers sometimes jump to conclusions about the evidence they see. The media often perpetuates distortions and exaggerations.

At the root of all this confusion is the fact that the mainstream of society has never regarded the occult as worthy of serious consideration. It has generally been seen either as entertainment or a flaky fringe pursuit. Now that attention is being paid to occult crime, few people understand the whole phenomenon of which the disturbing and threatening elements are just a part.

Many teenagers are now scaring others and themselves with a bizarre mish-mash of blood rituals, heavy metal rock music and ancient occult lore. Some murderers and other criminals are justifying atrocities in the name of Satan. At the same time, an increasingly vocal and visible group of people who call themselves witches are saying that their magic is for healing and their religion a return to earth-enhancing pagan beliefs.

Inevitably the two phenomena have been confused in some people's minds, while others refuse to believe that they are not connected. However much pagan witches maintain that they do not believe in the devil and that harming other people is contrary to their basic beliefs, popular suspicions persist that so called "white witchcraft" is just the public face of "black magic."

When I was setting out to contact witches in British Columbia, another writer warned me that the "white" witches are either themselves deceived about the true nature of the old religion or are deliberately concealing its dark secrets. She said she felt that people like the poet Robin Skelton were sincere in their beliefs, but were duped into participating in something fundamentally evil. She told me she had done some research to try to prove that this was the case, had not found any evidence, but was still convinced that there was more to witchcraft than meets the eye. A similar attitude was illustrated by an anecdote told to me by a Christian friend who had attended an ecumenical gathering in Vancouver. A Presbyterian woman told the meeting that she had been shocked and repulsed by a bumper sticker advocating witchcraft. She asked the group to pray for the misguided souls who were being lured into devil worship. When my friend asked the woman what the blasphemous slogan was, she explained that it read: "Witches Heal."

While many members of the public are suspicious of witches and frightened by what they think they represent, the present-day pagans are alarmed by what they see as a potential revival of age-old hatred and persecution. These fears were fuelled among witches in Canada by an incident in Edmonton that was widely reported and commented upon in pagan newsletters and magazines but received little public attention elsewhere. This occurred in 1987, the year of the devastating tornado that struck the city killing 27 people on July 31. Soon after that disaster, a woman who owned a local occult bookstore said she began to receive calls from someone who accused her of being a witch and having caused the tornado. A few weeks later her store was vandalized and in December of that year her home was destroyed by fire.

The Lion Serpent Sun case was another focus for these concerns, as are the frequent attacks on witches in some fundamentalist Christian publications. In the fall of 1987, a newspaper called *Battle Cry*, published by evangelist Jack Chick, who also produces tracts and comic books attacking Mormons and Roman Catholics, stated: "An old wickedness, masquerading as an innocent new 1980s style religion, is popping up on many police reports and in propaganda-like newspaper articles. Wicca, a form of whitewashed satanism, is drawing thousands into what appears at first to be a harmless 'back to nature' religion."

For some Christians and others, there is no distinction to be made between devil worship, witchcraft and other occult practices or new age therapies. They are all seen as examples of idolatry and falsehood which are therefore the works of the devil. Although this is obviously a minority view, it tends to be more widely propagated than other such extreme positions because of the lack of public understanding of the occult. Since fundamentalist Christians are among the few people in society who have taken an interest in satanism up until very recently, they do have a wealth of information about it and are therefore used as resources by police and media who might otherwise ignore their ideological viewpoints.

Christian evangelists who say that they used to be satanists have been frequent guests on television talk shows, which have found that audiences are intrigued with the highly emotive and controversial topics of satanic crime and ritual child abuse. The media sensationalization of this issue peaked with a Geraldo Rivera documentary on satanism, which was attacked by critics as "trash television" but attracted an audience of 50 million people, the largest ever to watch a documentary program.

This documentary presented the public with a confused but frightening message. It linked documented cases with allegations and suspicions to present a picture of an undefined and undifferentiated satanism as being responsible for a wide range of crimes. While it did serve to draw attention to some real issues, it also contributed to a self-perpetuating myth. A few days after the show aired, a teenager from Tampa, Florida, told police that he gained the "courage" to kill his mother after watching an earlier Geraldo daytime television special on satanist teenagers.

A strange case of a cult that was partly modelled on media distortions of black magic captured the public attention in April, 1989, when several mutilated bodies of ritually murdered victims, together with a cauldron containing boiled human brains, were found in Matamoros, Mexico. The group that committed these atrocities was a drug-smuggling ring that was ordered by its leader, who was known as "the godfather," to perform ritual human sacrifices in the belief that this would secure occult protection.

The leader's female companion was referred to by police as "the witch."

The rituals that this group performed were based on Palo Mayombe, a Cuban sect of Santeria. Santeria, like Voodoo, is a mixture of African and Christian beliefs that involves offerings to and supposed oracular communications with African gods. Although Santeria and Voodoo are popularly known for the negative magic that some practicioners indulge in, they are primarily legitimate religious faiths. Palo Mayombe, as followed by many Latin American drug gangs, is a corruption of these, which seems to serve a primary function of keeping followers in line and terrifying enemies and followers alike.

However, it appears that one of the sources for the rituals of the Matamoros cult was a Hollywood movie. A cult member told police that the form of Santeria that they practiced was that depicted in the film *The Believers,* which their leader made them watch repeatedly on videotape. The film, which was in fact shot in Canada, was itself a distorted version of a novel about murders committed by followers of Santeria.

By a strange paradox, the murders in Matamoros, which, more than any other case in recent history, alerted the public to the reality of occult-related crime, were partially inspired by fiction. This, I believe, is typical of the phenomenon that we label satanic or occult crime. Ever since the period of the witch-hunts, when some rebels and psychopaths espoused the myth of the devil worshipper that the Inquisition had propagated, deviants have been drawn to the images of black magic projected by our culture.

Many of the people who dabble in satanism and black magic, or commit crimes in their name, are influenced more by their own fantasies, the myths of popular culture, or even graphic condemnations of evil in religious texts, than by the actual beliefs that have come down through historical traditions. However, it is necessary to understand these beliefs in their original form in order to come to grips with the satanic rebellion of many young people today, the dangers that this poses and the challenge that it presents to society.

Satanism and black magic, though often linked together in practice, are essentially different phenomena. Satanism is a philosophy based on a reversal of Judeo-Christian concepts, while black magic is the practice of witchcraft and other forms of magic for negative or selfish ends.

I think it is important to point out that, in considering black magic, we are looking at something that comes from the dark side of human nature and is not peculiar to magical practice. The dark side of Christianity was very much in evidence in the barbaric practices of the witch-hunts, which were far more palpably evil than the real or imagined devilry that they were designed to crush. It was also there in the Crusades and other religious persecution that continues to the present day. One could characterize the 1978 mass suicides at Jonestown in Guayana, at the behest of the leader of a fanatical Christian sect, as an example of black Christianity.

The practice of black magic is probably as old as that of magic itself. Unless motives such as jealousy, malice, ambition and revenge were completely unknown in the earliest human societies, it is likely that there were some people who acquired magical skills and were inclined to use them for negative purposes. There are records of black magic being practiced in the earliest European civilizations. In Mesopotamia in 1800 B.C., there was a law by which black magicians or sorcerers were to be put to death. In ancient Egypt, people used to wear amulets to counteract evil spells. Wherever witchcraft or sorcery has been practiced, people have invariably recognized that the herbs that heal can be deadly poisons, and the spells that help crops grow can also be used to blight them.

There is an old belief that one still hears voiced today that there are two paths of witchcraft, the right-hand path of white magic, and the left-hand path of black magic. The origin of these terms is obscure, but they correspond with old associations of the right hand with strength, directness and rectitude and the left with weakness and duplicity. In Latin *sinister* means "left," and the Old English word from which the modern *left* is derived meant "weak." (This use of right and left to denote good and evil has nothing to do with the political categories right-wing and left-wing, which are derived from the fact that more progressive elements traditionally sat on the left-hand side of the chairperson in various European political assemblies.)

Most magicians and witches maintain that there are not, in fact, two different forms of magic. They say that the difference between black and white magic lies not in the magical techniques or the energy that they summon up, but in the people who practice it and the purpose for which it is applied. This is largely true, and the point that one should judge the magician, not the tools, is a valid one.

However some practices are peculiar to black magic. The most obvious of these is the practice of human or animal sacrifice, or any other sadistic act, as a means of raising energy through the pain suffered by the victim and the state of emotional frenzy aroused in the magician. There is also an ancient belief that blood is the medium in which energy flows through the body and therefore that shedding of blood, drinking it or smearing it on a ritual object are ways of releasing, capturing and transferring that energy.

From a practical perspective the act of performing such a sacrificial ritual hardens the resolve of the magician, fixing evil intentions and brutalizing the sensibilities. Anyone who perpetrates such an act is obviously to be feared, both because of what they might do and because of the kind of person they are striving to become.

Necromancy is another magical technique that is generally considered to be only the province of black magicians. This is the evocation of spirits of the dead for the purpose of fortune telling. It can be done in a symbolic form, but may involve exhuming a dead body. This is supposedly a very dangerous ritual, which may result in attracting a host of undesirable spirits. Akin to this is the Voodoo legend of the zombie, an empty body raised by a sorcerer to act as a slave. The idea of spirits of the dead returning to the world of the living occurs in Jewish folklore in the legend of the dybbuck, a restless soul that takes possession of a living body and can only be expelled by conjuring the divine name.

Some fundamentalist Christians attack spiritualism by confusing it with necromancy, but this is an erroneous association. Spiritualism is a belief in human abilities to contact the spirits of dead people and receive information from them, but it is not a form of magic. It involves cultivating a receptive state and waiting to be contacted by spirits who are willing to communicate. Necromancers use magic in an attempt to compel spirits to appear for interrogation.

Some forms of ceremonial or ritual magic involve summoning demons. These are usually thought of as black magic, as the purpose is often to derive personal power from the demons or use them for negative purposes, but this kind of ritual can also be performed with the aim of forcing the demons to do good. The psychological basis for this ritual was described by one modern occultist as a way of bringing one's own evil tendencies out into the open and putting them under the command of the higher self. However, the writer, William Gray, noted this is dangerous because, "if anything goes wrong and they obtain mastery over the operator during the encounter, exactly the opposite would occur, and a much more sophisticated and efficient Evildoer would emerge to swell the ranks of the Wicked Ones."

Most people who perform either black or white ceremonial magic today regard it as a form of psychodrama designed to release their subconscious thoughts and feelings and realize their full potential. The fundamental difference between black and white magic is the purpose to which it is put. A black magician is concerned primarily with the liberation of desire and the exercise of will. White ceremonial magic may also involve liberating desire, but the purpose is to recognize unconscious feelings for what they are and attempt to put them in tune with the higher self and the guiding principles of the universe.

One of the fundamental beliefs that runs through most of the western occult tradition, including both witchcraft and ceremonial magic, is that the Judeo-Christian idea of God as being identified only with good, and not with evil, leads to a one-sided view of human nature and the world. According to this view, the Judeo-Christian tradition encourages people not to accept themselves as they really are, to brand some aspects of their nature as evil and attempt to cast them out and stamp them down. This is seen as a way of self-denial, leading to an objectification of evil, a desire to see other people or the world as bad, which in turn causes hatred and strife.

Aleister Crowley, whom many people regard as one of the inspirations behind present-day satanism, was well versed in all forms of ritual magic and also imported into this tradition sexual magical practices from eastern religions. He maintained that he was not a black magician, and did not believe in deriving energy from pain and torture, but he subscribed to the notion that blood was a conduit of magical energy and that one could harness the energy of any being by ritually killing it within a magic circle.

In a passage about blood sacrifices that was probably deliberately designed to shock, Crowley explained that for the greatest magical effect one should choose ''that victim which contains the greatest and purest force. A male child of perfect innocence and high intelligence is the most satisfactory and suitable victim.''

Crowley added in a footnote that he performed this sacrifice on average 150 times a year, and this, his present-day followers are quick to explain, is an indication that he was speaking metaphorically of the spilling of semen in an act of sexual magic. Crowley's doctrine of will, which he called Thelema, is now an underground religion practiced by some Canadians. Since Crowley was, to say the very least, obtuse in his use of metaphor, I am quite uneasy about the prospect of one day meeting a fundamentalist Thelemite who believes in a literal interpretation of his writings.

In the passage that I just quoted, Crowley went on to say that one can use incense as a substitute for blood, "But the bloody sacrifice, though more dangerous, is more efficacious; and for nearly all purposes human sacrifice is the best."

Crowley predicted the coming of a new age, an age of Thelema or will, whose ruler would be Horus, the Egyptian God of the sky. He wrote, "There is a magical operation of maximum importance: the Initiation of a new aeon. When it becomes necessary to utter a word, the whole planet must be bathed in blood. Before man is ready to accept the Law of Thelema, the Great War must be fought. This bloody sacrifice is the critical point of the World-Ceremony of the Proclamation of Horus, the crowned and conquering child, as Lord of the Aeon."

It is reassuring to know that Crowley and his followers believed that the new age was proclaimed with the outset of the First World War in 1914.

In looking at satanism as an influence on what is termed occult-related crime, one has to be aware that one is dealing with a very diffuse and ill-defined phenomenon. Satan is a powerful symbol of evil and rebellion in Christian culture and has been used in many different ways.

Witches and various heretical groups have been accused of devil-worship and linked in popular imagination with all kinds of atrocious crime since the early days of Christianity. In some cases these groups were gnostics who did not accept the Christian dualism of good and evil and saw Satan as embodying a partly positive spirit of knowledge and energy. Others, like many of the people accused of witchcraft, were pagans who became confused with devil worshippers. There have been in the past, as there are now, some psychopaths for whom Satan has become a powerful symbol for their own compulsions, as well as being an excuse for their crimes. One nineteenth century historian claimed that devil worship became a popular form of rebellion because of the harshness of social conditions in Europe during the period of the witch-hunts, when "hell itself could appear as a shelter, an asylum, a relief when compared to the hell of this world."

As long as Christianity has been the dominant religion in society, there have always been some people whose rebellion against it has taken the form of a desire to mock and defile Christian rituals and beliefs. The Black Mass, which became popular in France about 250 years ago, was the classical example of this. These were usually performed by defrocked priests, who would say the Latin prayers backwards over an altar on which a naked woman would lie. The host was consecrated by the priest and then defiled, and the ritual would turn into an orgy. The jaded tastes of members of the French aristocracy probably inspired these rituals more than any spiritual goals. There were allegations that babies were sacrificed at these rituals, but these claims were made in the context of court intrigues and it is impossible to know to what extent they were based on fact.

Modern satanism often takes the form of a simple rebellion by teenagers who burn Bibles to symbolize the rejection of the religion and culture of their parents. It may be the personal fantasy of someone whose antisocial tendencies are mingled with religious imagery. It is also a modern philosophy that has been formulated in Anton LaVey's *The Satanic Bible*, a supposedly humanistic religion of self-expression, selfishness and sexual liberation.

Satan was the "adversary" in early Hebrew tradition, one who would accuse men before God. He came to be identified with the serpent, who tempted mankind with the fruit of the Tree of Knowledge in the Garden of Eden, and with Lucifer, the Archangel of Light, who rebelled against God, was thrown out of heaven, and became the Prince of Darkness. LaVey's satanists worship the devil as representing the rebel who rejects the hypocrisy of all organized religions and accuses God before mankind. Satan is seen as the principle of enlightenment and knowledge.

LaVey claims that satanists are witches of the left-hand path and that they are the only true witches. He sees the so-called white witches as merely mimicking Judeo-Christian morality. LaVey advocates the use of rituals as a means of overcoming guilt and inhibition. The Black Mass is an example of such rituals, but LaVey suggests making up ones that are relevant to the fantasies of the people involved and that will help them achieve their goals. He suggests that men should dress for rituals in black robes while women should wear sexually suggestive clothing. For him, a ritual is a form of magic that is directed towards achieving a practical result. He sees the purpose of magic as always being a selfish one, since he rejects all forms of altruism as hypocrisy.

The Satanic Bible does not condone sexual violence, animal sacrifice or violence towards any unwilling victim. It also opposes the murder of children. However it does say that it is quite acceptable to perform rituals in which a victim is symbolically sacrificed.

"The only time a satanist would perform a human sacrifice would be if it were to serve a two-fold purpose; that being to release the magicians's wrath in the throwing of a curse, and more important, to dispose of a totally obnoxious and deserving individual," LaVey writes. After explaining that babies and animals should not be killed he asks, "who, then, would be considered a fit and proper human sacrifice, and how is one qualified to pass judgment on such a person? The answer is brutally simple. Anyone who has unjustly wronged you—one who has 'gone out of his way' to hurt you—to deliberately cause trouble and hardship for you or those dear to you. In short, a person asking to be cursed by their very actions."

Once he begins to describe symbolic sacrifices the fact that he is not advocating actual murder or violence is easy to miss. The curses that he provides to his readers include passages such as this: "I call upon the messengers of doom to slash with grim delight this victim I hath chosen. Silent is that voiceless bird that feeds upon the brain-pulp of him (her) who hath tormented me."

I cannot resist noting, in passing, that LaVey does violence to the English language in his misuse of the antique form *hath,* which was never employed in the first person. This is the kind of mistake that Crowley, who greatly influenced LaVey's thinking, would never have made.

The Church of Satan, founded by LaVey in the late 1960s, is a public religious organization that does not advocate violence or illegal activity. It claimed 10,000 members in the 1970s, but does not disclose any information about its present membership. In the 1970s, the Temple of Set, a smaller, more elitist satanic organization, a sort of high church of Satan, was founded by a leading member of LaVey's church Michael Aquino, a lieutenant colonel in the U.S. Army Intelligence who is a specialist in psychological warfare. Another leading satanic organization is the Church of Satanic Liberation, whose leader, Paul Valentine, an English teacher from New Haven, Connecticut, appears particularly interested in the sexual aspect of satanic rituals and claims that most of his thousands of followers around the world are young middle-class women.

The Process, Church of the Final Judgement, a cult that worshipped Satan as well as Jesus Christ, and believed that motorcycle gangs would be the instruments of bringing about the apocalypse, had its headquarters in Toronto in the 1970s. This cult did social service work among youth, obtaining a government grant for one project. It folded in the late 1970s and one can only speculate as to what, if any, lasting impact its satanic beliefs might have had on the hundreds of people who came under its influence during their formative years.

One man from Montreal who told me that he used to belong to the Church of Satan said most of the members of the church were mainly interested in sexual orgies and later gravitated towards swingers' clubs. He said that some people who were seeking sadistic satisfaction found it too tame and subsequently joined underground satanic groups with links to prostitution and pornography. This man told me that he and other members who were more interested in the spiritual aspects of satanism called themselves Luciferians. He said he has since spent several years studying pornography as a form of religious mysticism. This line of research got him thrown out of a university theology department, he told me.

Followers of Aleister Crowley, members of a highly secretive group called the Ordo Templi Orientis (OTO), practice ritual or ceremonial magic in lodges in several Canadian cities. This is not a satanist organization, although Crowley's works were a strong influence on many people who now call themselves satanists. Crowley also denied being a black magician, in spite of his descriptions of sacrificial blood rituals. I have talked to OTO members in Victoria, Edmonton and Montreal who say they do not try to emulate Crowley's vicious lifestyle or indulge in blood rituals.

A member of an OTO lodge in Edmonton said his group uses a non-profit theater group as a front, which he said is appropriate in that ritual magic is a form of theater. He told me that his group had published in a newsletter some rituals involving animal sacrifice. He said in a telephone conversation that they would not indulge in such practices, but do like to shock people. Members of his lodge are mostly involved in the computer industry or working at the university, he said.

He told me that he used to be a member of the Church of Satan but had been thrown out of that organization. He also told me that he was involved with the Temple of Set, which he said held a secret convention in Toronto in 1988.

After talking with the Edmonton OTO member, I received some copies of the lodge's newsletter, which mostly contained very dry academic material about the history of the OTO. One issue contained a letter from a friend of the lodge suggesting that it would be a good idea if they began to admit women to their rituals.

Other OTO members I interviewed presented a much more sober view of the organization. One man told me that they had recruited too many people in the 1970s and were now trying to weed out the more undesirable element. He mentioned that he had been concerned to hear that someone had been practicing blood rituals in Trenton, Ontario, and that the organization was investigating this allegation.

The OTO, which is a very hierarchical organization requiring deep commitment from its members, has a Masonic principle of fraternity that differs from the aggressive individualism of LaVey's satanism. According to OTO members, Crowley's dictum, "Do what thou wilt shall be the whole of the law," is not a formula for licence. They believe that a person's "true will," what they really want to accomplish in life, is something akin to destiny. OTO members say that they engage in a disciplined program of self-examination in order to discover their "true will." Love, a concept that has no place in satanism, is also a key element in Crowley's philosophy. Love is viewed by OTO members as an ordering principle in the universe, but they see it as something that can only be realized when people are fulfilling themselves by following their will.

The leader of the Montreal OTO group, called the Church of the Starry Wisdom, told me in a letter that they share their temple with a group devoted to Wicca. He wrote, "The kids on the street are intrigued by our posters in the front hall windows, but their mothers have absolutely nothing to worry about."

Since the OTO is a closed and secret organization, it is not possible to say with complete confidence that there is no reason to be uneasy about its activities. I found most of the members I encountered to be rather earnest people with a serious interest in ritual magic and Crowley's philosophy. Some of them obviously derive some satisfaction from the shock value of Crowley's more outrageous statements about blood sacrifices. It is my impression, however, that the greatest risk one runs in encountering these people is of being offended by their humour and bored by their opinions.

On the other hand, I do believe that there is something to worry about with respect to satanism and black magic, with their emphasis on selfishness and personal power. The more public followers of Anton LaVey and members of various satanic religious organizations are apparently law-abiding people who do not pose any direct threat to society. But satanic ideas can exercise a pernicious influence, particularly on young people. There are many potential dangers in black magic, which sets out to evoke evil spirits and, in so doing, conjures up the darker side of human nature.

CHAPTER ELEVEN

The Problem of Satanism

On the cover of a record album called *Killers*, a skeletal human figure with long white hair and large teeth bared in a demonic grin, wields an axe that is dripping with blood. The figure is dressed in jeans and a t-shirt, which is being clutched by the hands of its victim. The background of the picture shows a bleak urban environment, an apartment building and a row of shops, which include a sex shop. The skeletal figure is Eddie, the mascot of the heavy metal band Iron Maiden, whose songs speak of Satan, murder, madness and despair.

In 1985, a Toronto couple and their seven-year-old daughter were shot to death by a fourteen-year-old boy who believed that Eddie had told him that the killings would set him free. The boy was a fan of the rock band and was dabbling in satanism. He had conjured up the character of Eddie in his own mind, and it had taken over his personality.

The murder of Arthur Bruce Irwin, his wife Joyce and their daughter Kelley became the subject of a major controversy three years later when the boy was released from custody after serving the maximum sentence for first degree murder under the *Young Offenders Act*. As a young offender, the law prohibits the disclosure of his name or identity. Members of the public were concerned that a murderer could be set free so soon after committing such a brutal crime, without apparently having had any psychiatric treatment and with no evidence of rehabilitation. The fact that the youth was a satanist tended to make people even more alarmed at the prospect of meeting him on the street.

There are, in fact, many young satanists walking the streets of most Canadian cities today. One often sees their graffiti on the walls of derelict buildings—symbols like the inverted cross or pentagram, and the number 666, the Sign of the Beast. With such symbols, one sees slogans like "Hail Satan" or "Kill Jesus," and words like Amen or Murder spelled backwards. It may seem reassuring to see 1960s-style peace signs in the midst of such graffiti, but satanists call that symbol the Cross of Nero, a cross with broken arms representing the defeat of Christianity. Though the symbol is still used primarily as a peace sign, it appears as a satanic symbol on rock music paraphernalia, skateboards and, sometimes, in jewellery.

Satanism is now a popular fashion among teenagers. It is an "innocent" form of rebellion and entertainment for most of the young people, who listen to albums like *Killers* and enjoy songs like "Mandatory Suicide" by the band Slayer. One young skateboarder I know, who is not seriously involved in satanism, has designed a logo comprised of a Baphomet, an inverted pentagram that incorporates a goat's head, surrounded by other occult symbols and accompanied with the words "Urban Retaliation Device." Of course, such material does not seem innocent to older people, but the whole point of a teenager's cultural rebellion is that it should shock. The heavy pounding sound of the music and morbid subject matter of the songs may not seem like entertainment, but that is a matter of taste.

Most young people who enjoy the music of rock bands that use satanic symbolism probably have no deeper understanding of the symbols than that they are emblems of their favourite band. But for some it is part of a philosophy of life, what one expert on youth culture has called, "a theology of chaos, violence and rebellion."

Some fundamentalist Christians, and others who have spoken of satanism in rock music, exposed themselves to ridicule a few years ago with the absurd notion that the lyrics of some bands contained "backward masked" lyrics. They suggested that if you listen to tapes or records of various bands backwards you hear messages like "Come to Satan." Few people took these theories seriously for the very good reasons that it is actually difficult to listen to tapes backwards, that most rock fans do not have the equipment to do so, and that the demonstrations of backward-masked messages were not very convincing anyway.

In talking about the explicit satanic messages of some heavy metal music, it is important to state that one is referring to something very simple and clear that anyone can see for themselves by browsing in a record store or going to a newsstand and picking up a copy of *Power Metal,* which proclaims itself to be "the nastiest magazine on earth."

"Death metal" or "black metal" are names given to the style of heavy metal music and lyrics associated with Slayer, Celtic Frost, which dedicated one of its albums to Aleister Crowley, and a host of other bands, with names like Rigor Mortis, Death Angel, Hellhammer, Forbidden Evil, Deathrow and Sodom. The term "thrash metal" is also used to describe a frenzied form of music comprised of fast driving rhythms and loud vibrating noise. That is the way some people regard all rock music, but listen to Slayer, if you can, and you will think that the Rolling Stones, or even Led Zeppelin, sound like Mozart in comparison. Some teenagers listen to thrash metal bands through Sony Walkman headsets, with the volume cranked up high, for hours on end, often playing the same songs over and over again. They are proud to be called Headbangers, Rivet Heads, Hell Rats and Metal Maniacs.

Angel Ripper, the leader of the Sodom, claims that his band has gone beyond a simple preoccupation with death and Satan, as they now also sing about political subjects with titles like "Electrocution" and "Nuclear Winter." An article in the popular skateboarding magazine *Thrasher* described Slayer as having set the standard for thrash metal music with an album called *Reign in Blood*. This album was faster, louder and heavier than anything that had preceded it. The article stated, "It also marked Slayer's move from the land of sadism and Satan to the land of social issues, sadism and Satan."

The songs of Slayer, Iron Maiden and other similar bands are predominantly expressions of despair in what is presented as a world of violence, cruelty and hypocrisy. They describe the meanness of urban wastelands, rife with senseless violence and sexual exploitation. They speak of hatred, oppression and war. This is the world that young people have inherited from their parents, the songs say. These problems are often seen in simplistic terms: they are the products of a hypocritical Christianity that masks a mean and grasping greed. The young people who grow up in the midst of all this are represented as "the children of the damned."

This vision of the bleak side of society is not unlike the view that many young rebels had in the 1960s, but the response is completely different. The death metal bands hold out no idealistic visions of an alternative society. The solution that they offer is to identify with the violence and chaos, and seek salvation in hell's fire.

"Blood's cheap. It's everywhere," Slayer says in "Mandatory Suicide," which can be seen as an anti-war song, but is interpreted by some young people as an invitation to self-destruction. "Silent Scream," another song by the same band, describes "a child's dream of death." It says "guidance it means nothing," and refers to the "shattered adolescent" going insane with "embryonic death embedded in your brain."

"We're always asked if we sit around thinking up the most disgusting things we can imagine," Tom Araya, bassist and vocalist for Slayer said in an interview in *Power Metal*. "The fact is we don't have to think that hard to come up with 'em. We naturally have sick minds, that's the only way I can figure it. We sit around thinking about our songs and we just come up with the ideas of rotting corpses and murderers.''

A teenager in Hamilton, Ontario, told newspaper reporters who were doing a story on street kids:''It all rhymes and it sounds great when you're stoned. It's like it gets into your blood and you think that way. It all sounds like the same thing that's happening to you.''

Although one or two of these bands openly acknowledge themselves to be satanists, the majority say that they are not and they are merely presenting their audience with an outlet for their fantasy. They disclaim responsibility for the fantasies of sexual violence, brutal murder and self-mutilation that they feed, saying that they are merely catering to a popular demand.

''It's ridiculous when bands have to worry about the way every word they sing is going to be interpreted,'' said Araya, whose band sang on a recent album:

Spill your blood let it run on me,
Take my hand and let go of your life.
Close your eyes, and see what is me,
Raise the chalice, embrace for evermore.

You've spilt the blood
I have your soul.

Ozzy Osborne, one of the pioneers of black metal music and still the greatest star of the genre, denies that he is a satanist and also disclaims responsibility for the suicide of an American teenager that was inspired by his song, ''Suicide Solution.'' He maintains that the song is about the dangers of alcoholism and that it is not his fault if some young people misinterpret it. He said in an interview in *Hit Parader* magazine, ''What possible motive would I have in trying to kill off the people who have made me rich and famous?''

In the same way, the author of *The Satanic Bible,* Anton LaVey, has disclaimed responsibility for a new trend in crime that ranges from petty vandalism in cemeteries to sadistic killings in the name of Satan. LaVey told a *Newsweek* reporter, "What's happening today is not Satanism. It's totally sick and distorted. A nut is a nut."

Psychiatrists at the Royal Ottawa Hospital, who have been conducting a study of youths involved in satanist groups, have found that most of the young satanists who have come into conflict with the law or school authorities do indeed have symptoms of psychiatric disturbances.

However, Rob Tucker, of the Council on Mind Abuse, who has counselled dozens of satanist youths, told me, "If you get a crazy kid and a crazy belief system, it's like putting fire and gasoline together."

The Satanic Bible is so popular among teenagers that bookstores report that it is hard to keep up with the demand. It is easy to understand this book's appeal to a rebellious teenager. It says that it is okay to take drugs and enjoy sex. It contains blasphemous material, which would be shocking to Christians. Its philosophy of selfishness and its contempt for human ideals would be equally shocking to parents who grew up with the values of the 1960s. It echoes the sentiment of generations of young rebels in stating, "I stand forth to question the wisdom of the world; to interrogate the 'laws' of man and of 'God'!"

For many of its young readers, *The Satanic Bible* is simply a means of getting a rise out of their parents. For others it represents an iconoclastic philosophy that they can use to test the values of a society in which they are struggling to find their place. But some use it as a taking off point for practical experiments in the occult.

In all parts of Canada, from Nanaimo, B.C., to Sackville, Nova Scotia, in cities and rural areas, there are reports of teenagers getting together to perform makeshift satanic rituals. In barns, graveyards, parks and rec rooms, young satanists gather to experiment with drugs and ouija boards to make sacrifices to the devil and attempt to summon up demonic entities.

It may be no more than a dangerous game for most of them, but the dangers are real and some succumb to them.

Police, social workers and psychiatrists are becoming increasingly concerned about crime, violence and insanity associated with satanic practices. The trappings of satanism have been espoused by outlaw biker gangs and, in the United States, by some urban teenage street gangs who are followers of some of the more brutal heavy metal bands. The presence of occult symbols at crime scenes and satanic connections in the backgrounds of some perpetrators have caused police forces in Canada, as in the United States, to organize seminars and workshops on occult-related crime investigation.

There have been reports from various parts of Canada of an increase in incidents of vandalism at cemeteries, including attempts to dig up graves and steal remains from mausoleums. Mutilated remains of cats and birds have been found in conjunction with graffiti and other evidence of satanic ritual. This phenomenon has become of sufficient concern to humane societies that they now issue warnings to people who own black cats suggesting that they keep them indoors on Halloween.

In Victoria, B.C., in December, 1988, four teenage girls allegedly tied a 14-year-old girl to a bed and cut an inverted cross on her forehead. In Nanaimo, a member of a satanist group died after a ritual in which the young people consumed drugs that they had stolen in a break-in, not realizing that they were experimental heart drugs. In Thunder Bay, Ontario, a 15-year-old boy who stabbed his father eight times in the chest in a frenzied attack was described by a judge as being under the influence of alcohol, heavy metal music and a preoccupation with the devil.

A 25-year-old man, who said he had made a pact with the devil that had to be sealed in blood, raped and stabbed his 12-year-old sister in Brantford, Ontario, in October, 1988. The girl's life was, ironically, saved by the fact that the knife was partially deflected by a metal satanic medallion that she was wearing around her neck. Her brother had given it to her for protection.

The man called an ambulance after stabbing the girl, and waited for police to arrive. He was wearing a T-shirt that read, "Your Worst Nightmare." He told police that Satan had instructed him and his brother through a ouija board to kill someone before Halloween: "It told us to kill, to kill would bring us life. If she would have died, we would have been rewarded."

He also told police that he expected to burn in hell. He said, "Hell ain't a bad place to be. You can do anything you want and no one will arrest you."

The man, who had been heavily involved in drugs since the age of 12, was sentenced to 14 years in jail. The judge who heard the case said the evidence recalled "the events of a horror movie. But this is a real event that occurred in our community."

Satanism has inspired or reinforced suicidal tendencies in some teenagers. Some of the death metal lyrics emphasize two themes: one is the old concept that Satan will demand the offering of the life of someone who has surrendered himself to his power and the other is that hell fire represents a cleansing, a fulfillment of all desires. There have been two high-profile cases in Canada of teen suicide linked to satanism in recent years, one in Sackville, Nova Scotia, and the other in Kitchener, Ontario.

In the Nova Scotia suicide case the victim, 16-year-old Dereck Shaw, had been performing satanic rituals with the help of instructional materials that included a package from a Montreal-based organization called the Continental Association of Satan's Hope (CASH). This group, which makes the dubious claim that it has 42,000 followers, is essentially a mail order company that sells material purporting to teach people how to use the infernal powers of Satan to achieve wealth, find love and cure sickness. On the day before he shot himself with his step-father's hunting rifle, Shaw had spoken about Satan appearing to him in a blue light and demanding his soul.

In the Kitchener case the victim also shot himself with his father's gun. His father was an avid hunter and the 16-

year-old boy had earlier stolen antlers and mounted animals from his home to use as sacrifices in satanic rituals. Among the personal effects left in the boy's room was a drawing of a ghoulish figure holding a gun, beside which he had written, "I want to kill."

Both of these cases came to public attention because the parents wanted to alert others to the dangers of satanic influences. Normally suicides are not reported, though statistics indicate more than 70 teenagers kill themselves in Ontario each year. There is no way of knowing how many of these cases involved satanic or heavy metal influences. However, several social workers have told me about cases of satanist teenagers who are either threatening suicide or are prone to self-mutilation. In some such cases the children also threaten to kill their parents.

The boy who killed the Irwins and their daughter had read the *Satanic Bible* and was an avid fan of heavy metal music. He had two posters of Iron Maiden's mascot Eddie in the bedroom of his suburban home. He used to write the number 666 on his body and once carved it on his chest with a knife. In this he was perhaps inspired by the Iron Maiden album *The Number of the Beast,* the cover of which shows Eddie rising out of the flames of hell.

The lyrics to the title song of that album say, "in my mind it's always there, the evil face that twists my mind, and brings me to despair."

A psychiatrist at the boy's trial attributed his violence to hostility towards his parents, who travelled extensively when he was young and treated him like a toy when they did have time for him. He was described as lonely, joyless and sad. Eddie, the evil twisted face that revels in violence, often became the dominant force in his personality.

He told police that he committed the murders to vent anger stemming from an argument he had with his parents over smoking and girls. He walked into the Irwins' bedroom at dawn on April 12, 1985, with a loaded hunting rifle. He had smoked a whole pack of Arthur Irwin's cigarettes that night and was afraid he would get into trouble for it. Two days earlier he had taken Irwin's gun from a closet and practiced loading and unloading it.

The boy later told police that the man and woman were asleep when he went into their room. He said, ''I stood over the bed for about five minutes with the gun two or three feet from [the woman's] head. I screamed, 'Fuck' and pulled the trigger. He was waking up as the smoke cleared. I put another shell in from the cartridge thing and shot [the man] in the head.''

He then went downstairs to the family room where the seven-year-old girl was watching television. He loved the child, but decided that he should kill her because he did not think that she could live with the fact that he had killed her parents. He later told a nurse that he felt he couldn't shoot her, but Eddie whispered to him that he could. The girl was shot in the chest and drowned in her own blood.

The boy took some money from Arthur Irwin's wallet, went out to meet a friend and spent the day playing video games, buying record albums and getting his ear pierced. Later he took four of his friends to the house to show them the bodies. While he was showing them the body of the little girl, he held her hand and put a Cabbage Patch doll in it. He said he was sorry, that he loved her and didn't mean to do it. He was quoted as saying, ''I hope you go to heaven and I go to hell.''

What members of the public found most scary about this story was the fact that a court did not find that the boy was insane. The *Young Offenders Act*, under which the maximum penalty is three years, has provisions for moving a more serious offense like murder to an adult court where a murderer can be sentenced to life imprisonment. But the crown and defense lawyers in this case expected that the Youth Court would accept their joint submission that he be found not guilty by reason of insanity. This would have meant that the boy would have been sent for psychiatric treatment and not released until it was considered he was no longer a threat to himself and others.

The judge rejected this submission on the grounds that the crime was premeditated and the boy was aware of what he was doing when he killed his three victims. The judge recommended that the boy receive psychiatric treatment during his three-year jail term, but the young offender has apparently refused such treatment and has held on to his satanic beliefs.

Cases such as these have alerted the public and police to the pervasive and potentially dangerous influence of satanism. There is also a growing concern about the equally disturbing phenomenon of ritual abuse of children. Concerns have been voiced by child protection workers and social agencies in several parts of Canada, but particularly in Ontario, about cases in which children have apparently been abused in connection with the rituals of satanic cults or some other similar groups. The evidence for this has come mainly from victims — children and adults who remember abuse inflicted on them as children — but there are nevertheless strong indications that this does represent a real threat, though no-one yet understands what lies behind it.

This issue surfaced in Canada with a case in Hamilton, Ontario, in which two young girls disclosed that their mother, father and another adult had subjected them to extreme sexual abuse, forced them to participate in pornographic video-making sessions, and involved them in bizarre sadistic rituals at graveyards and other sites. The descriptions of graveyard rituals, which involved chanting and dancing by people in hooded robes, included shocking allegations about murders of small children and cannibalism. After a lengthy family court case, a judge found that the children had been sexually abused and should be protected from their parents. He was not required to make a finding of fact on the more bizarre allegations, but did state that he did believe the children were describing things that they believed they had experienced and that their descriptions suggested cult activity.

A strikingly similar case was brought before the courts in Oshawa, Ontario, in the spring of 1989 and others are under investigation. Some people believe that these cases point to the existence of a loosely organized network of satanic cults, engaged in sadistic child abuse, pornography and other violent crime. Others dismiss the whole phenomenon as an unwitting conspiracy of deluded child care workers feeding one another's expectations and putting words into the mouths of children.

Having observed the Hamilton case first hand and done further research and investigation of the issue, I do not accept the theory that child care workers have invented the concept of ritual abuse or that the child victims have imagined or fabricated their allegations—but I do not know what it all means. Rather than accept the idea of a network of cults, for which there is little evidence, I am more inclined to believe that this kind of abuse is perpetrated by disturbed individuals who have been influenced by satanism or some other similar beliefs. I think it is also possible that people are using the trappings of satanism either as a theme for sadistic pornography or as a means of frightening children into complying with sexual abuse.

Observers of the current satanist trend usually divide modern satanists into four categories. The first of these is the religious satanists, members of groups like the Church of Satan, who have no overt criminal involvement. The second category is members of satanic cults, shadowy groups whose existence has not been proven, but which many people suspect of being behind ritual child abuse. The other two categories are the young dabblers in satanism and criminals who cite satanism as a motive or rationalization. These two groups merge at the point where some dabblers get involved in serious crime.

The criminal element are known as self-styled satanists, violent deeply disturbed individuals who seize upon satanism as a justification for releasing their inner demons. Charles Manson, the leader of a cult responsible for the brutal ritual murder of movie star Sharon Tate in California in 1969, was the first of a series of murderers and psychopaths during the last two decades who have espoused some elements of satanism as a rationale for their crimes. Serial killer Richard Ramirez, known as the Night Stalker, who said he was influenced by a record album called *Highway to Hell*, is a more recent example of this.

"They were outcasts, shunned by their peers and tormented by their own failures and visions of others' success," wrote U.S. author Arthur Lyons in his book *Satan Wants You*. "Put that kind of hostility into a cauldron, mix in the eye of a newt and the blood of a bat, stir in a little LSD and a few Reds, maybe a pinch of Angel Dust, and you have a recipe for murder, whether the murderer calls himself a Satanist, a Nazi, a Klansman, a Yahweh, a Black Muslim or a Jesus freak."

Rob Tucker, who is widely recognized as an expert on satanism and spends much of his time counselling disturbed teenagers, told me that he sees two distinct types of young people getting involved with satanic ideas. One group is made up of middle-class youths, often successful in school, who become fascinated with satanist ideas as a form of rebellion, then begin to change dramatically. The members of the other group, he says, have already been identified as problem kids, often children without a conscience who have a history of cruelty to animals and other children. For such teenagers satanism represents, according to Tucker, "a belief system which enables them to act out what they want to act out anyway. They are attracted to the core ideal of destruction of conscience or compassion."

One social worker described satanism as "a magnet for adolescents with problems." He said, "Teens need to separate from their parents, and reject old values in order to stand alone. But they also need order and a sense of belonging. Satanism gives order, secrecy, group identity, sense of power, permission — for drugs, sex, to do what you want — and it also reinforces self-destructive, suicidal tendencies."

The young dabblers in satanism often experiment with satanic rituals and ouija boards, attempting to call up demonic entities. Sometimes they become convinced that they have made contact with such entities. Psychiatrists and occultists may have different explanations for this but the effects on the young people are just as real whichever way you look at it.

One traditional witch was disturbed because his daughter was into satanism. That she had discovered a form of rebellion, which would get to her father was evident in the way he railed about her betraying "everything our family stands for." But what worried him most was that she was what his tradition described as a Merryweather, someone with the psychic ability to predict the weather. He was afraid that her psychic powers would make it more likely that she would be successful in contacting demonic entities.

An occult store manager told me she is often getting frightened youths coming to her and saying that they called up an entity and it came. She said she would ask them, "What did you expect, a wrong number?"

Some teenagers, like the boy who killed the Irwins, find that the entity that they called up begins to take over their own personality. They feel out of control and they frighten parents, friends and other people they come in contact with. They indulge fantasies, like those embodied in the drawings of one youth who depicted himself as a werewolf tearing out the heart of a priest, then cutting off his limbs and his head and sacrificing the body to Satan. This fantasy concluded with the priest rising out of the water, reborn, but with werewolf face, and then attacking someone else.

Complaints about headaches are common among such youths. The cause of these is quite likely drugs and constant exposure to loud heavy metal music. But they believe that the demons are literally inside their heads and growing bigger and more powerful. Parents have described children throwing themselves around as if they are possessed by demons.

According to Robert Tucker, many of these cases do not fit the normal psychiatric profiles for mental illness, and it is important in dealing with such teenagers not to dismiss their hallucinations as insanity, but to attempt to understand them as things that the kids believe they are experiencing as a result of their psychic experiments. In less extreme cases, he said, it is important not to overreact to satanic beliefs or dismiss them as nonsense. He said, "Their experience is something very real and must be heard. The experience is just as potent as that which a born again Christian will speak of, a potent life changing event. Unless you deal with that, the kid will clam up."

People in this society are not used to dealing with devil worship or demonic possession. It is very easy either to dismiss the real problems that arise from some young people's infatuation with satanism, or to overreact to them. The story of what happened in Delhi, Ontario, when some children came to believe that they were possessed by the devil is a fascinating example of the kind of confusions and distortions that can occur in such cases.

In May, 1986, Delhi, a small town in the tobacco belt of south-western Ontario, was gripped with hysteria over rumours of teenage gangs bent on human sacrifice. Police warned parents to keep their children home at night and vigilante groups began to form. An atmosphere that recalled the seventeenth century witch-hunts of Salem, Massachusetts, had been evoked. The cause was similar to the one that precipitated the hysteria at Salem, the strange behaviour of some children who had been dabbling in devil worship.

"I know evil exists, and this was some kind of evil. I dealt with it as best I could," said Grant Darling, an Anglican priest who counselled the children involved.

Darling believed in the devil as much as any other Christian, but he was not the type to go looking for demons. He was a low-key country chaplain, close to retirement, who had built up a reputation for doing good work in his community, particularly with young people. He had never before had cause to look up the text of the rites of exorcism.

The trouble started with a teenager who became fascinated with the occult. This was, according to Darling, a good-looking charming boy who was looked up to by his peers. He obtained a copy of LaVey's book *Satanic Rituals* and became the self-styled leader of a little cult, in which his girlfriend was designated as the "queen." They painted symbols in a barn and performed rituals to call up eight demonic spirits.

The leader fell out with his "queen" and she laid a curse on him. The boy became frightened and decided to leave the group that he had started. Two girls left with him and for about a month the three of them struggled with the demons that they believed they had summoned in their rituals. They could not eat or sleep.

After they consulted a Roman Catholic priest, who told them to see a psychiatrist, they decided to go to Darling for help. As they told Darling their story, one of the girls fainted and the boy fell into convulsions on the floor. They said they believed that something was going to happen to them at nine o'clock that night. This gave Darling an idea for defeating the devil with a piece of honest trickery. He knew that his kitchen clock lost time and that he had not reset it for several days. So, after praying with them for a while, he took them into the kitchen.

Darling and his wife suggested that they all play a game of cards. The teenagers insisted that they take all the sixes and nines out of the pack. When the clock struck nine, Darling told them that it was slow and the fateful hour had already passed. He persuaded them to put the nines and sixes back in the pack and played for a while longer.

"It is irrelevant whether the devil is real or not. He was real to them," Darling told me.

The three teenagers came to church the next day and were again suffering from convulsions and fainting spells.

Darling had found some prayers that he thought might be appropriate and said them with the children. He told them that God is more powerful than the devil and the battle with Satan was won 2,000 years ago. Although Darling does not generally believe in dramatic signs of faith and conversion, he told me, "I saw a glow on them after those prayers."

More members of the group came to Darling for help. With prayer and counselling, their problems appeared to be resolved and that should have been the end of the matter.

Meanwhile, however, some other teenagers, who had nothing to do with the original satanic rituals, heard about what had been happening and thought that it would be fun to scare little kids by telling them that they were going to be the next to be sacrificed to the devil.

The police became involved as a result of these threats. The media were informed and parents were afraid. In the ensuing uproar, the barn at which the teenagers had performed their rituals was burned down.

Darling said he was disturbed to realize that the spirit of the witch-hunts could so easily be invoked in his peaceful rural community. He felt that a lynch-mob mentality had taken hold of some of his parishioners. He said, "I felt they would be capable of stringing someone up, if they knew who to put the finger on."

In what was for Darling an amusing postscript to this story, his daughter returned from university announcing that she had joined a Wiccan group. She told her father that the witches had said she could dedicate herself to any god or goddess she chose and that she had chosen Jesus Christ.

Occult-related crime and the deviant behaviour of some young satanists have become a matter of serious concern for police. The trend has also been alarming to Wiccans and other law-abiding occultists, as it tends to tarnish their public image and put them under suspicion for things that they simply do not do.

One witch I talked to had two grounds for concern. Constable Kerr Cuhulain, a twelve-year veteran with a major police force in British Columbia, has practiced witchcraft for more than eighteen years. He is a feminist, a healer and a Goddess worshipper. But he also carries a gun and a badge, and is dedicated to fighting crime.

As a witch and a policeman, Cuhulain is particularly upset when his religion is confused with satanism and suspected of involvement in occult-related crime. He has become concerned that much of the information used by police investigators in that field is distorted and misleading. He is alarmed about some law enforcement newsletters, written by fundamentalist Christians in the United States. These feed police false information about Wicca, he says, and target innocent groups for investigation.

Cuhulain is his Craft name, the name he uses in Wiccan circles, both because it has some personal religious significance to him and because his job would be in danger if he publicly identified himself as a witch. Some of his close associates in the police force know about his religion. But others would not understand and could create serious trouble for him. He agreed to an interview on condition that his identity not be disclosed.

There is certainly nothing in his physical appearance or manner that would make him stand out from his fellow officers. On the contrary, most people who met him off-duty would probably guess that he was a cop from his clean-cut face, courteous self-assured manner, and alert, but wary, look.

"He looks like a real cop," observed one young witch, "the kind you'd be scared of, if he stopped you for speeding."

For many years Cuhulain has led a spiritually isolated life. While few other police officers have any understanding of his religious beliefs, he has found it difficult to win the trust of other witches.

"People think that you are the enemy trying to infiltrate," he said.

Witches tend to be cautious of outsiders, no matter who they are. They usually have good reasons for not wanting to be publicly identified as witches. They are often approached by people who want to get involved in the Craft for the wrong reasons. In British Columbia, many witches are feminists and less inclined to trust men. It is hardly surprising that they would be suspicious of a policeman who said he was a witch.

Cuhulain said he is sometimes asked, "Why are you a police officer anyway. Doesn't that conflict with your beliefs?" He explained that his religion is derived from that of ancient Celtic tribes who placed great emphasis on family. In that society, he said, one of the most respectable positions was that of the warrior who defended hearth and home.

The warrior tradition runs deep in Cuhulain's family. His father was an air-force veteran and also a freemason. He seldom went to church and did not push his son to go. But there was some pressure on him to join the cadets and join the armed forces, as every other male member of his family had done before him.

When he was a boy, Cuhulain's interest in paganism was sparked by a book he received as a present, *The Siege and Fall of Troy* by Robert Graves. His father, who gave him the book, probably thought of it more as military history than pagan mythology. But Cuhulain fell in love with the myths. He said the book told of a world that seemed familiar to him and the poetic myths were voicing something he already knew. He read more books on mythology while he was in high school and came across a book on witchcraft.

After reading this book and deciding that he had found a religion that felt right for him, Cuhulain started trying to locate people who followed Wicca. The search was fruitless, he said, "A guy with short hair about to go into the air force—they were probably saying, 'No way. He looks too much like a cop.' I stood in a bookstore for two hours getting courage to ask people. Then I decided that, if I'm not going to find anyone, I'd collect as much material as I could. I became a solitary practitioner.''

Although Cuhulain did not openly practice his religion in the armed forces, he did suffer a severe beating because of his beliefs. He was at a base where church attendance was compulsory. He and about half a dozen other young men who were atheists reached an understanding with the chaplain that it was okay for them to sit at the back of the church and read quietly during the service. This did not sit well with another group of men who were fundamentalist Christians. The non-believers were invited to a party, which they went to without realizing that it would be a gathering of the fundamentalist group who were seeking an opportunity to persuade them of the errors of their ways. Cuhulain was not amenable to their arguments, and he still has several scars on his body as a result of the religious dispute that ensued.

Cuhulain eventually decided that the armed forces were not for him. He had joined because it was what his family expected of him. He decided that he should do something he wanted to do. He chose a career in the police force, he said, because ''I like doing things to help people.''

After joining the police force, he again tried to make contact with other Wiccans, but still to no avail. He continued to practice witchcraft on his own. It was not until after he began working with a Wiccan anti-defamation group based in the United States, that Cuhulain became friends with other witches in his own area. Eventually, he said, they came to the conclusion that ''this guy is probably okay, although he's a cop.''

Now that he does have the trust and respect of other members of the Wiccan community, Cuhulain occasionally joins with other people, but remains essentially a solitary witch. He has written his own rituals, which he says come from the heart, rather than following any formula. He describes his own form of worship as eclectic and Dianic.

That means that he draws from many different sources and puts a lot of emphasis on the goddess Diana. Awareness of self, kinship with nature, creativity, psychic skills and sensitivity are key ingredients of the Wiccan tradition that he has adapted for his own use.

"I'm sworn to help people. And healing and compassion are a part of my faith. It's a great source of strength and inspiration," Cuhulain said, "It has helped me to manage stress. I have learned how to meditate, how to change things. It has given me a much broader perspective on things."

This broader perspective helps in solving crimes, he said, because he understands that it is possible to see the same reality in different ways. He said it helps him put things together. The fact that he has had difficulties because of his unconventional beliefs also makes him more sensitive to other people's personal problems. He understands that the prostitutes on the streets are also abused children who have, perhaps, been thrown out of their homes or forced to leave with no other resources to call upon.

"You tend to get a lot better results when you are willing to treat everybody as human beings no matter who they are," he said. "A couple of times on the streets my partner and I have been in trouble and the street people have helped us."

Cuhulain said he occasionally amazes his colleagues with the accuracy of his hunches. He has developed his psychic skills through Wicca and is able to let his unconscious mind work on problems when logic and police procedures do not provide the answers. He said he has a habit of saying "go that way," when everyone else is saying that a fugitive has gone in the other direction. On one occasion, he said, he and his partner were driving to see a woman whose stolen driver's licence had been recovered. The licence had a change of address listed on it. Cuhulain told his partner to try the old address first. The woman was there and explained that she had moved to a new address but then moved back to her old home.

''How do you do that?'' his partner asked him afterwards.

''Don't worry about it,'' Cuhulain replied.

He has not used his psychic abilities to solve any major cases, but that is not something that an ordinary constable, even if he is a witch, often gets an opportunity to do. On the street, however, the people with whom he deals on a daily basis have a nickname for him. They call him ''The Wizard.''

Cuhulain feels that nothing in the religion that he practices is inconsistent with his doing a good job as a police officer. He is frustrated that he cannot be open about his beliefs. He has not been encouraged by the response he has received to some tentative steps that he has made towards exercising his religious freedom.

When he appears in court or goes before a Justice of the Peace for a search warrant, he chooses to make an affirmation rather than swear on the Bible. He says this bothers some of his colleagues and some JPs. They ask him why he is not religious, unable to fathom how a white Anglo-Saxon police officer might follow a spiritual and ethical code that is not based on the Bible.

On one occasion a JP refused to issue a search warrant to Cuhulain on the grounds that the form for applying for a warrant contained the words ''Wherefore the informant prays that a search warrant may be granted . . . '' The JP said the use of the word ''pray'' indicated that a warrant could not be issued to someone who does not pray to God. This dispute was resolved after some legal research revealed that the word ''pray'' is used in such documents in its original English meaning of ask or petition.

''I'm fine and upstanding. What's that got to do with religion?'' said Cuhulain, observing that there is a common perception that someone who wears a uniform as a representative of society must automatically belong to an organized religion.

He encountered a similar attitude in a witch who was the victim of a sexual assault that he was once called on to investigate. The male assailant told him that he shouldn't believe the woman who was making the accusation because she was "nuts, a satanist, into black magic." When he approached the victim to get a statement from her, she said she didn't think there was any point in talking to him because he was obviously going to side with the man and couldn't possibly understand that the fact that she was a witch did not make her evil, crazy or manipulative.

Most police officers probably would not have understood the woman's point of view. Like other members of society, they have confused and distorted notions of what witchcraft is. It is inevitably associated in many people's minds with satanism and occult crime. It is certainly not an atmosphere in which a declaration from a police officer that he is a witch will meet with much public approval.

Cuhulain's own job would be a lot more secure if there was a greater public understanding of Wicca. This was one of the considerations that led him to seek ways of promoting the religion's public image, without going public himself. He contacted an organization called The Witches League for Public Awareness. This group, based in Salem, Massachusetts, the scene of the most notorious witch-hunt in American history, was gathering data on what it believed was a religious campaign to sew the seeds of a form of bigotry that has not appeared in North America since the Salem witches were hanged in the 1690s.

In working on Wiccan public relations, Cuhulain became aware of distortions and confusions that were constantly appearing in information disseminated to police as aids to the investigation of occult crime. He discovered that the sources of much of this material were fundamentalist Christian police officers.

For example, one police training manual produced by a California police department suggested that witchcraft originated when Adam and Eve ate the forbidden fruit in the Garden of Eden and has been involved in human sacrifice ever since. The author of this manual warned other Christian occult investigators that it is not safe to keep non-

Christian books on the occult in their houses as this would leave them and their families vulnerable to attacks from the devil.

Another California police officer circulated a letter, allegedly intercepted by Mexican police, containing a detailed plan for a conspiracy by witches to undermine society through influence on schools and political institutions. No evidence has been advanced to lend credibility to this document, which closely resembles the forged Protocols of the Elders of Zion that were used by Nazis to discredit Jews in pre-war Germany. However, the text of the letter has been reprinted in a widely circulated newsletter that purports to inform members of the law enforcement community on occult crime.

File 18 is a confidential newsletter containing what it describes as "restricted access information for official law enforcement use only." It is edited by a police lieutenant in Boise, Idaho, financed through Trinity Fellowship Church and sent to hundreds of police officers and other law enforcement personnel in the United States and Canada. It provides details of occult crimes, suspicions of occult involvement in criminal activity, and gives general information on aspects of the occult.

One role that *File 18* has assigned itself is offensive, not only to witches, but to many civil libertarians. The editor stated in a May, 1986, issue that the newsletter will include "information on cults, sects and deviant movements (political and religious), found in the United States. Emphasis will be placed on those which present aggravated law enforcement problems or potential threats."

But the newsletter does not limit itself to groups in the United States. Groups and individuals in Canada are also included. Names and addresses of individuals are given. Feminists are named along with neo-nazis, satanists and convicted criminals.

The June 10, 1987, issue quoted from a flyer advertising a workshop in British Columbia to be given by Starhawk. The flyer stated that the workshop would be "an opportunity to study Feminist Ritual, Magic and Political Change.'' *File 18* printed the home address of the Vancouver woman who had been listed as a contact person for this seminar. It also included a post office box number in San Francisco as an alternate contact address. The newsletter commented: ''Just the wording of this flyer gives some indication of the orientation of these sessions. It would be informative for each of us to send for an application and more information as well as those of you in the area of the two addresses doing a little background check to see who's connected etc.''

The December, 1986, issue of *File 18* contained information about Toronto witch Charles Arnold's labour arbitration seeking paid holidays to celebrate Wiccan festivals. The account of this case, which stressed the fact that Arnold worships nude, was juxtaposed with information about an unrelated murder case in Buffalo in which a 16-year-old was arrested for killing an 11-year-old boy. The same issue also warned police officers to keep an eye on activities associated with the harmonic convergence, when millions of members of the new age movement were planning a ''World Healing Meditation.'' The editor commented, ''What 50 to 500 million minds can accomplish if cohesively organized is yet to be seen. Be alert to 'strange going's on' in your area. This may be just a practice organizational event to see how many people they can bring 'on line.' ''

The same issue of the newsletter drew readers' attention to another information service, Christian Apologetics Research and Information Service, which under the name US Citizens Committee on Crime and Narcotics distributes names, addresses and phone numbers of 1600 groups or individuals who make up what it terms ''A Sorcery Iceberg in America.''

An Ontario witch, a spiritually inclined woman who devotes much of her energy to healing, was horrified to find that her group and her own postal address were listed by this organization. Although she had nothing to hide, she was alarmed at the thought that her address might find its way onto a local police list of occult crime suspects.

An article in *Police and Security News* on satanism and its relationship to crime stated: "The kidnapping and sacrificial murder of unbaptized infants, rape, sodomy, corpse theft, forced homosexuality, animal sacrifice, unlawful burial, dismembering and more crimes too heinous to describe are the elements of a new threat to law enforcement. These actions are the main ingredients of Satanism, devil worship, witchcraft, the occult and related pagan religious lore."

In a letter to the editor, Cuhulain responded, "I am extremely upset by this statement since I've dedicated my life to the apprehension of the perpetrators of such crimes. . . . Such acts have never been the main ingredients of my beliefs. I've done years of volunteer work for the Society for the Prevention of Cruelty to Animals and for the Orphaned Wildlife Rehabilitation Society saving animals. I want these murderers, rapists, kidnappers, etc. as badly as you do. More, in fact, since certain groups and individuals keep associating these heinous practices with my faith. There is no question that there are individuals out there reading cheap occult literature and forming do-it-yourself groups for all manner of purposes. Let's catch those criminals together, OK."

Cuhulain has written many such letters seeking to correct misleading impressions of his faith. He reports varying degrees of success. He said he has found several Christian theologians very supportive. But he has not convinced some police officers who are also lay preachers. He believes many people are trying to do a good job, but don't have access to good information. These he finds are willing to revise their position.

Assuming a public role in trying to correct other police officers' misunderstandings of Wicca involves some risk for Cuhulain, even though he does it under a pseudonym. He said, "If I didn't feel strongly about the religion, I wouldn't be taking chances. I have big problems with job security if I go public. But I am willing to do this kind of work and take the risk.''

Cuhulain said he is not trying to suggest that occult-related crime doesn't exist, but he believes the concept that a mass satanic conspiracy is behind it all is absurd, although that is the belief of some fundamentalist Christians. From a religious standpoint, Cuhulain cannot accept this theory and, as a policeman, he does not believe that any of the evidence points towards a conspiracy of satanic cults.

He maintains that the conspiracy theory is built up by putting together different incidents that happened over a period of years in different locations. If there was such a conspiracy, he questions why there have been no informants. Police can infiltrate bike gangs and the Mafia, he said, and there is no reason they could not get inside information about a satanic conspiracy, if there was one. He is skeptical about the only source of inside information on these satanic cults, people who claim that they used to be satanic priests and have since made a career out of telling their stories. If they had committed a small portion of the crimes they claim, Cuhulain maintains, they should be in jail.

Cuhulain attributes most occult-related crime either to the young dabblers in satanism or individuals suffering from psychiatric problems who sometimes adopt ritual or occult trappings and perform horrible crimes. The dabblers, he said, meet out of some common goal, such as the opportunity to use drugs or escape from parental abuse. Usually the groups fall apart because they become involved in crime and are arrested.

While Christians see satanism as the dark side of witchcraft, Wiccans, like Cuhulain, tend to see it more as the dark side of Christianity. It is a part of the Christian world-view, and a natural form of rebellion for people who are still bound to a religious system that they are unhappy with.

''When dabblers use the satanic mythos as part of their rebellion, it doesn't surprise me. It's a means of getting back at people they are annoyed with, who have control and power over their lives. Latin males justify crimes with Santeria. There is always someone who finds some sort of justification by using satanism. I run into kids downtown with Megadeth t-shirts, upside down pentagrams, 666. I ask them about it. They don't understand anything about it. It's part of the image."

Cuhulain was anxious to make it clear that he did not put Wiccans or people who call themselves such above suspicion. He said he doesn't believe that somebody who truly followed Wiccan beliefs would get involved with crime, but recognizes that anyone can call themselves a witch. Each case should be taken on its own merits, he said, bearing in mind that it's easy for criminals to get hold of satanic or occult material and use it as a red herring to confuse investigators.

While trying to dispel the bad images created by what he sees as fundamentalist propaganda in police newsletters, Cuhulain and the other witches working with him are also offering their expertise to assist in occult crime investigations. To this end, Cuhulain is working on a law enforcement manual on occult-related crime. He has also produced a detailed guide to Wicca in order to help police officers recognize the key ingredients of Wicca, its symbols, rituals and beliefs, and thus distinguish them from satanism and other occult practices.

Many of the public concerns about occult-related crime have come to a focus around the issue of ritual child abuse. Like other members of the public and many police officers, some Wiccans were at first inclined to deny the existence of this problem, seeing it as part of the fantasy of a satanic conspiracy conjured up by fundamentalist Christians. But many witches—who are also often parents, teachers, social workers or therapists — have since begun to accept that ritual abuse is a reality that should be taken seriously. They have come to realize that for them the problem is not that a false scare has been created but that their religion is in some quarters being falsely implicated.

Several networks of witches and pagans have attempted to co-ordinate a unified response to this issue. This has taken the form of a resolution endorsed by several coalitions of Wiccan groups. The resolution states: ''We, as practitioners of Pagan and Neo-Pagan religions, including Wicca (also known as Witchcraft) practice a positive, life affirming faith that is dedicated towards healing, both of ourselves and others, and of the Earth. As such, we do not advocate or condone criminal activities. We absolutely condemn the practices of child abuse, sexual abuse, substance abuse, and any other abuse that does harm to the bodies, minds or spirits of individuals. We offer prayers, therapy, and support for the healing of victims of such abuses. We recognize the divinity of Nature in our Mother the Earth, and we practice our rites of worship legally, and in a manner that is ethical and compassionate. We will not tolerate slander or libel against our churches, clergy or congregations, and are prepared to defend our civil rights with such legal action as we deem necessary and appropriate.''

While this resolution was widely endorsed, it also met with opposition from some witches, including one group in Canada, who did not agree with rejecting the use of drugs or forswearing illegal activity in relation to civil disobedience. Other Wiccans in Canada and the United States responded by offering their services as therapists to ritual abuse victims.

Various Wiccan organizations have considered launching slander suits or hate literature prosecutions against some of the more rabid publications, but the legal difficulties of any such suit and lack of funds have made this route seem unappealing. Most groups have concluded that the positive approach of entering into dialogue with and offering help to law enforcement agencies is a better way to counter the effects of the defamation.

One Wiccan magazine quoted the Bible in advocating this kind of response: ''After all, it was Jesus who said 'By their fruits you shall know them.' Hatred, Bigotry and Slander are bitter fruits. Let ours be those of Reason, Tolerance and Truth instead.''

Many witches fear that Wicca is compromising its own morality, in trying to present an acceptable image to the public. These people argue that witches should conform to the laws of nature and the ethics of their own craft, which are not necessarily the same as the standards of society, and certainly differ in some aspects from Judeo-Christian moral codes. They fear that the anti-social attitudes and negativity of satanists are forcing witches to paint themselves white.

CHAPTER TWELVE

Real Magic: Spells and Curses

It was the night of a new moon, a time to clear away fragments of negative energy left over from a period of dissipation and decay. It was the beginning of a phase of building and new growth. In the basement of a suburban Toronto home, a grey-haired man in a crumpled white shirt concentrated intensely as he held a knife in both hands over three lighted candles on a cluttered table.

The table was an altar, similar in its layout to other witches' altars in that it had symbols of earth, air, fire and water arranged to correspond with the cardinal directions, north, east, south and west. But, unlike any altar I had seen before, it also held what seemed like a haphazard collection of bits of paper, watches and jewellery, some of it rather junky looking.

Earth was represented not by a pretty crystal, such as most Canadian witches have, but a large chunk of limestone, beside which were two shrivelled rotted apples. The water was not in an elegant bowl, but a grimy old bottle. There were some beautiful objects there too, an old clay incense holder with a primitive Goddess figurine, a black cat carved in stone, and a collection of feathers that represented the air. The overall effect was casual rather than ceremonial. Standing as it did against the wall of a basement workshop, this altar did not look like a place of worship, but a somewhat disorganized work space.

Three shadows on the ceiling came together as the knife was slowly raised. Alf Marron, witch, reflexologist, palmist, exorcist and a devout Roman Catholic was showing me a symbol of the Triple Goddess.

Witchcraft, for Marron, is not a religion but a craft. He is not a pagan, and insists, with the kind of logic that is typical of an Irish catholic, "If you are not any good at your own religion, how can you expect to be any good at practicing anybody else's?"

The Virgin Mary, Saint Bridget and Mother Teresa are, for Marron, earthly manifestations of the Mother Goddess. The forces of the four directions that he invokes in his magic circle are the female aspects of the archangels. His magic is associated with prayer, and he advises the many clients who consult him for readings and rituals to say the prayers of whatever religion they were brought up in.

For most of the other witches I had met, Wicca was a religious belief or an attitude to life that separated them from the culture in which they lived and from the religious values with which they were brought up. Here was someone who had retained the Christian faith he grew up with, and read palms for other people who also considered themselves devout practicing Christians.

I had first met my namesake (but not my relation) a few months earlier, when I heard him give a talk about witchcraft at a meeting of the Toronto Psychic Society. In spite of its esoteric name, this is a very unpretentious group, an odd assortment of down-to-earth people who meet every week for a talk in a slightly run-down community centre, followed by a few beers at a nearby pub. One would never guess from the manner and appearance of the members that most of them were psychics, except perhaps from the way they tend to say "I know" when you tell them something.

Marron was born in Belfast in 1921 and grew up in a family that practiced witchcraft. This involved a simple, but profound, set of traditional teachings that were, as he put it, "a wee bit older" than the revival of witchcraft and paganism in the 1950s. The witchcraft of Marron's family was a combination of herbal lore, spells and techniques for divination, remnants of pagan practices that many would call superstitions that had survived in the Irish countryside for centuries. This was the magic of the common people, a popular tradition that is sometimes referred to as "folk magic." Folk magic is a basic component of all witchcraft, but in most modern versions of Wicca it has been absorbed into new philosophical systems, based on contemporary feminist thought, the mysticism of nineteenth century ceremonial magic or attempts to reconstruct ancient pagan beliefs.

According to Marron, magic can exist within a Christian framework. Some of its symbolism is shared with Christianity, but it also harkens back to something older, more universal. Although he refers to the Mother Goddess more often than the male Christian deity, Marron sees no conflict in continuing to observe the sacraments, beliefs and forms of prayer that are as much a part of his own Christian heritage as his knowledge of how to work on natural forces for magical ends. In this he differs from witches of other traditions, more in his cultural background than anything else.

Witches generally hold that all religions are paths to understanding the universal divine principle, but the Christian church in England, Scotland and other parts of Western and Northern Europe has tended throughout history to view witchcraft as incompatible with Christianity. In Ireland, however, the church was tolerant of the old pagan folk beliefs. Christian missionaries who arrived in Ireland in the fifth century A.D. found a remote rural community that was not amenable to the forcible imposition of a new religion. They also found a deeply entrenched pagan religion led by a learned priestly class of Druids. The missionaries showed respect for the pagan beliefs and gradually assimilated them into a Christian framework.

Once the Christian church was established, it continued to tolerate the surviving tradition of folk magic, rather than attempt to eradicate it through persecution. Typical of this attitude is a statement in a twelfth century Christian text *The Conversation of the Old Men,* attributed to Saint Patrick, the first archbishop of Armagh and patron saint of Ireland. In discussing the value of music that contained the "lilt of fairy sorcery," Saint Patrick was quoted as saying that one should not reject it altogether but "only that we should not believe in it too much."

Old forms of folk magic and elements of old pagan ways survived alongside Christianity in many other predominantly rural regions of Europe where the witch-hunts were either less draconian or less successful. They still survive in Canada today among members of various immigrant communities. Practicing Catholics from southern Italy and various parts of eastern Europe still use old herbal remedies, consult fortune tellers and continue to preserve old magical beliefs. People from Africa, the Caribbean and Latin America continue to practice a mixture of Christianity, paganism and magic. Marron showed me that folk magic remains a living tradition in some pockets of contemporary Canadian society.

The pile of paper and the junky jewellery on Alf Marron's altar is a testimony to the survival of these beliefs. The jewellery and the watches are items that different people, usually devout Christians, had brought to him believing that they were contaminated by spells or evil spirits. The pieces of paper each contain a wish from someone wanting him to perform candle magic to assist them with health problems, marital difficulties or in finding a job or a new house. While I was visiting, he had several calls from people whose palms he had read in the past asking for counselling about current difficulties. He consulted their palm prints from folders that contained the records of hundreds of clients, gave them his advice, reassured them by saying that the moon was entering a building phase, and urged them to pray to God and go to church regularly.

The magic that Marron practices is based on the forces of the moon, the influence of the stars and the changes in the seasons. He divides the year into the stages in the life of the Goddess, beginning at Candlemas when she is a young girl through to the period of old age that begins at Halloween. A spell for a woman who had problems with her children would work best, according to his calendar, in the fruitful autumn months of the Goddess's mother stage. But it is not always possible to wait for that, and one can find the stages of the Goddess also reflected in the astrological influences on the lunar month. The shrivelled apples on his altar were placed there, according to tradition, at Halloween after he and his wife had each taken a bite from them, and were to be buried on May Eve.

The power of the moon is the pivotal force of the magic practiced by most witches. The full moon has always been thought of as a time for magic. It is a time when emotional energies are at a peak. While the full moon inspires lovers and poets, police reports indicate that it also encourages drivers, drunks and criminals to act more wildly.

A very sane and stable friend of mine, who is not superstitious and has no interest in astrology or the occult, told me that he never goes out on the night of a full moon because he feels wound up and a little crazy. The word lunatic comes from the Latin word for the moon and it used to be believed that madness was associated with lunar phases. One of the most common old images of madness was of someone going out and baying like a hound at the full moon.

Witches believe that the growing or waxing phase of the moon is a time when things grow or can be built up, and the waning phase, when the moon appears to diminish in size, is a time when energies dissipate and things tend to fall apart. The waxing phase is a period for working positive magic, spells of healing and blessing. The waning phase is the banishing time, a period when negative spells would work best. The new moon is a time for building, and the full moon a time for releasing energy that has been built up.

Negative magic is not necessarily the same as black magic. Banishing implies drawing off or sending away bad energy, relieving pain, lightening emotional burdens, or keeping out bad influences. Another form of negative magic is the binding spell. This is a spell that is designed to limit someone's power to perform evil by symbolically binding the evildoer. A binding spell may be directed at warding off an attack or malign influence.

If a woman is being beaten up by her husband, for example, Marron says his first piece of advice would be for her to leave the house. He would then find out when the husband's birthday is, and, when his sign is in the moon, meditate and send power to calm him down a little. He would draw negative energy from him and hold that energy on his altar until the moon is full, at which time he would release it into the cosmos, and then wash his hands with running water.

In performing candle magic, Marron writes the purpose of the spell on a piece of paper, which he cuts in half. One piece is regarded as negative and burned while the positive half is placed under the candle. This simple formula recognizes that human desires and emotions are complex and invariably contain positive and negative elements. The act of cutting the paper and consigning the negative side to the flame is a framework that allows meditation and serious consideration of the selfish or perhaps irresponsible aspect of the wish. Creating the magical object is a means of clarifying one's intentions. The object that is created symbolizes a willingness to translate thought into deed. This object is what Marron, borrowing from his Catholic background, describes as a ''sacramental.''

A more complex form of ''sacramental'' object that he showed me were pentacles, five pointed stars drawn in the form of three interconnected triangles within a circle. In the spaces between the lines of the triangles and the circle were drawn symbols representing the astrological signs of the people for whom the magic was being worked and the different elements involved in the object they desired. For example, someone who was looking for a job had signs representing his need for discipline and order in his life. A woman looking for a house was also calling for heavenly blessing and happiness. This magic seemed to incorporate elements of self-help therapy and prayer.

Blasting spells are the kind that witches are not supposed to perform. These are curses or psychic attacks that are designed to work some harm on people or property. They offend against the witches' Threefold Law, that if you work magic to harm another the consequences will rebound on you with three times the force. It is also against the one ethical command that witches recognize, "Do what you will, if it harms none."

If a witch chooses to break these laws and casts a blasting spell, the best time to do so is when the moon is waning. People who stick pins in a photograph or wax image are, said Marron, "Taking a beautiful force given by God and using it to destroy somebody. They are going to lose that force, eventually."

Some people do perform black magic, however, and it can serve as a means of enhancing their commitment to malevolent ends. Magic is a way of focussing the will upon a certain goal. This involves clarifying one's intentions, and stifling self-doubt, psychological barriers and emotional distractions. The magical practitioner visualizes the desired result as something real and tangible, something that already exists and that one is simply moving towards. Incantations, candles, charms, cords, wax images or other magical devices are used to focus the intention and will, in the same way as many Christians use a crucifix as an aid to prayer.

People who do these things are performing a form of therapy on themselves, and, if their goals are not unreasonable, there is a good chance that their magic will help realize them. They can work the same kind of therapy on others who believe in their power or techniques. At this level, magic works in the same way that fostering personal ambition and team spirit can help in business or sports.

Groups like the Mafia or motorcycle gangs can also invoke team spirit and focus hostility or greed to achieve negative ends. Similarly, magicians can choose to dedicate themselves to black magic. Other people, who have faith in this power and believe that they have come under an evil influence, can feel their own will stifled by fear, their positive energies sapped and negative emotions aroused.

Unlike most other witches I have met, Alf Marron was prepared to admit, in fact anxious to demonstrate, that magic is a powerful but neutral force that can harm just as easily as it can heal.

One of the most primitive and universal forms of black magic is the practice of sticking pins in a doll made up to resemble the victim. This is a form of what is known as sympathetic magic, based on the belief that a likeness of a person takes on something of the spirit of that person. Again the form is not as important as the intention and the emotional energy that is focussed in the creation of an object that translates the purpose in the magician's mind into something that exists in the physical world.

This form of black magic is still practiced today, and the only difference is that the magicians do not usually bother to make a doll, if they can find a photograph.

Marron showed me such an object. He assured me that it was okay to touch it as it had been left on the altar for six months in order to dissipate its power. It was a photograph of a young woman, bordered with a gaudy twine of red and blue synthetic thread, and taped over a photograph of a man. Four pins were stuck in the forehead of the woman and two more were pointing towards the man's head.

The woman in the photograph was a Sicilian immigrant, and the man was her husband. She had approached Marron for help after she had been to another magical practitioner who had taken her money but failed to help her. Marron, who makes a living from his reflexology practice, is like other traditional witches in that he does not seek payment for working magic. The woman told him that she was having emotional problems with her husband and things had got to the point where she could hardly think of him without getting a headache. She suspected that this had something to do with a former lover, who had sworn when she left him that he would never let her marry another man.

She said she had seen her former lover near her home and thought that he might have worked some magic against her. Marron believed that in order for such a powerful spell to work over a period of time it would have to be embodied in a talisman or charm that would have been hidden somewhere close to the woman. He told her to search her apartment for such an object. She did not find one, and phoned him to ask for further advice. He had not been to her home, but suggested that she look again in her bedroom dresser. On his instructions, she took the drawers out of the dresser, and found the photographs with the pins in them hidden behind one of the drawers. The woman said that her headaches ceased after she had turned the talisman over to Marron for purification on his altar.

Like anthropologists who have studied such cases in Africa, I must confess I do not know what to think. I believe in the reality of the physical object I saw and have no reason to doubt Marron's story of how he came by it. One can no doubt attribute the woman's response to her belief in the efficacy of the spell. But that does not really explain why she felt the headaches before she knew that the talisman existed. Whether it is an example of black magic or psychological manipulation, it seemed quite astonishing to me that such practices exist in suburban Toronto.

Two spells, performed by a feminist coven in Vancouver and described in articles in the Summer and Fall, 1988, issues of the magazine *Witchwords,* used the same technique of image magic but for a different purpose. These were ostensibly binding spells. But there is sometimes a very thin line between binding—preventing people from doing something harmful—and blasting—putting a curse on them. The spells involved a very sensitive and emotional issue. Detailed accounts of the spells in a column that shares information and tips about "the nitty gritty of witches covens" provoked an outraged response from a traditional witch who saw it as black magic, which contravened the laws of the Craft and would be likely to give Wicca a bad name.

The first spell was laid against a man who had infected six women with venereal disease. The coven made a plasticine doll with a photograph of his face pinned to its head. The women asked the Goddess to limit the man's power and teach him a more humanistic way of living, stressing that they did not bear him any ill will. Then, they bound the head and loins of the doll with black wool, and wrapped it in a black cloth. The coven buried the doll, covered with stinging nettles, at the bottom of the garden where they used to dispose of dead rats and snakes that they confiscated from their cats.

The woman who described the spell in the column said she later heard from the man that his life was falling apart, that he felt surrounded by evil spirits, had lost his job and most of his friends, and was unable to find a girlfriend. "So, out of all of this, it is important to realize that we are not playing with dolls here, but that this powerful stuff works," she wrote.

A similar spell, described by the same woman in a second column, was designed to deal with a rapist. She said the coven members dressed in every piece of "power jewellery" and magical finery they owned, set the stage with music candles and sacred objects on the altar, and then cast a circle calling upon the power of the Goddess to create entities in the form of bloodhounds, with "eyes as big as burning plates, teeth of diamond, claws of ruby—to hunt, to sniff to seek and to hold." They also made a manikin of the rapist and pierced it with rose-thorns, accompanying each thorn with a curse such as "if you ever hold a knife for power, may your hand shrivel." The doll was sprinkled with hot peppers and again buried in the rats' graveyard. The columnist promised that a future article would contain news of the imminent capture of the rapist, but the controversy provoked by her columns was such that her next article was instead devoted to repudiating charges that she had been indulging in "black magic."

Another binding spell that got a little out of hand was described to me by a traditional witch who used to be a member of a coven in Montreal. A person in an occult community was misusing his power and inflicting a great deal of psychological damage on people around him. The members of the coven decided to do a binding spell to limit his power to do harm. They magically encircled him with a field of force. Perhaps doubting the efficacy of this magic, they also started a campaign to disorient him.

The coven was an underground one, and, although the victim of the spell knew the individuals in the group, he did not know that they were associated together in a coven. Thus he did not suspect a plot, when each one individually came up to him and asked him why he was behaving so oddly, why he had forgotten a certain appointment, why he had said something strange on the previous day, why he was looking so pale and unhealthy. The witch who told me this story said that the victim was last heard of in a psychiatric hospital.

These are examples of spells worked for honourable motives, but that were ethically questionable nevertheless. The image magic worked by the jilted Sicilian man was pure malice. Such magic appears to be the exception rather than the rule and my impression is that one has nothing to fear from black magic unless one puts oneself in a position of vulnerablity to it.

People who are vulnerable are those who dabble in magic, or who come from a cultural tradition that recognizes its power. From a skeptical point of view, all this means is that superstition feeds fear. But it is also clearly demonstrable that fear tends to create its own reality. Those who do not believe in the power of magic are unlikely to be affected by it. Magicians believe in creating a strong psychic barrier around themselves to defend against psychic attacks. But they also believe that someone who is oblivious to magical forces has a strong natural barrier against them.

Like most witches, Marron warned of the dangers of magic. If you summon a spirit, he said, it will not return empty handed, and, particularly if it is "one of the angry old gods," this could mean trouble. This is why it is always necessary to ensure that the object of the spell is a good one and realistic, because the magic that does not work will rebound on the magician.

It is also important, he said, to remain grounded. One's altar or circle should be at ground level, if possible, and psychically one should be conscious of the need to return the energy that one has invoked into the ground in the same way that electricity must be grounded to avoid a shock. Witches work within a magic circle that they believe serves to concentrate their positive power and keep negative influences out. In creating this magical working space they might use the simple traditional chant, "Broom, broom clean this room from anything that would cause our doom."

Hauntings by ghosts or malevolent spirits also tend to afflict only those who believe in them. Alf Marron does exorcisms when he is convinced that people have genuine concerns about hauntings. He does not take money for this work and only asks that people write him a letter afterwards to tell him if the exorcism has been successful. I saw dozens of these letters, which did little to strengthen my belief in ghosts, but did give me an insight into the power that such beliefs have in many people's lives.

He had taped a conversation with a woman who explained that her life had been disrupted by a presence that entered her house. She said that at first she would feel it breathing into her mouth and pressing against her body. She said that this entity disrupted her emotional life and caused bad things to happen to her, like accidents and break-ins at her home. She had visited various self-styled witches or psychics who had charged her hundreds of dollars for consultations and herbal baths but the problem persisted until Marron exorcised the being from her home.

She had let the spirit into her life by allowing it to make love to her, Marron explained, echoing an age-old belief in the power of demon lovers, succubi and incubi as they were called in medieval times. Once a malevolent spirit obtains entry into a home they attract evil energy, he said, so that thieves are more likely to break in and bad things happen between the people living in the house.

Spirits that haunt houses and people are usually the ghosts of people whose lives have been cut short by violence, often self-inflicted, and have not been allowed into the next world until their proper time has come, Marron explained. They can also be demonic and dangerous to the person attempting to exorcise them, he said. He described seeing large rats appear in the corner of a room during an exorcism, and realizing that, if he gave into his fears and stepped out of his circle of protection, he could be felled by these forces.

Exorcism involves compelling or persuading such spirits to leave, he said. Sometimes the spirits may be harmless and simply need to be convinced that they are causing trouble and do not belong where they are. Benign spirits are sometimes allowed to stay. One woman said in a letter that she was glad that the spirit of a little girl had been allowed to remain and that she occasionally heard the ghost bouncing a ball around in the attic.

The practice of witchcraft is not illegal in Canada, but it is an offense to fraudulently pretend to practice it. When the laws against witchcraft were repealed in Britain in 1951, Canada took the more cautious approach of amending its legislation.

Under the Canadian Criminal Code it is an offense "to fraudulently pretend to exercise or to use any kind of witchcraft, sorcery, enchantment or conjuration."

In the Toronto area, there are about 30 cases of this kind of fraud every year. Police believe that, for every victim of psychic fraud who comes forward, there are about

30 more who are embarrassed to admit that they have been bilked. In many people's eyes, any fortune telling is fraudulent by definition, but the majority of psychics or witches who charge fees for readings are not prosecuted under this legislation. Whether their services are viewed as entertainment or as genuine divinations, they do not come to the attention of police unless they seek to gain more from their clients than the standard fee that they advertise for their readings. Many psychics who consider themselves to be legitimate practitioners believe that the law serves to protect the standards of their profession.

One of the most foolish witches I have ever encountered was a Hamilton man who claimed to be able to put a hex on anyone within a 100-kilometre radius. When a woman asked him to do something about a troublesome brother-in-law in Brantford, Ontario, he explained that his normal fee for such things was $500 but offered to do a cut-rate curse for $20.

The man grunted and pointed three times in the general direction of Brantford, and then said, "There, that should take care of the bastard for the rest of his life."

His psychic powers had not been sufficient to alert him to the fact that his client was an undercover policewoman. He also told the officer that he could cure cancer and sold her a $10 bottle of Thursday Plantation Key Oil, which he said would kill everything from herpes to a boil.The bargain basement Hamilton witch was fined $250.

Some people pay large sums of money to self-styled witches or fortune tellers who persuade them that they can cure ailments or remove curses. In 1986, a Toronto fortune teller was jailed for six months for a $17,000 fraud perpetrated on three women, by persuading them that they had to pay larger and larger sums to remove curses that she had discovered them to be suffering from. She also wrecked two of her victims' love lives by telling one that she could guarantee a long-term relationship by giving her boyfriend urine-soaked cookies, and instructing the other to put oil on her mate's hairbrush. She advised the third woman that she could bring about a favourable outcome in a child custody case by pouring oil and chili peppers over her ex-husband's car.

The policeman who arrested this fortune teller, says that he was not affected by a curse she laid on him when she buried a photograph of him in a cemetery. The judge in this case praised the "rare form of courage" shown by the three witnesses who had been prepared to testify to the fact that they had been made fools of.

These women were apparently exceptionally gullible, but underlying their susceptibility was a belief that is rooted in old traditions and is not in its own terms irrational. In many immigrant communities, the witch serves the functions of healer, psychiatrist and counselor, offering people a practical way of working on their own personal problems.

People from the Caribbean and Latin America also follow traditions of folk magic that many see as compatible with their Christian beliefs. Like European witchcraft, they involve magic and herbal medicine that can be used for malevolent purposes, but, contrary to the popular image, they are primarily ways of worship and healing. The spiritual leaders in these African-based religions also play the role of unofficial therapists and practical advisors to the members of their communities. They can be very powerful figures in that they claim to contact the deities by going into trances and speaking on their behalf. Their advice is thus seen as coming directly from supernatural sources.

Tamarra James, owner of the Toronto Occult Shop, has studied African religion and has used it in combination with Wicca to compile a collection of spells designed mainly for the Caribbean clientele of her store. The spells employ candles, herbal remedies and aromatic cosmetics that are named after their function, such as Fast Luck Soap and Success Oil, Immigration Bath Salts, Jinx Removing Spray, Protection Soap and Just Judge Oil. This practice is common in Caribbean folk medicine, although the names vary from one practitioner to another. The spells also involve readings from Psalms and offerings to the Seven African Powers. These deities all have human emotions and peculiarities and are believed to each have a favourite food or drink. Oggun, the hunter and warrior, for example, is thought to have a partiality for rum and cigars and these are traditionally left for him as offerings.

Lady Tamarra's White Witch Book of Spells provides magic for almost every conceivable everyday purpose. There are spells for finding a job, persuading someone else to look for work, for business success, for making children behave, for love, for insomnia, for causing a neighbour to move away, for mail that has been tampered with, for the successful outcome of immigration hearings, and, if the last of these fails, for escaping official notice. For those whose sleep is "disturbed by evil spirits of a sexual nature" there is a spell for warding off an incubus or succubus. A wide array of oils, bath salts, lotions, shampoos and conditioners, together with promises of food, drink and other treats for each of the seven African powers, is prescribed in one of the most complicated spells in the collection, a spell "to succeed in a court case when you are guilty."

In all these spells the people performing them are instructed to meditate on their situation. The prayers and meditations that are suggested contain practical and therapeutic advice. In the introduction to this collection, James wrote, "Magic is born in the mind of the practitioner. It takes its strength from our will to see it succeed."

"Magic is prayer," James told me. "We do it in different ways. Every faith has it, and even people who are not essentially religious have little rituals of magic."

The Toronto witch Charles Arnold made a similar point when he told me, "Magic works in a thousand different ways, and the Craft doesn't have the inside track. I once went to a hymn sing in a black Baptist church in Oklahoma City. Five choirs came to sing gospel music. I have never in my life been to a pagan ritual where they could get one percent of the energy that about 80 to 90 people in that church worked up."

Alf Marron also sees magic as a form of prayer. Whether he lights a candle to the Triple Goddess on his altar at home or in front of a statue of the Virgin Mary at his parish church, Alf Marron believes he is making two different magical supplications to one undivided mystical force.

CHAPTER THIRTEEN

The Old Religion in a New Age

''What is now proved was once only imagined,'' wrote William Blake, an English poet and mystic. The borderline between new age science and science fiction sometimes appears to be a thin one, but twentieth century discoveries in areas like quantum mechanics and brain chemistry have, in fact, flown in the face of the conventional scientific thinking of the past 400 years. Scientist Niels Bohr, one of the pioneers of the new physics, echoed Blake by saying that there is no hope for any speculation that does not look absurd at first glance.

Physicists studying the movement of subatomic particles, a field known as quantum mechanics, have discovered that, contrary to Newton's laws upon which all previous physics was based, it is not possible to predict the direction and momentum of these pieces of matter. They have found that there is no such thing as objectivity, in this field, as one cannot observe reality without changing it.

Research in brain chemistry has shown that we can produce chemicals that have an effect similar to morphine in killing pain. This provides a beginning to our understanding of the phenomena of faith healing and the magic that people can work to heal themselves or others, escpecially when the other person is conscious that the healing spell is being cast. The discovery of electro-magnetic activity within the brain holds out the possibility that there may be a scientific explanation for ESP and the kind of magic that involves influencing other people's minds "over the ether." If electro-chemical reactions can take place within the human body, it is possible, although not proven, that the mind could emit energy that has an impact on external reality.

Many scientists no longer look at humanity and the universe as a series of separate units governed by natural laws. They see reality as a series of systems in which everything interconnects. Instead of breaking everything down into its component parts, one current trend in science is to see everything as a part of a whole, and that whole as a living organism called Gaia, the concept that the pagans would refer to as Mother Earth.

The ancient pagan notion of the circle as being the central symbol of all life is coming back into fashion after two thousand years of allegiance to the form of the cross.

A more connected way of approaching problems is also to be seen in present-day business and social organizations. This is partly due to the influence of computer technology, which makes it easier to relate numerous variables together into systems.

In the past Western society has taught people to value book learning and logical, linear thinking above any other form of knowledge. Folk wisdom passed on from generation to generation has often been dismissed as old wives' tales. The written word has been the basis for the culture of at least the last thousand years. The word of God as written in the Bible is the foundation of Christianity. At first this was interpreted through the authority of the Roman Catholic Church, then, with the invention of printing and the Reformation it became available for everyone to interpret individually. Our society became one in which people lived relatively isolated private or family lives, and eventually interrelated better in large organizations than on a community level.

But, as our thoughts on the value and nature of empirical knowledge change, so too do our notions of divinity and worship. Robert Ellwood, a religious historian who is an expert on new religious movements, has argued that, in order to survive into the next century, organized religions will have to undergo a ''New Reformation'' in which they will renew their commitment to social justice, take a more holistic view of the universe and become based on small communities rather than large structured groups. If this does not happen, he warned, the religions of the future will be ''folk religions,'' like the polytheistic paganism of pre-Christian times.

The idea that this sophisticated information age has something to learn from the myths of primitive cultures is hard to accept. However, I have found that simply entertaining this idea, without necessarily endorsing it, has given me a better perspective on what our own civilization represents. In this context, I was quite intrigued by a comment about witchcraft that came from someone who had grown up with native Indian beliefs. Cornwoman told me that discovering Wicca made her realize that white people have a tradition as rich and complex as native culture. This insight is a startling one as it challenges deeply ingrained notions about the superiority of Western civilization.

For hundreds of years white people regarded the cultures of indigenous people all over the world as savage and unsophisticated. One of the prime justifications for taking their land and exploiting its resources was the belief that it was a sacred trust to convert these primitive people to Christianity and bring them up to a European level of civilization.

The people of North America, however, came to see the arrival of the Europeans as a catastrophe, not only for themselves but for the land. The Mohawks prophesied that, seven generations after the white people came, the elm trees would die, and then the maples. They predicted that birds would fall from the sky and fish die in the water. Then, they said, ''man would grow ashamed of how he had treated his mother and provider, the earth.''

The current search for alternate spiritual values may be seen as a response to the great crises that confront our times. We live in a world in which values seem to be constantly failing us and the structures on which many people have based their lives are shifting. The global threats of overpopulation, disease, deforestation, ozone depletion and the greenhouse effect are of a scale and complexity unimaginable even twenty years ago. These problems are so great that they have even displaced the fear of nuclear war as a prime cause for public concern. In their everyday lives people are facing radical economic and technological change, and are becoming increasingly concerned about pollution and violence in their communities.

Teacher and author Joseph Campbell, an expert on mythology, has observed that it is becoming more and more difficult to believe in the myths contained in the old religious texts. He says that the consequences of this are dire: ''With our old mythologically founded taboos unsettled by our own modern sciences, there is everywhere in the civilized world a rapidly rising incidence of vice and crime, mental disorders, suicides and dope addictions, shattered homes, impudent children, violence, murder and despair.''

Responding to the same social problems, modern witches and pagans come to the conclusion that the Judeo-Christian belief system is not only irrelevant to present-day needs but that it is partly responsible for having led Western society astray. Their response is to revive a form of spirituality in which they see a potential for healing the wounds that civilization has inflicted on the world.

However, the problems and uncertainties of modern times only provide a partial explanation for the current occult revival. These could equally well be offered as reasons why many adherents of organized religion are rejecting established institutions in favour of either liberation theology or fundamentalism. There must be some other conditions which make magical beliefs so attractive to many people today.

I was pondering this issue one night in front of a television set, idly switching channels as a substitute for creative thought, when I gained some insight from an unlikely source. My attention was arrested by a rock video that showed a bleak urban streetscape dissolving into a scene of frenzied dancing around a primordial fire. As I considered the significance of this ritual, the scene changed again to documentary footage from the First World War, and then through a series of images almost too rapid for the conscious mind to grasp.

After sitting in a dazed state through several such videos, I realized that I was absorbing messages in a completely different way from the literate tradition in which I had grown up. In a written or printed text, ideas and details of a narrative or description are generally arranged in a sequence that follows the orderly rules of grammar. People who have been educated largely through the written word tend to understand and explain reality within the framework of linear logical structures. These videos were displaying potent symbols and linking disparate aspects of reality and myth, through a series of images, each containing several layers of meaning. The videos did not provide the logical connections, explanations and explicit statements that one expects in a culture based on the written word. I felt that the videos were communicating messages that I was processing unconsciously and responding to emotionally but could not easily explain or analyse.

It then occurred to me that it is almost inevitable that the kind of connections made through myth, ritual and magic, which existed in the earliest human cultures, should again appear in what has in many ways become a post-literate age.

Confronted with rapid change and an overload of information from a variety of sources, people are looking for new ways of making sense of reality and creating enduring values in their lives. Religions based on written texts, rigid codes and authoritarian structures are suddenly at a disadvantage to those which are based on flexible oral traditions, which change with each generation, and base their teachings on the multiplicity of meaning embodied in ritual and myth.

The generation that came of age in the 1960s was the first to grow up with television and it asserted very strongly that experience and intuition were more important than intellectual understanding. It is hardly surprising that some of them should have been drawn to religions like Wicca, in which the teachings are learned through the experience of acting out rituals.

Witchcraft is a religion based on an oral tradition and its origins are in a tribal society. The basic unit of Wicca is still the coven. In a society in which television has undermined the importance of the written word, and in which new technologies are promising to encourage the proliferation of smaller communities, it is perhaps to be expected that Wicca and other tribal-based religions rooted in the spoken word might become more popular.

The dawning of a new age at the time of the birth of Jesus Christ was something that had been predicted by astrologers. The New Testament records that the Three Wise Men from the East knew of the birth of the Messiah by looking at the stars. Astrologers believe that the earth takes about two thousand years to pass through each sign of the zodiac. The direction of this movement is the opposite of the progression of the year through the twelve planetary houses. At about the time Christ was born, the earth moved from the house of Aries, the sheep, which was a predominant symbol in the Old Testament, into the house of Pisces, the fish, a predominant symbol in the New Testament. The Greek letters of Christ's name also spell fish, and the simple line rendering of a fish is still used as shorthand identification for Christ and Christianity today.

Now astrologers are announcing the dawning of yet another new age, and for witches, and many other people who have adopted magical beliefs, the new age is the great myth of our times. According to this myth, the planet is beginning to leave the influence of Pisces and move into the sign of Aquarius. The Age of Pisces is seen by astrologers as one that has emphasized the separation of man from God, good from evil, male from female, and man from nature. It is seen as an age of authority, male domination, regimentation and nationalism. Aquarius is the sign of the water bearer, seen as symbolizing flow and the quenching of an ancient thirst. The Aquarian age is heralded as a time of peace and unity, when occult knowledge and extra sensory perception will be common and people will feel at one with one another, the earth and the universe.

The diverse and vaguely defined New Age movement is founded on the belief in the arrival of the Age of Aquarius, which was prematurely proclaimed in the 1960s musical "Hair" and which will begin at the end of this century. The present time is seen by astrologers as a period of transition between the two ages, when both sets of attitudes exist side by side, sometimes vying with one another, and sometimes becoming fused together.

The new age movement is an odd compendium of cosmic consciousness and self-absorbed middle-class ambitions. On the one hand the new age symbolizes an idealistic attempt to create a new spirituality rooted in the interconnectedness of all things, and, on the other, it is a quest for meaning and fulfillment on the part of people who have achieved most of their materialist goals. It is a movement made up largely of voracious consumers and innovative entrepreneurs. Much of the current new age phenomenon is comprised of commercial exploitation and superficial faddism, but the movement also includes some profound new interpretations of scientific concepts and religious experience.

Visualization, and even shamanic journeying, are increasingly being used as motivational aids in business and professional sports. This, like the commercialization of magical tools on the new age market, is a trend that disturbs many witches and pagans. It is an indication that a philosophy that witches see as having the potential to transform society can easily be absorbed and used to bolster the very elements that it was supposed to be changing.

A Wiccan therapist told me, "You can call it visualization or witchcraft, and, as long as you don't put the word *witchcraft* on it, professionals love it."

The commercialized new age culture takes beliefs and practices from traditional religions, including witchcraft, and use them in non-traditional ways, usually cutting out much of their original significance and sometimes distorting their purpose. But some witches like Charles Arnold regard this as an opportunity to market traditional skills under a new name. One witch told me that the main significance of the new age to her was that, "as long as stockbrokers are buying crystals they are less likely to persecute witches."

Most bookstores now have a new age section, and record stores have a category for new age music. In almost every major city in North America there are specialty new age bookstores and workshops on subjects ranging from the Kabbala to visitations from outer space. Now that the so-called Yuppies of the baby-boom generation have acquired their condominiums and BMWs, they are picking up on the search for the meaning of life that many of them abandoned in the 1970s. New age has come to represent one of the most booming service industries of the new post-industrial era.

While much new age thinking is just a repackaging of traditional practices, it also includes innovative uses of new technology for spiritual development. Equipment used in medical research to measure electical activity within the brain is now being used by many new age therapists and self-development groups in a technique known as *biofeedback*. This involves monitoring the frequency of one's brain waves during meditation sessions in order to discover what methods of meditation are most effective. Other equipment can be used to create patterns of light and sound that stimulate the same brain wave frequency that is achieved in meditative states.

These examples of New Age technology promise to provide anyone who can afford the equipment a key to controlling the powers of the mind and, even, gaining access to the astral plane. I heard one salesman telling a group of business and professional people that with the aid of such machines it would take about fifteen minutes to achieve mystical states of oneness with the cosmos that people have been trying to reach for centuries by dancing, chanting and meditating, or by means of herbs, drugs and ritual. The salesman promised his audience that the machines would help them return to the more relaxed way of life that existed in earlier, simpler societies. He said people who use the devices also cut down on use of tobacco, are more self-accepting, more spontaneous, more open to warm and sensitive relationships. They have fewer inhibitions, are more likely to succeed in their careers and increase their productivity.

The same combination of achieving a cosmic unity and business success is offered by a very popular series of courses in mind control known as the Silva Method, named after Jose Silva, who developed it in Texas in the late 1960s. The Silva Method teaches people to put themselves into meditative states of lower brain wave frequency and to use this state to project their consciousness into what witches would call the ether or astral plane. A Silva teaching manual reflects occultists' hopes for the Age of Aquarius by making the claim that "perfecting the means to communicate at this dimension will begin the second phase of human evolution on this planet."

This manual refers to twentieth century research establishing the validity of Extra Sensory Perception as a scientific basis for the belief that one can obtain "psychically perceived knowledge gained through our connection or oneness with all that is." This is exactly what witches believe, and the manual also teaches the magical technique of visualization, which it calls affirmation. This involves seeing one's goals, not as shadowy objects of desire, but as clearly defined accomplishments that one has already created out of one's will. However, the Silva Method looks down on magic and advises people that they should "cancel'' erroneous beliefs about ESP, occult or voodoo, and base their beliefs on scientific research.

Like Wicca, the Silva Method imparts the notion that one should work for the common good, when one is operating in sympathy with the forces of nature at a deeper level of consciousness, although it offers a rather broad interpretation of what constitutes the common good. These are examples of affirmative statements taken from a Silva Method manual:

''My increasing mental faculties are for serving humanity better.''

''A lot more money is coming into my life. I deserve it and use it for my good and that of others.''

''Every dollar I circulate comes back to me multiplied.''

Abraham Altman, a Toronto electronic technician, who has studied the Silva Method for six years and is also enthusiastic about biofeedback equipment, told me that he uses these techniques for developing his own personal power, his own magic. This magic, he said, involves control of pain, and developing an ability to heal oneself. His claims are similar to those of most witches I have talked to, in that he believes he has developed this power to the point of being able to heal some minor ailments, but does not pretend to be able to cure more serious diseases.

It makes no difference, he said, whether one acquires this ability through technology like biofeedback devices or through traditional occult methods. The ultimate experience is essentially the same.

One of the prime tenets of both Wicca and the new age movement is that there are many paths leading to the same place. They believe that everyone must find their own Goddess and God in their own ways. They see this as being particularly important in a world where belief in only one version of the truth has not only caused war and hatred, but has also led to error. The idea of ''the one and only way'' no longer fits with scientific thinking as it is now believed that there can be different answers depending on which questions one chooses to ask.

Louise, a Vancouver witch, told me, "I have a vision that one day people will be more appreciative of diversity of life on the planet. Diversity is our greatest strength. As paganism and witchcraft become more and more known to the public, I can see people saying, 'This other way of living is not providing me with the answers,' and realizing that you have to make your own answers."

I agree with Louise that an acceptance of diversity and a tolerance of other people's beliefs and peculiarities is one of the most valuable things that Wicca and paganism have to contribute to society. I think it is, however, something that many witches have first to teach themselves. Wicca prides itself on being a religion that does not blow its own horn or seek to make converts, yet some "evangelical" witches rail against Christianity or other Wiccan sects.

The respect for nature that is shown by all genuine witches and pagans, together with the honour that they give to the female principle in the universe, is also in my view something of the utmost importance — but it is not something that is an exclusive preserve of witches. Reverence for the earth was a common attitude among country people, before the advent of agri-business.It was reflected in the use of the term *Mother Earth,* which represented more a figure of speech and an attitude than any deep-seated religious belief. A respect for the female at its deepest level is undoubtedly less common, and it is probably something most men could afford to develop. These things are important for all people to strive towards, but I would not like to give the impression that one has to become a witch to do so. One could probably find people from many diverse religions espousing these attitudes.

Witches and pagans, who see the earth as the Goddess or regard trees as sacred, do have a unique perspective, though, and have much of value to contribute. They celebrate the benevolence of nature and the Gods, but they also have an appreciation for their wildness and indifference. As Sam Wagar of Pagans for Peace told me, witches know that humanity is not in control of the natural world and that, if we do not stop polluting, the world will stop us.

People who believe that the universe is permeated with a form of energy that can be harnessed for magical purposes have seen confirmation of their beliefs in research in the field of nuclear physics. In 1905, Albert Einstein expounded the theory that time and space are part of one continuum and that energy and mass are names for the same thing. More recently, some scientists have questioned the distinction between matter and human consciousness, and suggested that all nature is interconnected in, what physicist David Bohm has called, "an unbroken wholeness." Such speculations seem less than a quantum leap away from the magical notion that human consciousness can alter the fabric of reality.

Like magic, nuclear energy is an amoral force, and one that can be seen as having potential for evil as well as good. It has great value when applied in medicine and other scientific and technological uses, and has become widely regarded as indispensible as a source of electrical power. But it is accompanied by untold risks and, if used as a weapon, could destroy all human life. It is, perhaps, an indication of a certain lack of moral perspective on these issues that it is not customary to apply the terms black and white to scientists as to magicians.

I am somewhat relieved to be able to say that in all my encounters with witches and magicians I did not ever feel that I had come under a spell or suffered a curse. I did, however, learn to respect magic, not as a supernatural force, but as a way of dealing with the world that exerts considerable influence on many people today.

People who use magic in their daily lives often find that it gives them confidence and energy, and makes them feel vitally connected with the world around them. Magic can also have devastating consequences for people who try to use it for negative effects. Those who attempt to use magic for evil purposes have a good reason to be afraid. However, what they need fear is not so much magic as themselves, and the psychological consequences of a deliberate pursuit of malevolent goals. If you evoke demons, it is quite likely that they will appear. It does not make any difference whether they come from hell's fire or your own subconscious, as in either case they may have the power to possess you.

The distinctions between satanism and witchcraft should by now be obvious, but running through both there is a common thread of magical thinking, a belief in psychic energies that flow beneath the surface of reality and can be harnessed for practical purposes. The question of why these light and dark sides of occult beliefs should both be so popular today is important, because in trying to answer this question we can gain some insights into the nature of modern society and culture.

Witches and some other modern pagans employ magical practices as an expression of the divine principles of nature and to tap that psychic energy for positive works. Satanists use magic for personal power in a world that they see as governed by indifferent or destructive forces. For some young people, it makes more sense to see the world as prey to forces of chaos and confusion than ordered by a benevolent God. Satanism provides them with explanation and it also gives them a principle to live by, albeit one based on self-gratification and greed. Others get involved with satanism primarily as a rebellion against conventional values and as an expression of their powerless rage against what seems to them a cruel and hypocritical society. For some, this rebellion is simply a cultural statement, but for others it represents a desire to explore the intriguing realm of the occult. Some people working with teenage satanists have found that many such youths are not aware of the positive aspects of magic and are happy when they are presented with such alternatives.

In a book called *The Black Arts,* British writer Richard Cavendish summed up the attitude of most magicians to satanists, when he wrote: "Satanism is as harshly rejected by most magicians as it is by Christians. But where the churches, which brought the Devil to life in the first place, condemn his worship as the adoration of evil, magicians despise it as a failure to understand the true nature of the universe."

In discussing the values that witchcraft and a magical consciousness have to contribute to society, one cannot lose sight of the "dark side" that satanism and black magic represent. One should also keep them in perspective.

I think it is time that we got away from the notion of a black and white world. The greatest atrocities of history were committed by people who thought that they were "white" and somebody else was "black." While our civilization has been busy putting labels on the world, it has also come close to destroying it.

I believe that the only other reason to fear magic is if one is susceptible to the influence of a proponent of black magic. The obvious reason to fear such a person is that he or she might be inclined to inflict some real harm in a practical way, but one would also be vulnerable to psychological manipulation, if one believed in that person's magical powers.

When we strip away the veil of mystery from magic and look at it without fear, we can see something that is quite simple and ordinary. What we see is a way of harnessing the natural energies of mankind, strengthening the will, focussing the intellect, tapping spiritual and emotional depths, and directing all this towards the realization of practical goals. Magic is essentially a neutral force. Good and evil are not inherent in the capacities of mankind but are attached to the moral context in which these are used.

Witchcraft and modern paganism provide their adherents with a way of understanding the world that they feel is more in touch both with eternal life-forces and present day needs than conventional organized religion, but the most important insight that I have received from the magicians, witches and modern pagans whom I have met is that we should try to understand and accept all aspects of our human nature. People who recognize that there is a light and a dark side to all things do not have to strive to make themselves into either saints or devils. They can live on their own terms in an ambiguous and complex society without doing violence to themselves, to others or the earth.

BIBLIOGRAPHY

ADLER, MARGOT, *Drawing Down the Moon*, Beacon Press, Boston, 1986.

ARROWSMITH, NANCY, *A Field Guide to the Little People*, Hill and Wang, New York, 1977.

BRIGGS, KATHARINE, *The Fairies in Tradition and Literature*, Routledge and Kegan Paul, London, 1967.

BUCKLAND, RAYMOND, *Buckland's Complete Book of Witchcraft*, Lewellyn Publications, St. Paul, Minnesota, 1987.

CAMPBELL, JOSEPH, *Myths To Live By*, Bantam Books, New York, 1973.

CAREY, JOHN, ''Listening to the Celts,'' in *Gnosis*, Fall 1988.

CAVENDISH, RICHARD, *The Black Arts*, G.P. Putnam's Sons, New York, 1967.

COLQUHOUN, ITHELL, *Sword of Wisdom: MacGregor Mathers and the Golden Dawn*, G.P. Putnam's Sons, New York, 1975.

CROWLEY, ALEISTER, *Magick*, Routledge and Kegan Paul, London, 1973.

CROWLEY, ALEISTER, *The Book of the Law*, 93 Publishing, South Stukely, Quebec, 1975.

CUNNINGHAM, SCOTT, *Wicca: a Guide for the Solitary Practitioner*, Llewellyn Publications, St. Paul, Minnesota, 1989.

DE WAAL MALEFIJT, ANNEMARIE, *Religion and Culture: an Introduction to the Anthropology of Religion*, Collier-Macmillan, London, 1968.

ELLWOOD, ROBERT S., *Religious and Spiritual Groups in Modern America*, Prentice Hall, New Jersey, 1973.

ELLWOOD, ROBERT S., *History and Future of Faith*, Crossroad Publishing Company, New York, 1988.

FARRAR, JANET and STEWART, *A Witches Bible Compleat*, Robert Hale, London, 1981.

FERGUSON, MARILYN, *The Aquarian Conspiracy*, J.P.Tarcher, Los Angeles, 1980.

THE FINDHORN COMMUNITY, *The Findhorn Garden*, Harper and Row, New York, 1975.

FRAZER, SIR JAMES GEORGE, *The New Golden Bough*, Theodor H. Gaster (ed.), Anchor, New York, 1962.

GARDNER, GERALD B., *Meaning of Witchcraft*, Aquarian Press, London, 1959.

GORDON, HENRY, *Channeling into the New Age*, Prometheus Books, Buffalo, New York, 1988.

GRAVES, ROBERT, *The White Goddess*, Faber and Faber, London, 1961.

GRAY, WILLIAM, *Between Good and Evil: Polarities of Power*, Llewellyn Publications, St. Paul, Minnesota, 1989.

HARNER, MICHAEL, *The Way of the Shaman*, Bantam, New York, 1982.

HUGHES, PENNETHORNE, *Witchcraft*, Penguin, London, 1965.

HUYSMANS, J.K., *Là-Bas*, Trans. Keene Wallace, Dover Publications, New York, 1972.

KAHANER, LARRY, *Cults That Kill: Probing the Underworld of Occult Crime*, Warner Books, New York, 1988.

KEESING, FELIX M., *Cultural Anthropology: the Science of Custom*, Holt, Rinehart and Winston, New York, 1965.

LELAND, CHARLES G., *Aradia or the Gospel of the Witches*, David Nutt, London, 1899.

LAVEY, ANTON SZANDOR, *The Satanic Bible*, Avon Books, New York, 1969.

LAVEY, ANTON SZANDOR, *The Satanic Rituals*, Avon Books, New York 1972.

LYONS, ARTHUR, *Satan Wants You: the Cult of Devil Worship in America*, The Mysterious Press, New York, 1988.

MALINOWSKI, BRONISLAW, *Magic, Science and Religion*, Doubleday Anchor Books, New York, 1954.

MARTELLO, LEO, *Black Magic Satanism Vooodoo*, H.C. Publishers, New York, 1973.

MICHELET, JULES, *Satanism and Witchcraft: A Study in Mediaeval Superstition*, The Citadel Press, New York, 1939.

PAZDER, LAWRENCE, *Michelle Remembers* Pocket Books, New York 1981.

REGARDIE, ISRAEL, *The Eye in the Triangle: an interpretation of Aleister Crowley*, Falcon Press, Phoenix, Arizona, 1970.

ROSE, ELLIOT, *A Razor for a Goat: A Discussion of Certain Problems in the History of Witchcraft and Diabolism*, University of Toronto Press, Toronto, 1962.

TREVOR-ROPER, H.R., *The European Witch Craze of the Sixteenth and Seventeenth Centuries and other essays*, Harper and Row, New York, 1969.

RUSSELL, JEFFREY, *A History of Witchcraft*, Thames and Hudson, London, 1980.

SANDILANDS, KATE, *Spirituality and Praxis: Witchcraft and Neo-paganism in Canada*, York University, Toronto, 1988.

SKELTON, ROBIN, *The Practice of Witchcraft Today*, Robert Hale, London, 1988.

SPRETNAK, CHARLENE (ed.), *The Politics of Women's Spirituality*, Anchor Books, New York, 1982.

STARHAWK, *Dreaming the Dark: Magic, Sex, and Politics*, Beacon Press, Boston, 1982.

STARHAWK, *Truth or Dare: Encounters with Power, Authority and Mystery*, Harper and Row, San Francisco, 1987.

STEWART, LUIS, *Life Forces: A Contemporary Guide to the Cult and Occult*, Andrews and McMeel, Kansas City, 1980.

SUSTER, GERALD, *The Legacy of the Beast*, W.H. Allen, London, 1988.

TALBOT, MICHAEL, *Beyond the Quantum*, Bantam, New York, 1988.

WEINSTEIN, MARION, *Positive Magic: Occult Self-Help*, Phoenix Publishing, Custer, Washington, 1981.

WILSON, COLIN, *Mysteries*, Grafton Books, London, 1979.

WILSON, COLIN, *The Occult*, Panther Books, London, 1979.

ZUKAV, GARY, *The Dancing Wu Li Masters: an Overview of the New Physics*, Bantam, New York, 1979.

ACKNOWLEDGEMENTS

I am very fortunate to have an extremely talented editor in Sarah Silberstein Swartz, who has the insight to envision bold structural changes and the tact to make such proposals delicately. I would like to thank her for the intelligent and sensitive work she has done on this manuscript. I would also like to thank Dean Cooke and everyone else at Seal Books who have worked on preparing this book, together with Susan Rutledge who got the project under way and Greg Ioannou, who is a meticulous copy editor.

I probably would not have written this book without the advice and encouragement of Joanna Chapman, and I would like to thank her for all the time she spent reading my manuscripts and telling me to get back to work. Many other friends helped enormously in various ways. I would particularly like to thank Margaret Rees for anthropological information, Ellen Wolter for legal research and Pat Moore for her interest and support.

I am most grateful to all the witches, pagans and other people who agreed to be interviewed for this book, helped make contacts or gather background information. Many people also extended great kindness and hospitality to me during my travels and I would like to express my appreciation for that. I would especially like to thank Sam Wagar, Tamarra James, Dobhran, Seán Ó Tuathail, Charles Arnold, Kate Sandilands, Charles Taylor, blackWing, Rob Tucker, Linda Gibb, Bill Rodman and Howard Goldenthal.